STRATEGIC MARKETING MANAGEMENT

Alexander Chernev

Kellogg School of Management
Northwestern University

Eighth Edition

Strategic Marketing Management

Eighth Edition | June 2014

ISBN: 978-1-936572-19-9 (Paperback)

ISBN: 978-1-936572-20-5 (Hardcover)

ISBN: 978-1-936572-21-2 (eBook)

www.CHERNEV.com | www.G-STIC.com

Published by Cerebellum Press, USA

TABLE OF CONTENTS

About the Author

Alexander Chernev is a professor of marketing at the Kellogg School of Management, Northwestern University. He holds a PhD in psychology from Sofia University and a PhD in business administration from Duke University.

Dr. Chernev's research applies theories and concepts related to consumer behavior and managerial decision making to develop successful marketing strategies. He is an area editor for the *Journal of Marketing* and serves on the editorial boards of top research journals, including the *Journal of Marketing Research, Journal of Consumer Research, Journal of Consumer Psychology, Journal of the Academy of Marketing Science,* and *International Journal of Research in Marketing*. Dr. Chernev's research has been published in the leading marketing journals and has been frequently quoted in the business and popular press, including *Scientific American, Associated Press, Business Week, Forbes, Newsweek, The Wall Street Journal, Financial Times, The New York Times, The Washington Post,* and *Harvard Business Review*. He has written numerous articles focused on corporate planning, marketing strategy, and brand and customer management.

Dr. Chernev teaches marketing management, marketing strategy, product management, and behavioral decision theory in MBA, PhD, and executive education programs. He has received numerous teaching awards including the *Top Professor* award from the Executive MBA program at Kellogg. In addition to teaching, he advises companies around the world on issues of strategic marketing planning and analysis, business innovation, brand and customer equity, and new product development.

Acknowledgments

This book has benefited from the wisdom of many of my current and former colleagues at the Kellogg School of Management at Northwestern University: Nidhi Agrawal, Eric Anderson, Jim Anderson, Robert Blattberg, Ulf Böckenholt, Anand Bodapati, Miguel Brendl, Bobby Calder, Tim Calkins, Gregory Carpenter, Moran Cerf, Yuxin Chen, Anne Coughlan, Patrick Duparcq, David Gal, Kelly Goldsmith, Kent Grayson, Sachin Gupta, Karsten Hansen, Julie Hennessy, Dawn Iacobucci, Dipak Jain, Robert Kozinets, Aparna Labroo, Lakshman Krishnamurthi, Eric Leininger, Angela Lee, Sidney Levy, Michal Maimaran, Prashant Malaviya, Eyal Maoz, Blake McShane, Vikas Mittal, Vincent Nijs, Christie Nordhielm, Mary Pearlman, Yi Qian, Neal Roese, Derek Rucker, Mohan Sawhney, John Sherry, Jr., Louis Stern, Brian Sternthal, Rima Touré-Tillery, Alice Tybout, Rick Wilson, Song Yao, Philip Zerrillo, Florian Zettelmeyer, and Andris Zoltners.

I would like to thank Andrea Bonezzi (New York University), Aaron Brough (Pepperdine University), Pierre Chandon (INSEAD), Akif Irfan (Goldman Sachs), Mathew Isaac (University of Seattle), Ryan Hamilton (Emory University), Ajay

Kohli (Georgia Institute of Technology), and Jaya Sah (Goldman Sachs) for their valuable comments.

I owe a considerable debt of gratitude to Philip Kotler, one of the leading thinkers in the field of marketing, who through his insightful writings sparked my interest in marketing. I am also indebted to Jim Bettman, Julie Edell Britton, Joel Huber, John Lynch, John Payne, and Rick Staelin at the Fuqua School of Business at Duke University for their advice and support at the outset of my academic career.

Foreword

Marketing is both an art and a science. Many of its practitioners view marketing as an art, in which both intuition and creativity play a major role—a popular view, particularly in the advertising and sales spheres. Yet, if marketing plans were to be based primarily on intuition and creativity, they would be less effective and less credible to senior management and the company's stakeholders and collaborators. What gives marketing its growing respect and impact is the development and use of a broad range of scientific and analytic tools.

Over the past decades, the field of marketing has accumulated numerous tools. They help define goals and target markets, and facilitate positioning, differentiation, and branding. These tools, however, are usually scattered within marketing textbooks and fail to come together in a clear framework. Here lies the unique contribution of *Strategic Marketing Management*. This concise book presents the major tools and decision processes involved in planning and controlling marketing.

The theory presented in this book is based on three cornerstone ideas:

The first idea is that an offering's ultimate success is determined by the soundness of the five key components of its business model: goal, strategy, tactics, implementation, and control, or the G-STIC framework. This framework is used to streamline a company's marketing analyses and deliver an integrative approach to marketing planning.

The second idea is that when developing its offerings, a company should strive to create value for three key market entities: target customers, the company, and its collaborators. An offering's value proposition, therefore, should be optimized to deliver superior value to target customers in a way that enables the company and its collaborators to reach their strategic goals. These three types of value—customer value, collaborator value, and company value—comprise the 3-V framework, which is the foundation of strategic marketing analysis.

The third idea is that a company's marketing activities can be represented through the process of designing, communicating, and delivering value to its key constituencies. This framework offers a novel interpretation of the traditional 4-P approach to capture the dynamic nature of the value management process.

Strategic Marketing Management applies these ideas to common business problems, such as increasing profits and sales revenues, developing new products, extending product lines, and managing product portfolios. By linking the theory to practical applications, this book offers a structured approach to analyzing and solving business problems and delineates a set of methodologies to ensure a company's success in the market.

Student testimonies are evidence that this book is very helpful for analyzing marketing cases in the classroom. This book is also very helpful to managers involved in the development and implementation of marketing plans. I further recommend it to senior executives to improve their understanding of what constitutes great marketing analysis and planning.

A company's main focus should be on maximizing value for the customer, the company, and its collaborators. This can be achieved by applying the strategic marketing framework outlined in this book.

Philip Kotler
S. C. Johnson Distinguished Professor of International Marketing
Kellogg School of Management
Northwestern University

Part One

The Big Picture

Chapter One

Marketing as a Business Discipline

Marketing is the whole business seen from the point of view of its final result, that is, from the customer's point of view.

— Peter Drucker, founder of modern management theory

A great deal of confusion exists about the nature of marketing. This confusion stems from a more general misunderstanding of marketing as a business discipline. Managers often think of marketing in terms of tactical activities such as sales, advertising, and promotion. In fact, within many organizations marketing is thought of as an activity designed to support sales by helping managers sell more of the company's products and services.

The view of marketing as an activity designed to support selling is particularly common among organizations whose primary activity is selling large inventories of warehoused products. These companies often view the goal of marketing as "selling more things, to more people, more often, and for more money." Many managers find this view appealing because it is intuitive, clear, and succinct. The problem with this view is that it does not describe marketing but a related business activity—sales. Indeed, selling more things, to more people, more often, and for more money is a definition of sales, not marketing. This raises the question of defining the boundaries between sales and marketing.

Marketing as a business discipline is much broader than sales; it involves all aspects of developing the offering that is to be sold. The goal of marketing is to create a product that sells, not to sell a product. While marketing certainly can facilitate selling, this accounts for only a portion of its scope. *Marketing is not only much broader than selling, it is not a specialized activity at all,* writes Peter Drucker, business philosopher and writer, viewed by many as the founder of modern management science. *It encompasses the entire business. The aim of marketing is to make selling superfluous.*

Marketing is also regarded by many organizations as equivalent to advertising and sales promotion. Thus, marketing is frequently defined as a process of communicating the value of a product or service to customers—which is, in fact, a better definition of advertising than of marketing. Advertising is only one aspect of marketing, albeit its most visible aspect. Marketing begins long before advertising is conceived: marketing guides the development of the offering that will later be advertised. In the same vein, marketing is often equated with sales promotions such as price discounts, coupons, and rebates. Yet, sales promotions aimed at nudging customers to purchase a company's offerings reflect only one facet of marketing. This view of marketing as an activity that helps bring products to market is oblivious to marketing's role in creating the very products that need to be promoted.

Equating marketing with sales, advertising, and sales promotions share is a common misperception, whereby marketing is defined as a tactical activity. This myopic view of marketing as a tactical tool limited to creating awareness, incentivizing customers to make a purchase, and facilitating sales precludes companies from harnessing marketing's full potential to develop a comprehensive business strategy. What is missing is the understanding of how sales, advertising, and promotions fit together and how they relate to the other tactical aspects of the marketing process, including product development, pricing, and distribution. More important, the view of marketing as a tactical tool does not address the question of what drives the individual marketing activities, how the company creates offerings for its target customers, and how these offerings create value for these customers and the company.

Marketing is far more than tactics. In addition to specialized tactical activities that include sales, advertising, and sales promotion, marketing also involves strategic analysis and planning, which provide the foundation for the success of its tactical elements. As a strategic discipline, marketing is first and foremost about creating value; the different marketing tactics—such as sales, advertising, and promotion—are the means for achieving the company's value-creation goals. Focusing on value recognizes marketing as a central business function that permeates all areas of an enterprise. This view of marketing as a fundamental business discipline is the basis of the strategic marketing theory outlined in this book.

Marketing as a Value-Creation Process

There are many definitions of marketing, each reflecting a different understanding of its role as a business discipline. Some define marketing as a functional area—similar to finance, accounting, and operations—that captures a unique aspect of a company's business activities. Others view marketing as a customer-centric philosophy of business, or as a process of moving products and services from a concept to the customer. Yet others view marketing as a set of specific activities that marketers are involved in, such as product development, pricing, promotion, and distribution. And for some, marketing is simply a department in the company's organizational grid.

This diverse set of definitions attests to the multiple functions that marketing serves. Marketing is a business discipline, a functional area, a business philosophy, a set of specific business activities, as well as a distinct unit in a company's organizational structure. Although diverse, these views of marketing are conceptually related. Marketing as a business discipline is defined by the view of marketing as a philosophy of business, which in turn defines marketing as a set of processes and activities coordinated by the marketing department. Thus, the key to defining marketing is delineating its core business function, which can help define the specific processes and activities involved in marketing management.

The integrative nature of marketing as a business discipline calls for a definition that captures its essence and can serve as a guiding principle in managerial decision making. Because marketing studies consumer and business markets, its focal point is the exchange of goods, services, and ideas that takes place in the market. Furthermore, because the driving force for this exchange is the process of creating value, the concept of value is central to marketing. This view of marketing as an exchange that aims to create value for its participants is reflected in the following definition of marketing as a business discipline:

> *Marketing is the art and science of creating value by designing and managing successful exchanges.*

Marketing is an *art* because it is often driven by a manager's creativity and imagination. In fact, many brilliant marketers—Henry Ford, King Gillette, Ray Kroc, and Henri Nestlé, to name a few—have not formally studied marketing. Their marketing prowess is driven by their innate ability to identify unmet customer needs and develop products to fill those needs. Yet, marketing is also a *science* because it represents a body of generalized knowledge about value creation. By examining the successes and failures of different companies throughout time, marketing science has articulated a set of general principles that abstract from the idiosyncratic experiences of individual companies to capture the essence of the marketing process. The scientific aspect of marketing that distills the logic underlying the processes of creating and managing value is the focus of this book.

Marketing is a business discipline about markets; consequently, its focus is on the *exchange* of goods, services, and ideas—the defining activity of a market. In this context, marketing aims to develop and manage successful exchanges among the participating entities: the company, its customers, and its collaborators. Because the main function of the marketing exchange is to create *value*, the concept of value is central to marketing. Value is a strategic concept that captures the benefits that exchange participants receive from the market exchange. Optimizing value for target customers, collaborators, and the company is the key principle that guides managerial decision making and serves as the foundation for all marketing activities. The goal of marketing is to ensure that a company's offerings create superior value for target customers in a way that enables the company and its collaborators to achieve their strategic goals.

Marketing is not limited to maximizing monetary outcomes; rather, it is defined using the broader term *success*, which extends beyond monetary outcomes to include all forms of value created in the market. Indeed, success is not always expressed in monetary terms, such as net income, return on investment, and market share. For many organizations, success is defined in nonmonetary outcomes, such as technological leadership, customer satisfaction, and social welfare. Therefore, the goal of marketing is to create exchanges that are deemed successful—monetarily or otherwise—by the participants in the exchange.

The view of marketing as a process of creating and managing value has important implications for the way managers should think about the role of marketing within the company. Because it aims to create value for the key participants in the marketing exchange—customers, the company, and its collaborators—marketing plays a pivotal role in any organization. Consequently, marketing is not just an activity managed by a single department; it spans all departments. *Marketing is too important to be left to the marketing department*, advocates David Packard, the cofounder of Hewlett-Packard. *In a truly great marketing organization, you can't tell who's in the marketing department. Everyone in the organization has to make decisions based on the impact on the customer.*

The Role of Frameworks in Marketing

The rapid growth of technological innovation, ever-increasing globalization, and the emergence of new business models have made today's markets exceedingly dynamic, unpredictable, and interdependent. The increasingly complex environment in which companies operate underscores the importance of using a systematic approach to market analysis, planning, and management. Such a systematic approach can be achieved by using frameworks.

Frameworks facilitate decisions in several ways. Frameworks help identify alternative approaches to thinking about the decision task, thus providing managers with a better understanding of the problem they are trying to solve. In addition to helping formulate the problem, frameworks typically provide a generalized approach to identifying alternative solutions. Frameworks further enhance decision making by providing a shared vocabulary with which to discuss the issues, streamlining the communication among the entities involved in the marketing process.

Because of their level of generality, frameworks are not intended to answer specific marketing questions. Instead, they provide a general approach that enables managers to identify the optimal solution to a particular problem. Using a framework calls for abstracting the problem at hand to a more general scenario for which the framework offers a predefined solution and then applying this solution to solve the specific problem. By relying on the abstract knowledge captured in frameworks, a manager can effectively sidestep the trial-and-error-based learning process.

The role of frameworks in business management can be illustrated with the following example. Imagine that a client, a cereal manufacturer, asks your advice on how to price a new cereal. After analyzing the industry dynamics, you identify five key factors that need to be considered when deciding on the price of the cereal: customer willingness to pay for the cereal, the availability and pricing of competitive offerings, the cost structure and profit goals of the company, the margins that suppliers and distributors charge, as well as the more general context factors such as the current economic environment, consumption (health and diet) trends, and legal regulations concerning pricing strategies and tactics.

A month later you receive an assignment from a different client, a gas pipeline manufacturer, asking for your help with setting pricing for a new pressure valve. You diligently analyze the industry and end up suggesting the same five factors: customer willingness to pay, competitive pricing, company costs and goals, collaborator (supplier and distributor) margins, and the current context.

The following month you receive another assignment from a telecommunications company, asking for your advice on pricing its new mobile phone. By this time you have realized that the three recent requests are conceptually similar, calling for setting a price for a new product. Moreover, you realize that setting the price in all three tasks calls for analyzing the same five factors: customer willingness to pay, competitor prices, company goals and cost structure, collaborator prices and margins, and the overall economic, regulatory, technological context in which the company operates. (These five factors comprise the 5-C framework, which is discussed in the following chapter.)

As the above example illustrates, frameworks build on already existing generalized knowledge to facilitate future company-specific decisions. Thus, many of the business problems companies face on a daily basis can be generalized into a framework that can be applied to solving future problems. The role of frameworks as a problem-solving tool is captured in the words of French philosopher René Descartes: *Each problem that I solved became a rule which served afterwards to solve other problems.*

The effective use of frameworks as a managerial problem-solving tool involves three key steps. First, a manager needs to generalize the specific problem at hand (e.g., how to price a new mobile phone) to a more abstract problem that can be addressed by a particular framework (e.g., how to price a new product). Second, the manager needs to identify a framework that will help answer the specific problem (e.g., the 5-C framework) and use it to derive a general solution. Third, the manager needs to apply the generalized solution prescribed by the framework to the specific problem. The reliance on generalized knowledge captured in frameworks can help managers circumvent the trial-and-error approach to solving business problems (Figure 1).

Figure 1: The Role of Frameworks in Marketing Management

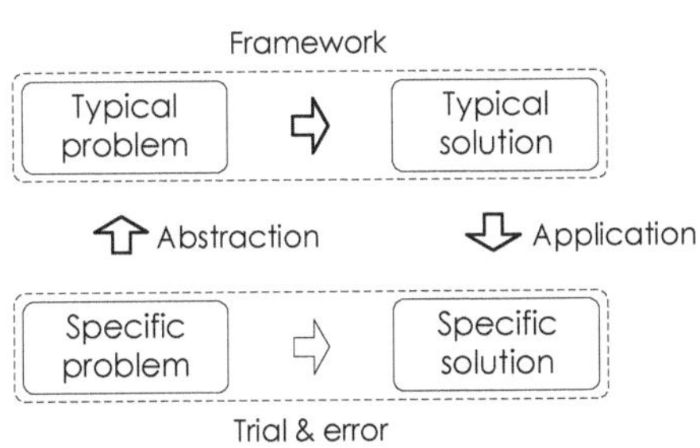

Frameworks vary in their generality. Some address more fundamental strategic issues, such as identifying target customers and developing a value proposition for these customers, whereas others deal with more specific issues such as product development, branding, pricing, promotion, and distribution. In this context, this book presents an overarching framework for identifying, analyzing, and solving marketing problems that incorporates both strategic and tactical aspects of marketing management. By offering an integrative view of the key marketing concepts and frameworks, this book offers a systematic and streamlined approach to marketing analysis, planning, and management.

ADDITIONAL READINGS

Drucker, Peter (1954), *The Practice of Management*. New York, NY: HarperCollins.

Kotler, Philip (1999), *Kotler on Marketing: How to Create, Win, and Dominate Markets*. New York, NY: Free Press.

CHAPTER TWO

MARKETING STRATEGY AND TACTICS

It is possible to fail in many ways,
while to succeed is possible only in one way.
—Aristotle, Greek philosopher

The success of an offering is defined by its ability to create market value. The particular way in which an offering creates value is reflected in its business model. The role of business models in marketing management and the two key components of a business model—strategy and tactics—are the focus of this chapter.

The Role of Business Models in Marketing Management

The term *business model* outlines the architecture of value creation by defining the entities, factors, and processes involved in delivering and capturing value in the marketplace. Because the business model defines the essence of the value-creation process, designing a viable and sustainable business model is the key to market success.

Business models vary in generality: Some are narrower, highlighting only the most important and unique aspect of the value-creation process, whereas others are broader, articulating all relevant aspects of value creation. The narrow business model describes fairly generic value-creation strategies related to a particular marketing activity, such as pricing, promotion, and distribution. For example, the *razors-and-blades model* describes a pricing strategy in which one offering is sold at a low price (or given away for free) to facilitate sales of a complementary offering; the *freemium model* describes a promotion strategy in which a basic version of the offering is given away for free to encourage users to upgrade to a paid (premium) version; the *bricks-and-clicks model* describes a distribution strategy that integrates both offline (bricks) and online (clicks) channels; and the *franchising model* describes the strategy of adopting (leasing) an already existing business model. Despite the intuitive appeal of these narrowly defined business models, their focus on a single aspect of the value-creation process limits their ability to serve as the basis for a more comprehensive analysis and planning of the company's business activities.

Accordingly, this book adopts the broader view of business models that encompass all relevant aspects of the value-creation process.

Three aspects of business models merit attention:

- Business models are **value focused**. The concept of value is central to any business model and can be associated with both monetary (e.g., profits) and nonmonetary (e.g., social welfare) outcomes. Thus, the focus on profits, albeit common, is a facet of the more general focus on value.
- Business models are **intangible**. They involve an idea, a subjective representation of reality, and as such they do not physically exist in the marketplace. Business models represent the way in which the organization conceptualizes the value-creation process.
- Business models are **universal**. There is a common misconception that only start-ups need a business model, whereas established companies can operate without one. This is incorrect: A viable business model is essential for the success of any organization, be it a start-up or an established market leader.

From a structural perspective, business models comprise two key components: strategy and tactics. *Strategy* identifies the market in which the company operates, defines the value exchanges among the key market entities, and outlines the ways in which an offering will create value for the relevant participants in the market exchange. *Tactics*, on the other hand, describe a set of activities—commonly referred to as the marketing mix—employed to execute a given strategy by designing, communicating, and delivering specific market offerings. Whereas strategy focuses on defining the target market and the value exchange among the relevant market entities, tactics describe the particular aspects of the offering that will ultimately create market value. The two components of the business model—strategy and tactics—are discussed in more detail in the following sections.

Marketing Strategy: Defining the Value Exchange

The term *strategy* comes from the Greek *stratēgia*—meaning "generalship"—used in reference to maneuvering troops into position before a battle. In marketing, strategy outlines the logic of how an organization creates market value. Marketing strategy involves two key components: the target market and the value proposition.

The Target Market

The market in which a company's offering competes is defined by five key factors: *customers* whose needs the company's offering aims to fulfill; the *company* managing the offering; *collaborators* working with the company on this offering; *competitors* with offerings that target the same customers; and the relevant economic, business, technological, sociocultural, regulatory, and physical *context* in which the company operates. These five factors are commonly referred to as the *Five Cs* and the resulting framework is referred to as the 5-C framework. The Five Cs are briefly outlined below.

- Target **customers** are the potential buyers, typically defined by the *needs* the company aims to fulfill with its offering(s). Target customers can be consumers (in the case of business-to-consumer markets) and/or businesses (in the case of business-to-business markets).

- **Company** is the organization managing the offering. In the case of organizations comprising a diverse portfolio of offerings, the term *company* refers to the particular business unit of the organization, often referred to as the *strategic business unit*, managing the offering. A company's ability to successfully compete in a given market is defined by its resources—core competencies and strategic assets—that enable the company to fulfill customer needs.

- **Collaborators** are entities that work with the company to create value for target customers. Common collaborators include suppliers, manufacturers, distributors (dealers, wholesalers, and retailers), research-and-development entities, service providers, external sales force, advertising agencies, and marketing research companies.

- **Competitors** are entities with offerings that target the same customers and aim to fulfill the same customer need. Competition is not limited to the industry in which the company operates. It also includes all entities that aim to fulfill the same customer need, regardless of whether they are in the same industry. Accordingly, a company's offering competes not only with offerings from entities operating in the same industry, but also with offerings (often referred to as substitutes) operating in different industries as long as they aim to fill the same customer need. To illustrate, Canon competes not only with manufacturers of digital cameras, such as Sony and Nikon, but also with manufacturers of camera-equipped mobile phones, such as Apple and Samsung. Starbucks competes not only with other coffee shops, but also with manufacturers of caffeinated energy drinks, such as Red Bull and Monster Energy.

- **Context** involves the relevant aspects of the environment in which the company operates. Six context factors are particularly relevant for the value-creation process: *economic* (e.g., economic growth, money supply, inflation, and interest rates); *business* (e.g., emergence of new business models, changes in the market structure, the balance of power, and information accessibility); *technological* (e.g., the diffusion of existing technologies and the development of new ones); *sociocultural* (e.g., demographic trends, value systems, and market-specific beliefs and behavior); *regulatory* (e.g., import/export tariffs, taxes, product specifications, pricing and advertising policies, and patent and trademark protection); and *physical* (e.g., natural resources, climate, and health conditions).

The choice of target customers is fundamental to defining the other aspects of the target market: It determines the scope of the competition, the range of potential collaborators, the core competencies and assets of the company that are necessary to fulfill the needs of target customers, and the specific context factors pertinent to the chosen target segment. Accordingly, different customer segments tend to be served by different competitors, require a different set of collaborators (different suppliers and distribution channels), are managed by different business units of the company, and operate in a different context. The fundamental role of target customers in defining the market is reflected in its central position in Figure 1.

Figure 1: Identifying the Market: The 5-C Framework

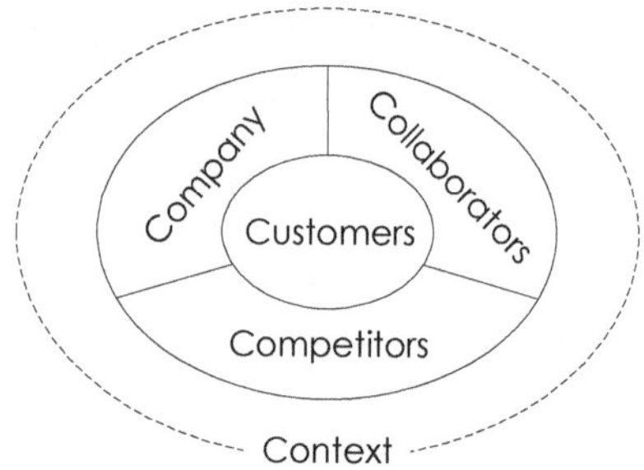

The central role of target customers further implies that a change in target customers is likely to lead to a change in all aspects of the relevant market. For example, a company's decision to target a new customer segment by moving upscale must not only account for the different needs of these customers, but also might involve collaboration with upscale retailers catering to these customers, require specialized core competencies and strategic assets that will enable the company to successfully serve these customers, face competition from a different set of competitors traditionally serving these customers, and be influenced in a different way by the economic, business, technological, sociocultural, regulatory, and physical context in which the company operates.

The Value Proposition

The value proposition defines the value that an offering aims to create for the relevant participants in the market. The key to designing a meaningful value proposition is to understand the value exchange defining the relationships among the different market entities. The key aspects of the value exchange and the offering's value proposition are discussed below.

Defining the Value Exchange: The 6-V Framework

The term *value exchange* refers to the value-based relationships among the different entities in a given market. Specifically, the target market is defined by four key entities—customers, the company, its collaborators, and its competitors—that operate in a given economic, business, technological, sociocultural, regulatory, and physical context. The interactions among these four entities define the six value relationships defining the 6-V framework illustrated in Figure 2.

Figure 2: Defining the Value Exchange: The 6-V Framework

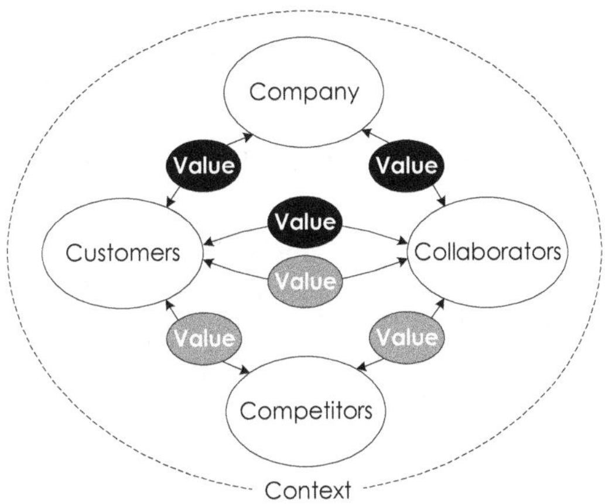

Each of the relationships shown in Figure 2 can be viewed as a process of giving (creating) and receiving (capturing) value. Thus, the relationship between the company and its customers is defined by the value the company creates for these customers as well as by the value created by these customers that is captured by the company. In the same vein, the relationship between the company and its collaborators is defined by the value the company creates for these collaborators as well as by the value generated by these collaborators that is captured by the company. Finally, the relationship between the company's customers and its collaborators is defined by the value these collaborators create for target customers as well as by the value generated by the target customers that is captured by collaborators.

To illustrate, consider the relationship between a manufacturer, a retailer, and their customers. The manufacturer (the company) partners with a retailer (the collaborator) to deliver products (value) to target customers. Customers receive value from the products (created by the manufacturer) they purchase as well as from the service (delivered by the retailer) involved in the buying process, for which they offer monetary compensation that is shared by both the manufacturer and the retailer. The retailer receives value from the customers in the form of margins (the differential between the buying and selling price) as well as value from the manufacturer in the form of various trade promotions. The manufacturer receives value from customers in the form of the price they pay for its products (net of retailer's margin) as well as from the retailer in the form of the various services that retailers perform on its behalf.

The three value relationships between the company, its customers, and its collaborators, however, reflect only the company side of the value exchange. No market exists without competitors that aim to create value for the same target customers, often working with the same collaborators as the company. The competitive aspect of the value exchange is symmetric to the company value exchange, and consists of three types of relationships: those between the company's target customers and its competitors, between the company's target customers and competitors' collaborators (some or all of whom could also be the company's collaborators), and between the competitors and their collaborators. Furthermore, as with the company value exchange, each of the competitive relationships is defined by the processes of creating and capturing value among market participants.

Developing the Optimal Value Proposition: The 3-V Principle

To succeed, an offering must create value for all entities involved in the market exchange—target customers, the company, and its collaborators. Accordingly, when developing market offerings, a company needs to consider three types of value: the value for target customers, the value for its collaborators, and the value for the company. Therefore, to evaluate the market potential of an offering a manager needs to answer three key questions:

- *Does the offering create superior value for target customers relative to the competitive offerings?*
- *Does the offering create superior value for the company's collaborators relative to the competitive offerings?*
- *Does the offering create superior value for the company relative to the other options the company must forgo in order to pursue this offering?*

The need for managing value for three different entities raises the question of whose value to prioritize. Surprisingly, many companies find it difficult to reach a consensus. Marketing departments are typically focused on creating customer value; finance departments and senior management are focused on creating company (shareholder) value; and the sales force is focused on creating value for collaborators, such as dealers, wholesalers, and retailers.

The "right" answer is that the company needs to balance the value among its stakeholders, customers, and collaborators to create an optimal value proposition. Here, the term *optimal value* means that the value is balanced across the three entities, whereby an offering creates value for its target customers and collaborators in a way that enables the company to achieve its strategic goals. Optimizing these three types of value—company, customer, and collaborator—is the key principle that drives market success (Figure 3).

Figure 3: The Optimal Value Proposition (OVP)

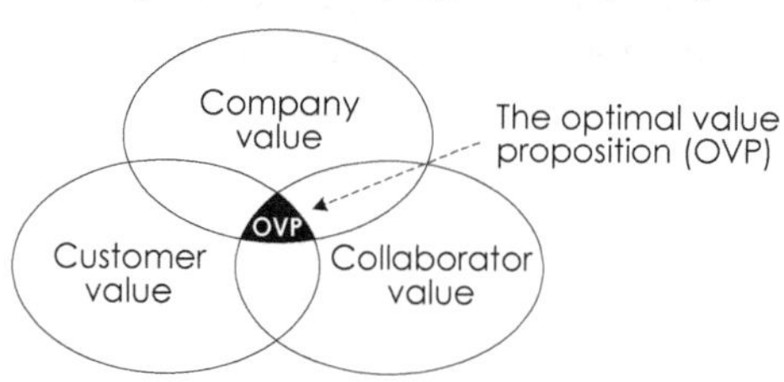

The 3-V Principle calls for creating superior value for target customers in a way that benefits the company and its collaborators. Thus, an offering's ability to create superior value for customers, collaborators, and the company is the ultimate criterion for achieving market success. Failure to create superior value for any one of the relevant market participants inevitably leads to an inefficient marketing exchange and market failure.

The value proposition reflects the company's expectation of the value that the offering will create for target customers. The value proposition is an ideal representation of the benefits that target customers will receive from the offering; the value proposition does not physically exist in the market. The value proposition is actualized through the specific offering(s) the company designs, communicates, and delivers to its target customers. The key aspects of developing an offering are discussed in the following section.

Marketing Tactics: Designing the Marketing Mix

The term *tactics* comes from the Greek *taktika*—meaning "arrangement"—used in reference to the deployment of troops during battle from their initial strategic position. In marketing, tactics refer to a set of specific activities, commonly referred to as the marketing mix, employed to execute a given strategy.

The strategy is an abstract depiction of the way in which an offering aims to create superior value for the relevant market entities. The company designs an offering that aims to fulfill customer needs, thereby creating value for these customers, the company, and its collaborators. Whereas the strategy defines the value exchange and the optimal value proposition, the tactics define the attributes of the actual offering that creates market value.

The Seven Tactics Defining the Marketing Mix

Tactics are defined by seven key elements, often referred to as the marketing mix: product, service, brand, price, incentives, communication, and distribution. The tactics represent the key marketing decisions that embody an offering's marketing strategy. The seven marketing mix factors can be summarized as follows:

- The **product** aspect of the offering reflects its key functional characteristics. Products typically change ownership during purchase; once created, they can be physically separated from the manufacturer and distributed to buyers via multiple channels.
- The **service** aspect of the offering also reflects its functional characteristics but, unlike products, services typically do not imply a change in ownership; instead, customers obtain the right to use the service for a period of time. Because they are simultaneously created and consumed, services are inseparable from the service provider and cannot be inventoried.

- The **brand** involves a set of unique marks and associations that identify the offering and create value beyond the product and service aspects of the offering.
- The **price** refers to the amount of money the company charges its customers and collaborators for the benefits provided by the offering.
- **Incentives** are tools used to selectively enhance the value of the offering for its customers, collaborators, and/or employees. Incentives may be monetary—such as volume discounts, price reductions, coupons, and rebates—and nonmonetary, such as premiums, contests, and rewards.
- **Communication** refers to the process of informing current and potential buyers about the specifics of the offering.
- **Distribution** defines the channel(s) through which the offering is delivered to customers.

The above seven factors are the means that managers have at their disposal to execute a company's strategy and deliver the optimal value proposition to the target market (Figure 4). These seven factors are referred to as the "7 Ts" because they define the 7 Tactical aspects of the offering; they are the 7 Tools that managers use to create value for target customers, the company, and collaborators.

Figure 4: The 7 Tactics Articulating the Offering's Value Proposition

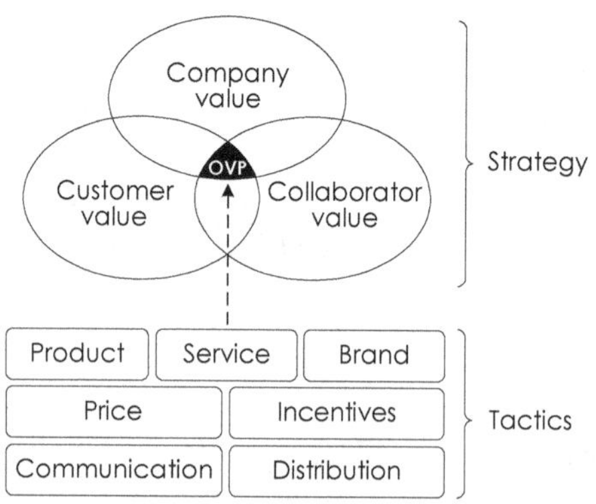

Consider the decisions that Starbucks had to make when launching its retail outlets. It had to decide on the product assortment it would carry and the specific attributes of each product (e.g., the type of coffee, roasting and brewing processes, and noncoffee ingredients), the type and level of service offered, the identity and the meaning of its brand, the set price for its offerings, the monetary and nonmonetary incentives offered to stimulate sales, ways to make customers aware of its offering, as well as store locations to make its products and services available to customers. Decisions based on these seven factors defined Starbucks' market offerings. Thus, the *product* aspect of Starbucks' offerings is the virtually endless variety of coffee drinks, complemented by a number of food items and noncoffee beverages. The *service* involves addressing customer inquiries and concerns and providing customers with an environment in which to consume the purchased foods and beverages.

The *brand* includes Starbucks' identity, such as its name and logo, as well as the associations that Starbucks' identity invokes in customers' minds. The *price* is the monetary amount that Starbucks charges customers for the offering. *Incentives* are the variety of promotional tools that aim to provide additional value for customers, such as Starbucks' loyalty program rewarding its frequent customers, coupons, and temporary price reductions. *Communication* is the Starbucks-specific information disseminated via different media channels, including advertising, social media, and public relations. Finally, *distribution* encompasses the channels though which Starbucks' offerings are delivered to its customers, including Starbucks-owned stores, franchised stores, as well as retail outlets licensed to carry Starbucks' products.

Tactics as a Process of Designing, Communicating, and Delivering Value

The seven marketing tactics—product, service, brand, price, incentives, communication, and distribution—are not a list of unrelated activities managers use to create value. On the contrary, the marketing tactics are interrelated because they represent different aspects of the same value-creation process. In this context, the relationships among the individual marketing tactics can be represented as a process of *designing, communicating,* and *delivering* value. Here, product, service, brand, price, and incentives compose the value-design aspect of the offering; communication captures the value-communication aspect; and distribution reflects the value-delivery aspect of the offering.

The last two aspects of the value-creation process—communication and distribution—are conceptually different from the first five aspects in that they serve as channels for the other marketing mix variables. Thus, communication can inform customers of the functionality of a product or service, share the meaning of its brand, publicize its price, apprise buyers of current incentives, and advise them about the availability of the offering. In the same vein, distribution can involve delivering a company's products through a series of retail outlets, delivering service through dedicated service centers, delivering its brand by offering customers a firsthand experience of the brand, delivering its price by collecting customer payments and processing refunds, and delivering communications through various channels, including television, radio, print, point of purchase, personal selling, and online. The view of the seven marketing tactics as a process of designing, communicating, and delivering value is illustrated in Figure 5.

Figure 5: Marketing Tactics as a Process of Designing, Communicating, and Delivering Value

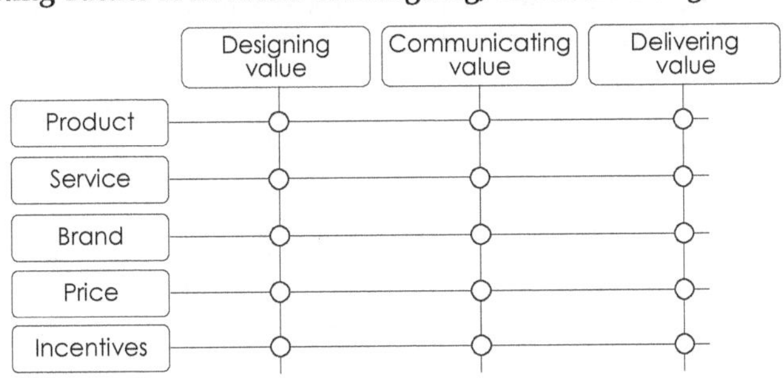

The different nodes in the value-creation process depicted in Figure 5 represent the specific decisions to be made in designing the offering's tactics. Thus, for each of the five factors—product, service, brand, price, and incentives—managers have to make three separate decisions concerning the design, communication, and delivery of the offering. In this context, product and service management calls for identifying the specific product/service attributes (value design), deciding how to communicate these attributes and the corresponding benefits to target customers (value communication), as well as determining how to deliver the product to these customers (value-delivery). In the same vein, brand management calls for identifying the key brand identity elements and associations and deciding how they will be communicated and delivered to target customers. Likewise, managing price involves not only deciding on the price level but also on how price will be communicated and money will be collected from customers and then delivered to the company. Finally, managing incentives involves defining the specific incentives, such as price discounts, coupons, and loyalty programs, as well as ways to communicate these incentives and deliver them to target customers.

Business Model Dynamics

The discussion so far has focused on the structure of a business model, its key components, and the relationships among them. An important question that has not been addressed concerns the dynamics of a business model—specifically, how a business model is created and when a business model is no longer viable and should be modified. These two issues—business model generation and business model reinvention—are discussed in more detail below.

Generating a Business Model

The development of a business model can follow different paths. The first approach—commonly referred to as *top-down* analysis—starts with a broader consideration of the target market and the relevant value exchange, which is then followed by designing a specific offering. In contrast, the second approach—commonly referred to as *bottom-up* analysis—starts with designing the specific aspects of the offering (e.g., developing a new technology or a new product utilizing an already existing technology), which is then followed by identifying the target market and developing an optimal value proposition. These two basic approaches to business model generation are illustrated in Figure 6 and discussed in more detail below.

Figure 6: Strategies for Generating a Business Model

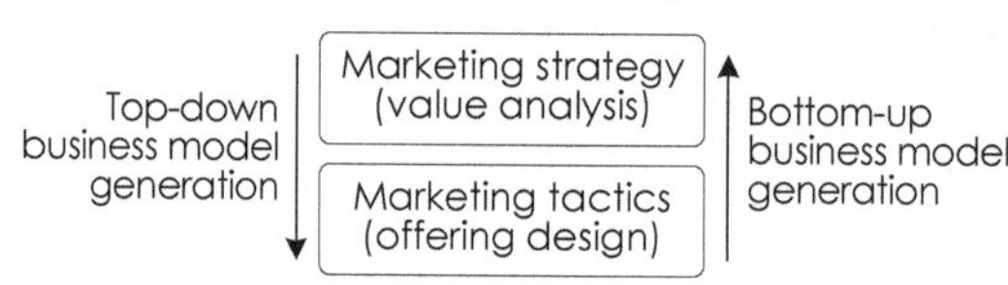

Top-Down Business Model Generation

The top-down approach typically stems from a strategic analysis aimed at identifying the target market and creating an optimal value proposition for the key players in that market. In this context, the top-down approach commonly follows one of two alternative paths: (1) by starting with a customer analysis that seeks to identify a need that has not been fulfilled by the competition or (2) by starting with an analysis of company resources that aims to identify core competencies and strategic assets that could potentially lead to a sustainable competitive advantage. Thus, in the former case, a manager can start by asking, *What are the key problems customers are facing?* and *Which of these problems can we solve better than the competition?* In contrast, in the latter case, a manager can start by asking, *What are our unique resources – strategic assets and core competencies – that we can deploy to create market value?* and *What unresolved customer needs can we can address with these resources?* Note that regardless of which question comes first, both questions – customer needs and company resources – need to be addressed in order for the company to develop a sustainable business model. The availability of unique resources without an unmet customer need or the existence of an unmet customer need that the company has no resources to fulfill is insufficient to create a viable business model.

To illustrate top-down business model generation, consider Apple's approach to developing new offerings. Most of Apple's products were designed to address a clearly identified customer need. Thus, the development of the iPod aimed to address the need for a user-friendly device that enables people to carry their favorite music with them. The development of the iPhone aimed to address the need for a user-friendly device that combines the functionality of several individual devices, such as a mobile phone, personal digital assistant, and a camera. The development of the MacBook Air aimed to address the need for a lightweight ultra-thin, fully functional computer. The development of Apple TV aimed to address the need for a device that connects users' digital libraries to their television set. Note that when developing offerings to address customer needs, Apple built on its existing strategic assets while at the same time developing new ones. One such newly created strategic asset was Apple's ecosystem, ensuring compatibility of the individual devices in a way that both complements and enhances the functionality of each product.

Other top-down business models include Procter & Gamble's Swiffer line of cleaning products, Herman Miller's Aeron chair, Dyson vacuum cleaners, and Tesla electric cars. Thus, Swiffer was designed to address the need for a cleaning tool that is more efficient than a mop, with less time spent cleaning. The Aeron chair was designed to address the need for an office chair that is both comfortable and stylish. The Dyson vacuum was designed to address the need for a vacuum that does not lose suction with usage. Tesla was designed to address the need for an environmentally friendly, high-end car that is fast, spacious, and stylish.

Bottom-Up Business Model Generation

The bottom-up approach starts with the design of a particular aspect of the offering and is followed by the identification of target customers whose unmet needs can be fulfilled by the offering. The development of a bottom-up business model typically stems from a deliberate research-and-development process, which leads to improvement of a particular product or product feature and/or the development of new ones. In this case, a manager can start by asking the question, *How can the current offering be improved?* without necessarily considering the business applications of such an improvement. The bottom-up business model can also stem from advancements in technology that are not company-specific and are available to all companies. In this case, a manager can start by asking, *How can the current product/service benefit from the new technological advancements?* and *How can the new technology be applied to develop new offerings?* In such cases, business model development begins with product development rather than with the desire to solve a particular customer need.

To illustrate, Groupon—the multibillion dollar deal-of-the-day company—started with an existing technological platform, a social media website designed to get groups of people together to solve problems. The real customer problem it ended up solving—finding deals—came later in 2008 when in the midst of the economic crisis many consumers were financially strained. Likewise, the development of the iPad was largely driven by the already existing technology used by the iPhone rather than conceived as an entirely new product to address an unmet consumer need. Note that in both cases, even though the products stemmed from a technological platform, their ultimate success was the result of bridging the technological solution with a relevant customer need.

In addition to being a result of a deliberate innovation process, new offerings can be the result of an accidental discovery. A classic example of a business model that began with an accidental invention is 3M's Post-it Notes, which stemmed from the discovery of less sticky glue. Likewise, Viagra—the multibillion dollar erectile dysfunction drug—was originally designed to treat high blood pressure and certain heart conditions. In the same vein, Rogaine (minoxidil)—the popular over-the-counter drug for treating hair loss—was originally used to treat high blood pressure. Other bottom-up, product-driven business models include Kellogg's corn flakes, Velcro, Teflon, and Super Glue. Note that, as with the offerings that are a result of a focused research-and-development process, the market success of offerings resulting from accidental discoveries is determined by their ability to create an optimal value proposition for target customers, the company, and its collaborators.

Updating the Business Model

Business models are not static; once developed they change throughout time. The most common factor necessitating business model change is that its value proposition for the relevant entities—the company, its customers and its collaborators—is no longer optimal. The suboptimal value proposition is often caused by changes in the underlying market. Specifically, the suboptimal value proposition can be traced to two types of factors: suboptimal business model design and changes in the target market.

- **Suboptimal business model design**. One of the key factors necessitating an update of the business model is the presence of flaws and inefficiencies in its design. In this case, a manager can start by asking the question, *How can the current business model be improved to maximize its market value?* For example, while seeking ways to make cars more affordable, Henry Ford perfected the concept of the conveyor-belt-driven assembly line that could produce a Model T in fewer than two hours, and at a price that made the car accessible for the average American.
- **Changes in the target market**. Another factor that calls for updating the business model involves changes in one or more of the five key market factors (the Five Cs): target customers, the company, collaborators, competitors, and context. To illustrate, in response to the change in the needs and preferences of its *customers*, many fast-food restaurants, including McDonald's, redefined their offerings to include healthier options. To respond to the new type of *competition* from online retailers, many traditional brick-and-mortar retailers, such as Macy's, Barnes & Noble, and Best Buy had to redefine their business models to become multichannel retailers. In the same vein, many manufacturers had to redefine their product lines to include lower tier offerings in response to their *collaborators'* (retailers) widespread adoption of private labels. The development or acquisition of *company* assets, such as patents and proprietary technologies, can call for redefining the underlying business models in many industries, such as pharmaceuticals, telecommunications, and aerospace. Finally, changes in context, such as the automobile, air travel, and the Internet, have disrupted the extant value-creation processes, forcing companies to redefine their business models.

To succeed, business models must evolve with the changes in the market in which they operate. A number of formerly successful business models have been made obsolete by the changing environment. Companies that fail to adapt their business models to reflect the new market reality tend to fade away, their businesses engulfed by companies with superior business models better equipped to create market value. According to Charles Darwin, *It is not the strongest of the species that survives, nor the most intelligent, but the one most responsive to change*. The key to market success is not only generating a viable business model but also the ability to adapt this model to changes in the marketplace.

SUMMARY

The goal of marketing is to create value by designing and managing successful exchanges. Consequently, a company's goal is to develop offerings that create value for all relevant participants in the exchange: customers, the company, and its collaborators.

Optimizing these three types of value—referred to as the 3-V principle—is the foundation for all marketing activities.

The essence of the value-creation process is reflected in the company's business model, which defines the key entities, factors, and processes involved in delivering and capturing market value. From a structural perspective, business models comprise two key components: strategy and tactics.

Strategy identifies the market in which the company operates, defines the value exchanges between the key market entities, and outlines the ways in which an offering will create value for the relevant participants in the market exchange. An offering's strategy is defined by two decisions: identifying target customers and developing a value proposition. The target market is defined by five factors (captured by the 5-C framework): customers, collaborators, company, competitors, and context. The value exchange is defined by the value relationships (captured by the 6-V framework) among the customers, collaborators, company, and competitors.

Tactics describe a set of activities—commonly referred to as the marketing mix—employed to execute a given strategy by designing, communicating, and delivering specific market offerings. Unlike the strategy, which focuses on defining the value exchange among the relevant market entities, tactics define the key aspects of the particular offering that will create market value. Tactics are defined by seven key components (captured by the 7-T framework): product, service, brand, price, incentives, communication, and distribution. Tactics can also be represented as a process of *designing*, *communicating*, and *delivering* value, where product, service, brand, price, and incentives compose the value-design aspect of the offering; communication captures the value-communication aspect; and distribution reflects the value-delivery aspect of the offering.

The development of a business model typically follows one of two paths. The first approach—commonly referred to as *top-down* analysis—starts with a broader consideration of the target market and the relevant value exchange, which is then followed by designing a specific offering. In contrast, the second approach—commonly referred to as *bottom-up* analysis—starts with designing the specific aspects of the offering (e.g., developing a new technology or a new product utilizing an already existing technology), which is then followed by identifying the target market and developing an optimal value proposition.

RELEVANT CONCEPTS

Marketing Myopia: Term coined by Theodore Levitt,[1] used to describe a company's exclusive focus on product development while losing sight of underlying customer needs. The myopic product focus blinds companies to the threat of cross-category competitors that can fulfill the same customer need. A classic example of marketing myopia is railroad companies whose decline was in part due to the fact that they considered themselves in the railroad business (rather than transportation) and consequently let other competitors—cars, buses, and airplanes—steal their customers.

Strategic Business Unit: An operating company unit with a discrete set of offerings sold to an identifiable group of customers, in competition with a well-defined set of competitors.

Substitutes: Products that fulfill a particular customer need traditionally addressed by products in a different category. For example, Gatorade can be viewed as a substitute for Coke. The term *substitute* is used primarily in the context of industry-based analysis (e.g., using the Five Forces framework discussed later in this chapter). Traditional marketing analysis defines competitors based on their ability to fulfill a particular customer need, rather than based on their belonging to the same industry and, accordingly, does not differentiate among cross-category competitors (substitutes) and within-category competitors.

RELEVANT FRAMEWORKS: THE 3-C FRAMEWORK

The 3-C framework was advanced by Japanese business strategist Kenichi Ohmae, who argued that to achieve a sustainable competitive advantage a manager should evaluate the following three key factors: company, customers, and competition. The 3-C framework suggests that managers need to evaluate the environment in which they operate: the strengths and weaknesses of their company, the needs of the consumer, and the strengths and weaknesses of their competitors. The 3-C framework is simple, intuitive, and easy to understand and use—factors that have contributed to its popularity.

Despite its popularity, the 3-C framework has important limitations that hinder its applicability to marketing analysis. A key limitation of the 3-C framework is that it overlooks two important factors: the company's *collaborators* and the *context* in which the company operates. The importance of collaborators in today's networked environment can hardly be overstated; virtually all business activities involve some form of collaboration to create the offering, communicate its benefits, and deliver it to consumers. In the same vein, the economic, business, technological, sociocultural, regulatory, and physical context in which the company operates plays a significant role in formulating its business model and can determine the ultimate success or failure of the company's offerings. Another important limitation of the 3-C framework is that it does not account for the interdependencies among its individual components, and specifically, the central role of customers in defining the other Cs.

RELEVANT FRAMEWORKS: THE 4-P FRAMEWORK

The 4-P framework identifies four key decisions that managers must make when designing and managing a given offering. These decisions involve (1) the functionality and design of the company's *product,* (2) the *price* at which the product is offered to target customers, (3) the company's *promotion* of the product to target customers, and (4) the retail outlets in which the company will *place* the product. The 4-P framework is intuitive and easy to remember—factors that have contributed to its popularity.

Despite its popularity, the 4-P framework has a number of important limitations. One significant limitation is the lack of separate *service* and *brand* components. Because it was developed more than a half-century ago with a focus on consumer packaged goods, the 4-P framework does not explicitly account for the service element of the offering—a key drawback in today's service-oriented business environment. Furthermore, the brand is not explicitly considered as a separate marketing mix variable and instead is viewed as part of a company's product and promotion decisions—a fact that is difficult to justify given the crucial role brands play in marketing.

Another limitation of the 4-P framework concerns the term *promotion*. Promotion is a broad concept that includes two distinct types of activities: (1) *incentives,* such as price promotions, coupons, and trade promotions, and (2) *communication,* such as advertising, public relations, social media, and personal selling. While considering these two activities jointly is common accounting practice, each has a distinct role in the value-creation process. Incentives aim to enhance the offering's value, whereas communication aims to inform customers about the offering without necessarily enhancing its value. Using a single term to refer to these distinct activities muddles the logic of the marketing analysis.

An additional shortcoming of the 4-P framework involves the term *place*. The increased complexity of delivering the company's offering to customers calls for a more accurate description of the entire process, not just the location where the company's offering is made available to buyers. Consequently, the term "place" is rarely used in contemporary marketing analysis and is most commonly substituted with the terms *distribution* and/or *channel.*

Some of the limitations of the 4-P framework can be overcome by describing the marketing mix in terms of seven, rather than four, factors—product, service, brand, price, incentives, communication, and distribution—as implied by the 7-T framework discussed earlier in this chapter. Note that the four "P"s can be easily mapped onto the seven "T"s, whereby the product, service, and brand comprise the first P; price is the second P, incentives and communication are the third P, and distribution is the fourth P (Figure 7). Thus, the 7-T framework can be viewed as a more refined version of the 4-P framework that offers a more accurate and actionable view of the key marketing mix variables.

Figure 7. The 7-T and the 4-P Frameworks

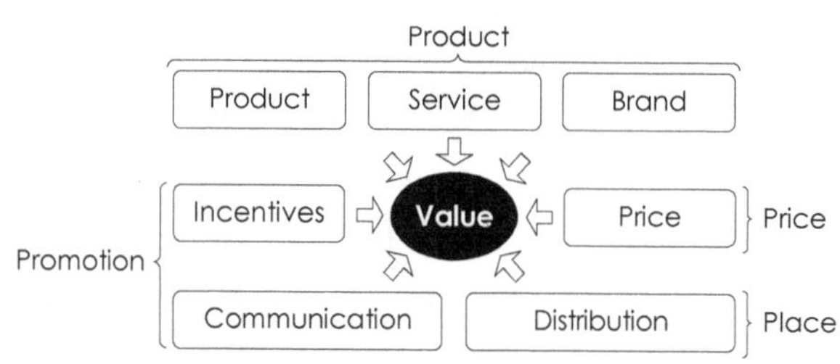

RELEVANT FRAMEWORKS: THE FIVE FORCES OF COMPETITION

The Five Forces framework, advanced by Michael Porter, is a conceptual approach for industry-based analysis of the competition. It is often used for strategic industry-level decisions, such as evaluating the viability of entering (or exiting) a particular industry. According to this framework, competitiveness within an industry is determined by evaluating the following five factors: bargaining power of suppliers, bargaining power of buyers, threat of new entrants, threat of substitutes, and rivalry among extant competitors (Figure 8). The joint impact of these five factors determines the competitive environment in which a firm operates and allows the firm to anticipate competitors' actions. In general, the greater the bargaining power of suppliers and buyers, the threat of new market entrants and substitute products, and the rivalry among existing competitors, the greater the overall industry competitiveness.

Figure 8. The Five Forces of Competition[2]

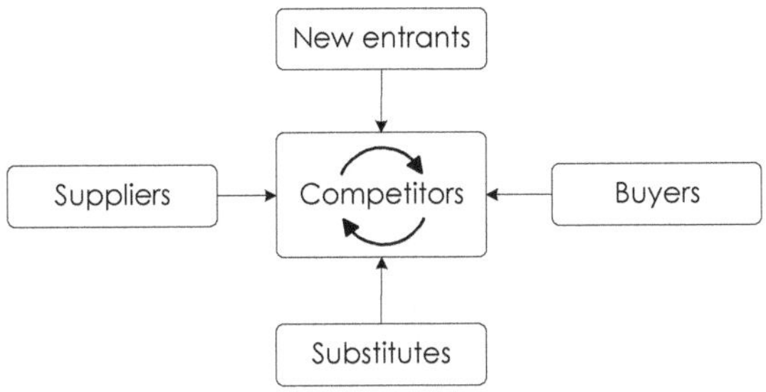

The Five Forces framework reflects an industry perspective whereby competitors are defined based on the industry in which they operate. According to this view, cross-industry competition occurs through substitute products that can fulfill the same customer need as the products of within-industry companies. Furthermore, as suggested by its name, the focus of the Five Forces framework is on the competition; the process of creating customer value is captured rather indirectly. In contrast, the marketing frameworks discussed in this chapter are explicitly focused on the value-creation process, whereby competitors are discussed from the standpoint of the value they create for the company's customers and collaborators. The customer-centric focus of value analysis discussed in this chapter is not industry-specific and does not depend on whether the company and its competitors operate within the bounds of the same industry. Because competitors are defined based on their ability to fulfill customer needs rather than on their industry affiliation, the concept of substitutes is not particularly meaningful here and is captured by the broader concept of competitive offerings.

ADDITIONAL READINGS

Aaker, David A. (2009), *Strategic Market Management* (9th ed.). New York, NY: John Wiley & Sons.

Johnson, Mark W., Clayton M. Christensen, and Henning Kagermann (2008), "Reinventing Your Business Model," *Harvard Business Review*, 86, (December).

Kotler, Philip and Kevin Lane Keller (2011), *Marketing Management* (14th ed.). Upper Saddle River, NJ: Prentice Hall.

Ohmae, Kenichi (1991), *The Mind of the Strategist: The Art of Japanese Business*. New York, NY: McGraw-Hill.

NOTES

[1] Levitt, Theodore (1975), "Marketing Myopia," *Harvard Business Review* (September–October), 2–14.

[2] Adapted from Porter, Michael E. (1979), "How Competitive Forces Shape Strategy," *Harvard Business Review*, 57 (March–April), 137–145.

CHAPTER THREE

THE MARKETING PLAN

Vision without action is a daydream. Action without vision is a nightmare.

—Japanese proverb

The increasing complexity of a company's marketing activities calls for the use of a systematic approach to marketing management. Such a systematic approach, which is outlined in this chapter, delineates the logic of strategic analysis and planning by advancing a comprehensive yet streamlined framework for developing actionable marketing plans.

The G-STIC Framework for Market Planning

An offering's marketing plan delineates the specific activities by which an offering creates market value. The core of the marketing plan is the offering's business model, which articulates the strategy and tactics of the offering to outline the logic of the value-creation process and define the specifics of the market offering. In this context, an offering's marketing plan can be defined by five key activities: setting a *goal*, developing a *strategy*, designing the *tactics*, defining an *implementation* plan, and identifying a set of *control* metrics to measure the success of the proposed action. These five activities comprise the G-STIC (Goal-Strategy-Tactics-Implementation-Control) framework, which is the cornerstone of market planning and analysis (Figure 1).

Figure 1: The G-STIC Framework for Market Planning and Analysis

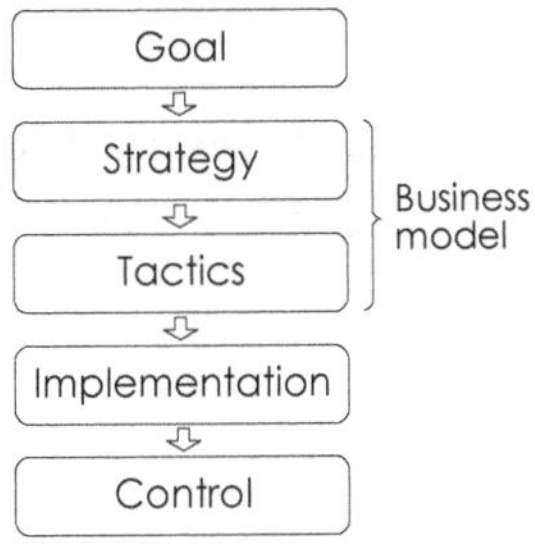

The individual components of the G-STIC framework are outlined in more detail below.

- The **goal** identifies the ultimate criterion for success that guides all company marketing activities. Setting a goal involves two decisions: identifying the *focus* of the company's actions and defining the specific quantitative and temporal performance *benchmarks* to be achieved.

- The **strategy** outlines the logic of the company's value-creation model. Defining the strategy involves two decisions: identifying the *target market* and developing the offering's *value proposition*. Identifying the target market involves identifying five key factors (the Five Cs): customers whose needs the company's offering aims to fulfill, the company managing the offering, collaborators working with the company on this offering, competitors with offerings that target the same customers, and the relevant context in which the company operates. The *value proposition,* on the other hand, defines the value that an offering aims to create for the relevant participants in the market—target customers, the company, and its collaborators. The development of a value proposition also involves the development of a *positioning* that singles out the most important aspect(s) of the offering's value proposition to create a distinct image of the offering in customers' minds.

- The **tactics** outline a set of specific activities employed to execute a given strategy. The tactics define the key aspects of the company's offering (often referred to as the marketing mix): product, service, brand, price, incentives, communication, and distribution. These seven tactics are the means that managers have at their disposal to execute a company's strategy and create the optimal value proposition for the target market.

- The **implementation** outlines the logistics of executing the company's strategy and tactics. Defining the implementation involves three key components: defining the business infrastructure, designing business processes, and setting the implementation schedule.

- The **control** defines criteria for evaluating the company's goal progress. Control involves two key processes: evaluating the company's progress toward its goal and analyzing the changes in the environment in which the company operates.

The key components of the marketing plan and the main decisions underlying each individual component are summarized in Figure 2 and discussed in more detail in the following sections.

Figure 2. The G-STIC Action-Planning Flowchart

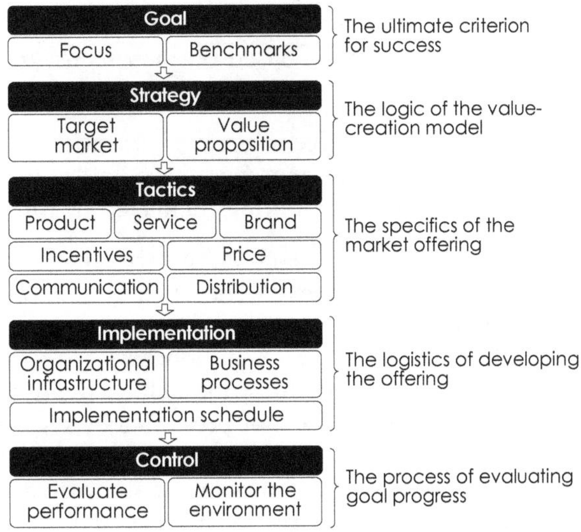

The G-STIC framework offers an intuitive approach to streamlining a company's activities into a logical sequence that can produce the desired market outcome. Note that even though the G-STIC framework implies a particular action sequence, starting with the definition of the company's goal and concluding with identifying controls for measuring performance, the process of marketing planning is an iterative activity. In this context, the G-STIC framework has a dual function: it describes the key elements of the iterative process of market planning (G↔S↔T↔I↔C) and, at the same time, it describes the outcome of the planning process, which is typically presented as a linear sequence of distinct marketing activities (G→S→T→I→C).

The key aspects of the action plan are discussed in more detail in the following sections. Because the offering's strategy and tactics were discussed in depth in the previous chapter, the focus here is on the remaining three aspects: goal, implementation, and control.

Setting a Goal

The action plan is formulated to achieve a particular goal; it starts with defining a goal and outlines a course of action that will enable the company to achieve this goal. The goal guides all the company's marketing activities; without a well-defined goal, an organization cannot design an effective marketing strategy or evaluate the success of its current activities. Setting a goal involves two decisions: identifying the focus of the company's actions and defining the specific performance benchmarks to be achieved.

Goal Focus

The focus identifies the key criterion for a company's success; it is the metric describing the desired outcome. Based on their focus, two types of goals can be distinguished:

- **Monetary goals** involve monetary outcomes and typically focus on maximizing net income, earnings per share, and return on investment. Monetary goals are common for offerings managed by for-profit companies.
- **Strategic goals** involve nonmonetary outcomes that are of strategic importance to the company. Nonmonetary goals are common for nonprofit organizations, which aim to achieve nonmonetary outcomes, such as promoting social welfare. Nonmonetary goals are also common in for-profit organizations by facilitating the achievement of other profit-related goals. Thus, an offering that is not profitable by itself might benefit the company by facilitating the sales of other, profit-generating offerings. An offering might also benefit the company's bottom line by enhancing the corporate culture, by boosting employee morale, and by facilitating talent recruitment and retention.

Note that monetary goals and strategic goals are not mutually exclusive: A company might aim to achieve certain strategic goals with an otherwise profitable offering, and a strategically important offering might contribute to the company's bottom line. One could argue that long-term financial planning must always include a strategic component in addition to setting monetary goals, and long-term strategic planning must always include a financial component that articulates how achieving a particular strategic goal will translate into a financial outcome.

Performance Benchmarks

Performance benchmarks define the ultimate criteria for success. The two types of performance benchmarks—quantitative and temporal—are discussed in more detail below.

- **Quantitative benchmarks** define the specific milestones to be achieved by the company with respect to its focal goal. For example, goals such as "increase market share by 2%," "increase retention rates by 12%," and "improve the effectiveness of marketing expenditures by 15%" include benchmarks that quantify the set goal. Quantitative benchmarks can be expressed in either relative terms (e.g., increase market share by 20%) or absolute terms (e.g., achieve annual sales of one million units).
- **Temporal benchmarks** identify the time frame for achieving a particular milestone. Setting a timeline for achieving a goal is a key strategic decision, because the strategy adopted to implement these goals is often contingent on the time horizon. The goal of maximizing next-quarter profitability will likely require a different strategy and tactics than the goal of maximizing long-term profitability.

To illustrate, a company's goal might involve generating net income (focus) of $1B (quantitative benchmark) by the end of the fourth quarter (temporal benchmark).

Market Objectives

Based on their focus, goals vary in their level of generality. Some goals reflect outcomes that are more fundamental than others. Therefore, a company's goals can be represented as a hierarchy headed by a company's ultimate goal, which is implemented through a set of more specific goals, referred to as market objectives.

Unlike the ultimate goal, which is typically defined in terms of a company-focused outcome, market objectives delineate specific changes in the behavior of the relevant market factors—customers, the company, collaborators, competitors, and context—that will enable the company to achieve its ultimate goal. The different types of market objectives are outlined below.

- **Customer objectives** aim to elicit changes in the behavior of target customers (e.g., increasing purchase frequency, switching from a competitive product, or making a first-time purchase in a product category) that will enable the company to achieve its ultimate goal. To illustrate, the company goal of increasing net revenues can be associated with the more specific objective of increasing the frequency with which its customers repurchase the offering. Because the customers are the ultimate source of a company's revenues and profits, a company's ultimate goal typically involves a customer-focused behavioral objective.

- **Collaborator objectives** aim to elicit changes in the behavior of the company's collaborators, such as providing greater promotional support, better pricing terms, greater systems integration, and extended distribution coverage. To illustrate, the company goal of increasing net revenues can be associated with the more specific collaborator objective of increasing the shelf space for the offering in distribution channels.

- **Company (internal) objectives** aim to elicit changes in the company's own actions, such as improving product and service quality, reducing the cost of goods sold, improving the effectiveness of the company's marketing actions, and streamlining research-and-development costs.

- **Competitive objectives** aim to change the behavior of the company's competitors. Such actions might involve creating barriers to entry, securing proprietary access to scarce resources, and circumventing a price war.

- **Context objectives** are less common and usually implemented by larger companies that have the resources to implement changes in the economic, business, technological, sociocultural, regulatory, and/or physical context in which the company operates. For example, a company might lobby the government to adopt regulations that will favorably affect the company by offering tax benefits, offering subsidies, and imposing import duties on competitors' products.

Defining market objectives is important because without a change in the behavior of the relevant market entities, the company's ultimate goal is unlikely to be achieved. Indeed, if there is no change in any of the five market factors (the Five Cs), the company is unlikely to make progress toward its goals. To illustrate, a company's ultimate goal of increasing net income by $1B by the end of the fourth quarter can involve different objectives. A customer-specific objective might involve increasing market share by 10% by the end of the fourth quarter. A collaborator-related objective might involve securing 45% of the distribution outlets by the end of the fourth quarter. An internal objective might involve lowering the cost of goods sold by 25% by the end of the fourth quarter. In this context, market objectives help the company articulate the course of action aimed at achieving its ultimate goal.

Defining the Implementation

The implementation component of market planning delineates the logistics of executing the offering's strategy and tactics. Implementation involves three key components: defining the business infrastructure, designing business processes, and setting the implementation schedule.

Business Infrastructure

The business infrastructure reflects the organizational structure and the relationship among relevant entities involved in creating and managing the offering. For example, a company can form the business unit managing the offering by organizing employees based on their function (e.g., research and development, manufacturing, marketing, accounting/finance, and human resources). Alternatively, a company might organize employees based on the type of product or market involved, such that each division is responsible for a certain product or market and is represented by different functions. Finally, a company might use a matrix approach by combining the functional and divisional approaches in a way that preserves the functional structure while simultaneously creating specialized teams responsible for a particular product or market

Business Processes

The business processes depict the specific actions needed to implement an offering's strategy and tactics. These processes involve managing the flow of information, goods, services, and money. In this context, there are three common types of implementation processes: market planning, resource management, and marketing mix management.

- **Market planning** includes activities involved in the development of the marketing plan. These processes involve gathering market intelligence, defining the company's goal(s), developing the strategy and tactics for achieving that goal, defining the implementation plan, and identifying a set of control measures to monitor goal progress.
- **Resource management** involves activities focused on acquiring and managing human resources (e.g., recruiting, evaluation, compensation, and professional development), functional resources (e.g., manufacturing capacity), and financial resources required for the implementation of a given offering.
- **Marketing mix management** involves activities focused on managing the marketing tactics. This includes designing (e.g., identifying the key attributes), manufacturing (e.g., procurement, inbound logistics, and production), and executing (e.g., installation, support, and repair activities) the product and service aspects of the offering; designing (e.g., determining brand identity) and managing an offering's brand, price setting (e.g., setting retail prices and wholesale price schedules) and price management (e.g., modifying existing prices) activities; designing and managing (e.g., processing coupons and implementing price discounts) an offering's incentives; designing (e.g., identifying the message, media, and the creative solution) and managing (e.g., producing the advertisement and placing it in the appropriate media channel) an offering's communications; and designing (e.g., determining the optimal channel structure) and managing (e.g., warehousing, order fulfillment, transportation) an offering's distribution system.

Implementation Schedule

The process of setting an implementation schedule involves deciding on the timing and the optimal sequence in which individual tasks should be performed to ensure effective and cost-efficient completion of the project. The implementation schedule can also identify the key personnel involved in managing individual tasks and delineate the time frame for beginning and completing these tasks.

Identifying Controls

The uncertainty and dynamics associated with most business markets necessitate that companies continuously evaluate their performance and monitor changes in the environment. Accordingly, marketing controls serve two key functions: to evaluate the company's progress toward its goal and analyze the changes in the environment in which the company operates.

Performance Evaluation

Performance evaluation involves evaluating the outcomes of the company's actions vis-à-vis its goals. Performance can be evaluated on a variety of metrics, such as net income, market share, and unit sales. Performance evaluation can lead to one of two outcomes: either a company is making adequate goal progress or there is a discrepancy (performance gap) between the desired and the actual performance. In cases when performance evaluation reveals a gap, the existing action plan needs to be modified to put the company back on track toward achieving its goal. The key principle in modifying a company's action plan is that the changes should be directly linked to the cause of the performance gap.

Environmental Analysis

Environmental analysis involves monitoring the environment in which the company operates to ensure that the company's action plan remains optimal, and adjusting the action plan as necessary to take advantage of new opportunities (e.g., favorable government regulations, a decrease in competition, or an increase in consumer demand) and counteract potential threats (e.g., unfavorable government regulations, an increase in competition, or a decline in consumer demand). Once the key opportunities and threats have been identified, the next step involves modifying the current action plan to take advantage of the opportunities and counteract the impact of threats. The basic principle in modifying the action plan is that the changes should directly address the identified opportunities and threats.

Writing a Marketing Plan

The marketing plan can be formalized as a written document that effectively communicates the proposed course of action to relevant stakeholders: company employees, collaborators, shareholders, and investors. Writing a marketing plan is different from market planning. Market planning is the process of identifying a goal and developing a course of action to achieve this goal. The marketing plan is the tangible outcome of a company's market planning process that documents an already identified goal and the decided-on course of action.

Most marketing plans follow a similar structure: They start with an executive summary, followed by a situation analysis; they then set a goal, formulate a value-creation strategy, delineate the tactical aspects of the offering, articulate a plan to implement the offering's tactics, define a set of control measures to monitor the offering's progress toward its goals, and conclude with a set of relevant exhibits. The key components of the marketing plan are illustrated in Figure 3 and summarized below.

Figure 3. The Marketing Plan

- The **executive summary** is the "elevator pitch" for the marketing plan—a streamlined and succinct overview of the company's goal and the proposed course of action. The typical executive summary is one or two pages long, outlining the key problem faced by the company (e.g., a market opportunity/threat or a performance gap) and the proposed action plan.

- The **situation analysis** section of the marketing plan aims to provide an overall evaluation of the company and the environment in which it operates, as well as identify the markets in which it will compete. Accordingly, the situation analysis involves two sections: (1) the company overview, which outlines the company's strategic goals and current progress toward these goals, its core competencies and strategic assets, and its portfolio of offerings, and (2) the market overview, which outlines markets in which the company operates and/or could potentially target.

- The **G-STIC** section is the core of the marketing plan. It identifies (1) the *goal* the company aims to achieve, (2) the offering's *strategy*, which defines its target market and value proposition, (3) the offering's *tactics* which define the product, service, brand, price, incentives, communication, and distribution aspects of the offering, (4) the implementation aspects of executing an offering's strategy and tactics, and (5) control procedures employed in evaluating the company's performance and analyzing the environment in which it operates.

- **Exhibits** help streamline the logic of the marketing plan by separating the less important and/or more technical aspects of the plan into a distinct section in the form of tables, charts, and appendices.

The ultimate goal of the marketing plan is to guide a company's actions. Accordingly, the core of the marketing plan is defined by the key elements of the G-STIC framework delineating the company's goal and the proposed course of action. The other elements of the marketing plan—the executive summary, situation analysis, and exhibits—aim to facilitate an understanding of the logic underlying the plan and provide specifics for the proposed course of action.

In addition to developing an overall marketing plan, companies often develop more specialized plans. Such plans include a product development plan, service management plan, brand management plan, sales plan, promotions plan, and communication plan. Some of these plans can, in turn, encompass even more specific plans. For example, a company's communication plan often comprises a series of activity-specific plans, such as an advertising plan, public relations plan, Internet plan, and social media plan. The ultimate success of each of these individual plans depends on the degree to which they are aligned with the overall marketing plan.

Updating the Marketing Plan

Once developed, marketing plans need updating in order to remain relevant. The dynamic nature of marketing plans is ingrained in the structure of the G-STIC framework, whereby the control aspect of planning (the "C" in the G-STIC framework) is explicitly designed to provide the company with feedback on the effectiveness of its actions and the relevant changes in the target market.

There are two common reasons to consider updating the marketing plan: (1) the presence of a performance gap reflecting a discrepancy between the company's expected and desired performance and (2) changes in the target market.

- **Performance gaps** involve a discrepancy between a company's desired and actual performance on a key metric, such as net income, profit margins, and sales revenues. Performance gaps typically stem from three main sources: (1) inaccurate information and/or assumptions about the target market, including unforeseen market changes, (2) logic flaws in the marketing plan, and (3) implementation errors, which involve poor execution of a viable marketing plan.

  Inaccurate information/assumptions. When developing the marketing plan, managers rarely have all the necessary information at their fingertips. It is often the case that, despite the voluminous amount of available information, certain strategically important pieces of information are not readily available (e.g., information about competitors' strategies, technological developments, and forthcoming government regulations). As a result, managers must fill in the information gaps by making certain assumptions. Because assumptions reflect uncertainty, updating the plan to reduce the uncertainty can increase its effectiveness.

  Logic flaws. Another common source of performance gaps is the presence of logic flaws in the design of the marketing plan. For example, the proposed strategy might be inconsistent with the set goal, whereby an otherwise viable strategy might not produce desired results. In the same vein, the offering's tactics might be inconsistent with the desired strategy, whereby product attributes might not create value for target customers, the price might be too high, and/or communication and distribution channels might be inadequate.

Implementation errors. Performance gaps can also stem from implementation errors, which involve poor execution of an otherwise viable marketing plan. This type of error is due to the fact that managers do not adhere to the actions prescribed by the marketing plan (e.g., because they are unfamiliar with the plan), because their intuition based (erroneously) on prior experience contradicts the proposed course of action, or because of lack of discipline (often imbued in a company's culture) to systematically implement the agreed-on marketing plan.

- **Changes in the target market** involve changes in one or more of the Five Cs: (1) changes in target customers, such as changes in customer demographics, buying power, needs, and preferences; (2) changes in the competitive environment, such as a new competitive entry, price cuts, launch of an aggressive advertising campaign, and/or expanded distribution; (3) changes in the collaborator environment, such as a threat of backward integration from the distribution channel, increased trade margins, and consolidation among retailers; (4) changes in the company, such as the loss of strategic assets and competencies; and (5) changes in the market context, such as an economic recession, the development of a new technology, and new legal regulations.

Updating a marketing plan involves modifying the company's current course of action and might involve the need to reevaluate the current goal; redesign the existing strategy (e.g., identify new target markets, and/or modify the overall value proposition of the offering for customers, company, and/or collaborators); change the tactics (e.g., improve the product, enhance the service, reposition the brand, modify the price, introduce new incentives, streamline communication, and introduce new channels of distribution); improve the infrastructure, processes, and/or schedules underlying implementation; and/or develop alternative controls (e.g., use more accurate performance metrics). The key principle in updating the action plan is that the changes in the plan should address the inefficiencies in the existing marketing plan and/or changes in the market environment.

SUMMARY

On the most general level, marketing planning can be viewed as a process defined by five main steps: setting a *goal*, developing the *strategy*, designing the *tactics*, defining the *implementation* plan, and identifying the *control* metrics to measure progress toward the set goal. These five steps comprise the G-STIC framework, which is the backbone of developing successful action plans. The core of a company's marketing plan is its business model, which encompasses its strategy and tactics.

The *goal* identifies the ultimate criterion for success that guides all the company's marketing activities. Setting a goal involves two decisions: identifying the *focus* of the company's actions and defining the specific quantitative and temporal performance *benchmarks* to be achieved. A company's goals can be represented as a hierarchy headed by a company's ultimate goal, which is implemented through a set of more specific goals, referred to as market objectives, which delineate specific changes in the behavior of the relevant market factors—customers, the company, collaborators, competitors, and context—that will enable the company to achieve its ultimate goal.

The *strategy* outlines the logic of the company's value-creation model. Defining the strategy involves two decisions: identifying the *target market* and developing the offering's *value proposition*. Identifying the target market involves identifying five key factors (the Five Cs): customers, collaborators, company, competitors, and context. The *value proposition* defines the value that an offering aims to create for the relevant participants in the market—target customers, the company, and its collaborators.

The *tactics* outline a set of specific activities employed to execute a given strategy. The tactics define the key aspects of the company's offering (the seven Ts): product, service, brand, price, incentives, communication, and distribution. These seven tactics are the means that managers have at their disposal to execute a company's strategy and create the optimal value proposition for the target market.

The *implementation* outlines the logistics of executing the company's strategy and tactics, and involves three key components: defining the business infrastructure, designing business processes, and setting the implementation schedule.

The *control* defines criteria for evaluating the company's goal progress and involves two key processes: evaluating the company's progress toward its goal and analyzing the changes in the environment in which the company operates.

In addition to structuring the managerial decision process, the G-STIC framework also serves as the basis for *writing a marketing plan*. The marketing plan identifies a specific goal and outlines a course of action to achieve this goal. The primary purpose of a marketing plan is to effectively communicate the company's goal and the desired course of action to relevant stakeholders. The marketing plan typically comprises four key components: (1) an *executive summary* that outlines the highlights of the marketing plan, (2) a *situation analysis* that examines the environment in which the company operates and identifies the target market(s) in which it competes, (3) a *G-STIC action plan* that outlines the proposed course of action to create value for its target customers, and (4) *exhibits* that provide additional information about specific aspects of the marketing plan.

ADDITIONAL READINGS

Chernev, Alexander (2011), *The Marketing Plan Handbook* (3rd ed.). Chicago, IL: Cerebellum Press.

Kotler, Philip and Kevin Lane Keller (2011), *Marketing Management* (14th ed.). Upper Saddle River, NJ: Prentice Hall.

Lehmann, Donald R. and Russell S. Winer (2007), *Analysis for Marketing Planning* (7th ed.). Boston, MA: McGraw-Hill/Irvin.

PART TWO

MARKETING STRATEGY

INTRODUCTION

All men can see the tactics whereby I conquer,
but what none can see is the strategy out of which victory is evolved.

—Sun Tzu, Chinese military strategist

An offering's strategy articulates the logic of the value-creation process. Specifically, strategy identifies the market in which the company operates, defines the value exchanges among the key market entities, and outlines the ways in which the offering creates market value. Accordingly, the key aspects of strategic analysis outlined in this book include (1) identifying target customers, (2) creating customer value, (3) creating company value, and (4) creating collaborator value. These four aspects of the value-creation process are briefly summarized below and discussed in greater detail in the following four chapters.

- **Identifying target customers** is the stepping stone for the development of a marketing strategy. Identifying target customers involves grouping customers into segments, selecting which segments to target, and identifying actionable strategies to reach the selected target segments. The key aspects of identifying target customers are discussed in Chapter 4.
- **Creating customer value** involves developing a value proposition that articulates the benefits and costs of the company's offering for target customers. The value proposition is augmented by a positioning that formulates the primary reason for customers to choose the offering. The process of developing a value proposition and positioning is discussed in Chapter 5.
- **Creating company value** involves optimizing the value exchange in a way that enables the company to reach its goal and create value for its stakeholders. The key approaches to creating company value are discussed in Chapter 6.
- **Creating collaborator value** involves identifying entities that will work with the company to create market value for target customers and optimizing the offering in a way that enables collaborators to reach their goals. The key approaches to creating collaborator value are the focus of Chapter 7.

These four aspects of the value-creation process stem from the key marketing principle: that the success of an offering is determined by its ability to create superior value for its target customers in a way that benefits the company and its collaborators. Accordingly, the following chapters take the perspective of each of the three market entities—target customers, the company, and its collaborators—to identify strategies for identifying a viable target market and developing an optimal value proposition for that market.

CHAPTER FOUR

IDENTIFYING TARGET CUSTOMERS: SEGMENTATION AND TARGETING ANALYSIS

The purpose of a company is to create a customer.

—Peter Drucker, founder of modern management theory

Understanding customer needs and identifying market opportunities is the starting point in formulating a company's marketing strategy. The cornerstone of developing a viable strategy is deciding which customers to target and how to reach those customers in an effective and cost-efficient manner. The process of identifying target customers is the focus of this chapter.

The Concept of Targeting

Targeting is the process of identifying customers for whom the company will optimize its offering. The logic of identifying target customers and the strategic and tactical aspects of this process are discussed in more detail below.

The Logic of Targeting

Imagine a company operating in a market in which there are two customers with different needs. Which of these customers should the company serve? The intuitive answer is—both. Indeed, all else being equal, the greater the customer base, the greater the company's profit potential. Should the company choose to target both customers it has two options to develop an offering. One approach is to develop the same offering for both customers (one-for-all strategy), and the other is to develop different offerings based on the needs of each one (one-for-each strategy).

The *one-for-all strategy* of developing the same offering for both customers might not be effective for customers with different needs because the offering will end up not creating value for at least one (and perhaps even both). For example, if the customers vary in terms of their price sensitivity, developing either a high-quality, high-priced offering or a low-priced, low-quality offering will inevitably fail to fulfill the needs of one of these customers because one will find the offering too expensive and the other will deem it of insufficient quality. Furthermore, developing a mid-priced, mid-quality offering will likely fail to fulfill the needs of both because the offering will still be too expensive for one of the customers and of insufficient quality for the other.

The *one-for-each* strategy of developing a separate offering for each customer might not be effective because the company might not have the resources to develop offerings that meet the needs of both customers. For example, the company might not have the scale of operations to develop a low-priced offering for the price-sensitive customer and the technological know-how to develop a high-performance offering for the quality-focused consumer. Furthermore, even if the company has resources to develop separate offerings, both customers might not be able to create value for the company. For example, the customer for the high-quality product might not have the financial resources to afford the company's offering, or might have needs that the company cannot fulfill without incurring costs that exceed the benefits received from serving this customer.

As a general rule, developing a separate offering for each individual customer is beneficial when the incremental value created by customizing the offering outweighs the costs of developing the offering. To illustrate, when the cost of customization is relatively high (as with durable goods, such as cars, household appliances, and electronic equipment), companies tend to develop offerings that serve relatively large groups of customers, whereas in industries where the cost of customization is relatively low (as in the case of delivering online information), offerings can be tailored for smaller groups of customers.

Individual and Segment-Based Targeting

The discussion so far has focused on a scenario in which a company operates in a market comprised of two customers. While such markets do exist, especially in a business-to-business context, they are the exception rather than the rule: Most markets comprise thousands and often millions of buyers. This scenario is different not only in the number of customers but also in that some customers are likely to have fairly similar needs that could be fulfilled by the same offering. In such cases, rather than developing individual offerings for each customer, a company might consider developing offerings for groups of customers—commonly referred to as *customer segments*—that share similar characteristics.

The concept of segment-based targeting is illustrated in Figure 1. Here, individual customers are represented by circles, which are shaded to reflect the differences in their underlying needs. For simplicity, consider a scenario in which customers' needs vary on a single factor that has three levels, represented by circles with different shades. For example, dark circles might represent quality-focused customers (Segment A), white circles might represent price-sensitive customers (Segment B), and gray circles might represent customers who are looking for a compromise between price and quality (Segment C). In this context, Figure 1 depicts a scenario in which a company targets quality-oriented customers by developing high-end offerings to fulfill the needs of these customers, while ignoring the other two customer segments.

Figure 1. Segment-Based Targeting

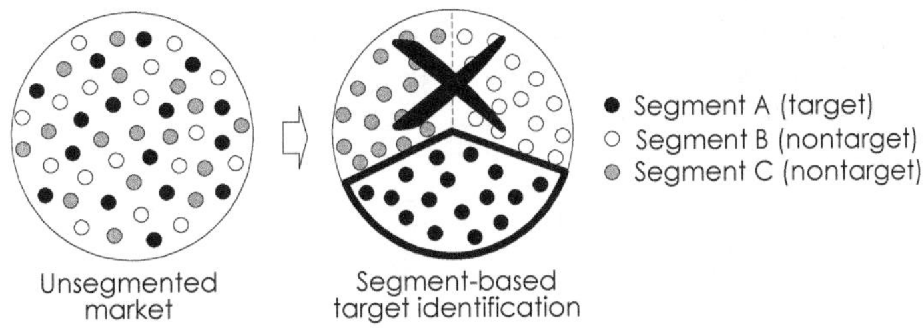

Grouping customers into segments enables a company to improve the cost efficiency of its marketing activities by not having to customize the offering for individual customers, usually with minimal sacrifice to the effectiveness of the offering. From a conceptual standpoint, the process of identifying target customers is virtually identical, be it individual customers or customer segments. The key difference is that in addition to identifying the needs of the target customers, segment-based targeting involves grouping customers with similar needs into segments—a process commonly referred to as segmentation.

Strategic and Tactical Targeting

Customers vary in two main aspects: (1) their needs and resources and (2) their readily observable characteristics. The first aspect captures *value-based factors* that reflect customer's needs and their willingness and ability to pay for the company's offerings. Unlike customer needs and resources, which are unobservable, the second aspect captures *profile-based factors* that reflect customers' readily observable characteristics such as their age, gender, income, social status, geographic location, and buying behavior.

The existence of these two types of customer characteristics—value and profile—raises the question of which one to prioritize in targeting. Focusing on the value is logical because value-creation is the essence of any business activity. The drawback of focusing on value is that value, as well as its drivers—customer needs and preferences—is unobservable, which makes it difficult for the company to develop an effective and cost-efficient action plan. Focusing on the customer profile, on the other hand, can be beneficial because it is observable, which enables the company to reach its customers, make them aware of the offering, and deliver the offering in an effective and cost-efficient manner. The downside of focusing on profile is that it provides little or no insight into customer needs and preferences, thus making it difficult for the company to create value for its customers. Because neither of the two customer descriptors—value and profile—is sufficient on its own to create customer value in an effective and cost-efficient manner, targeting must incorporate both factors.

Based on their focus, two types of targeting can be distinguished: strategic and tactical. *Strategic targeting* focuses on the value defined by customer needs and the potential to create value for the company. In contrast, *tactical targeting* focuses on customer profile, including factors such as age, gender, income, social status, geographic location, and buying behavior, to identify effective and cost-efficient ways to reach these customers. These two aspects of targeting—strategic and tactical—are discussed in more detail in the following sections.

Strategic Targeting

Strategic targeting involves identifying which customers to serve and which to ignore. The process of identifying target customers is guided by the company's ability to develop an offering that will fulfill the needs of these customers better than the competition and do so in a way that creates value for the company and its collaborators.

Because strategic targeting aims to optimize value for customers, on one hand, and for the company and its collaborators, on the other hand, when evaluating the viability of targeting a particular customer segment, a manager needs to answer two key questions: *Can the company create superior value for these customers?* and *Can these customers create value for the company and its collaborators?* The answer to the first question is determined by the degree to which the company's resources are compatible with the needs of target customers. The answer to the second question is determined by the ability of target customers to create value for the company and its collaborators. These two key targeting criteria—*target attractiveness* and *target compatibility*—are illustrated in Figure 2 and discussed in more detail below.

Figure 2: The Key Targeting Principles

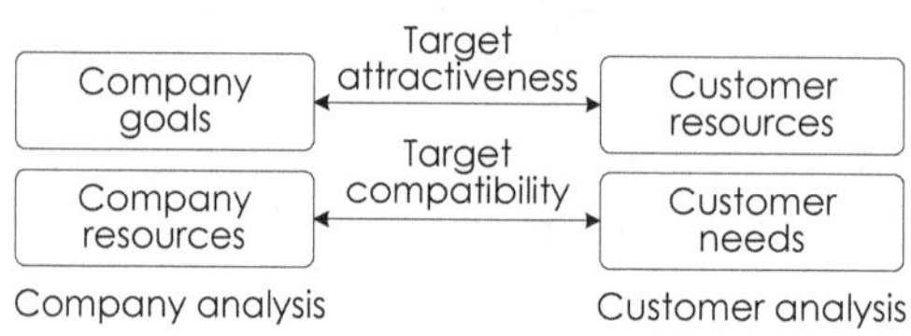

Target Attractiveness

Target attractiveness reflects the ability of a given segment to deliver superior value to the company. The two general types of company value—monetary and strategic—are discussed in more detail below.

Monetary Value

Monetary value refers to customers' ability to generate profits for the company. Monetary value is a function of the revenues generated by a particular customer segment and the costs associated with serving this segment.

- **Customer revenues** involve money received from customers for the right to own and/or use a company's offering. Customer revenues are influenced by a number of factors, including the size of the market and its growth rate; customers' buying power; price sensitivity; the company's pricing power; competitive intensity; as well as various context factors, such as the state of the economy, government regulations, and the physical environment.
- **Costs of serving target customers** involve expenses necessary to tailor the offering's benefits to fit target customers' needs as well as to communicate and deliver the offering to these customers. The cost of serving target customers can also include the expenses incurred in acquiring and retaining these customers (e.g., customer incentives, post-purchase support, and loyalty programs).

Strategic Value

Strategic value refers to customers' ability to create nonmonetary benefits that are of strategic importance for the company. There are four main types of strategic value: product-line value, scale value, communication value, and information value.

- **Product-line value** reflects the synergies between the focal offering and the other offerings in the company's product line. Popular examples of such synergies involve a manufacturer developing a low-priced, entry-level offering to facilitate the sales of a more profitable offering, a software company giving away a basic version of its product to encourage customers to upgrade to the premium, paid version (often referred to as the "freemium" strategy), and a retailer pricing a popular item at or below cost to drive store traffic (often referred to as the loss-leader strategy).
- **Scale value** refers to the benefits received from the scale of the company's operations. For example, a company might target low-margin or even unprofitable customers due to the economics of its business model, especially in the case of companies such as airlines, hotels, and cruise lines, which have large fixed costs and marginal variable costs. Furthermore, a company in its early stages of growth might target low-margin customers in order to build a product and/or user ecosystem that will serve as a platform for future growth. The success of Apple, Microsoft, eBay, and Facebook networks illustrates the benefits from building large-scale user networks.
- **Communication value** reflects customers' potential to influence other buyers. Thus, a company might target customers not because of their own buying power and the profits they are likely to directly generate for the company but to take advantage of their social networks and their ability to influence other buyers. For example, a company might target opinion leaders, trendsetters, and mavens because of their ability to create and/or expand the market for the company's offering.

- **Information value** reflects the worth of the information provided by customers. A company might target customers because they furnish the company with data about their needs and profile that can help design, communicate, and deliver value for other customers with similar needs. A company might also target customers whose needs precede those of the mass market and who are likely to be early adopters of the company's offering—commonly referred to as lead users—to benefit from their feedback on how to modify and enhance the offering.

Note that the attractiveness of different segments is a function of a company's goals. Companies with different strategic goals are likely to vary in the way they evaluate the attractiveness of different segments, such that the same customers might be viewed as attractive by some companies and as unattractive by others.

A segment's ability to create value for the company is a necessary but not sufficient condition for successful targeting. The second and equally important aspect of identifying target customers is the ability of the company to create superior value for these customers. Thus, in addition to being attractive for the company, the target must be compatible with the company's resources. The key factors involved in evaluating target compatibility are discussed in the following section.

Target Compatibility

Target compatibility reflects the company's ability to fulfill the needs of target customers better than the competition. Target compatibility is a function of the company's resources and the degree to which these resources enable it to create superior value for target customers. The key resources—also referred to as strategic assets—that are essential for the success of a company's business model include: existing business infrastructure, collaborator networks, human capital, intellectual property, strong brands, established customer base, synergistic offerings, access to scarce resources, and access to capital.

- **Business infrastructure** involves several types of assets: manufacturing infrastructure comprising the company's production facilities and equipment; service infrastructure, such as call-center and customer relationship management solutions; supply-chain infrastructure, including procurement infrastructure and processes; and management infrastructure, defined by the company's business management culture.
- **Collaborator networks** include two types of networks: vertical networks, in which collaborators are located along the company's supply chain (suppliers and distributors), and horizontal networks, in which collaborators are not a part of the company's supply/distribution chain but collaborate with the company in developing the offering (research and development, manufacturing, and promotion collaborators).
- **Human capital** involves the technological, operational, business, and customer expertise of the company's employees. For many organizations—such

as those involved in research and development, education, and consulting—human capital is a key value-creating asset.

- **Intellectual property** covers the legal entitlement attached to intangible assets. Intellectual property involves two types of assets: (1) industrial property, such as inventions, industrial designs, and identity marks (trademarks, service marks, commercial names and designations), and indications of source/appellations of origin; and (2) copyrights, such as literary and artistic works (novels, plays, films, musical compositions, drawings, paintings, photographs, sculptures, and architectural designs).
- **Strong brands** create value by identifying the offering and generating meaningful associations that create value above and beyond the value created by the product and service aspects of the offering. Brands are particularly important in commoditized industries where the differences between the actual products and services are relatively minor or nonexistent.
- **Established customer base** can facilitate the acceptance of a company's current and new offerings because loyal customers are more likely to buy other offerings from the same company. Loyal customers can also create awareness and favorable word of mouth among customers unfamiliar with the company's offering.
- **Synergistic offerings** are a strategic asset to the degree that they facilitate customer acceptance of related company offerings. For example, the Windows operating system can be viewed as a strategic asset for Microsoft because it ensures product compatibility, thus facilitating customer adoption of related software offerings.
- **Access to scarce resources** provides the company with a distinct competitive advantage by restricting the strategic options of its competitors. For example, a company can benefit from access to unique natural resources, from securing prime manufacturing and/or retail locations, as well as from acquiring a memorable web domain.
- **Access to capital** provides the company with resources to carry out different aspects of its strategy and tactics, including sustaining a price war, developing new products, or implementing a communication campaign. Access to capital can also enable a company to develop and/or enhance its other assets necessary to create value for target customers.

A company's resources are target-specific: resources compatible with one segment might not be compatible with another segment. In fact, assets that are a source of customer value for one segment can become liabilities for a different segment. For example, a brand associated with a casual image is likely to be an asset when targeting customers seeking to convey a casual image and a liability for customers seeking to project a more upscale, exclusive image. Therefore, when choosing a target market a company needs to evaluate its assets from the viewpoint of the particular target segment to ensure the compatibility of customer needs with its own resources.

Strategic Targeting: Competitive Perspective

A key principle of strategic targeting is that the choice of customers should be driven by the company's ability to create an offering that delivers superior value to these customers relative to the competition. A company's ability to create a superior offering stems from its resources and the degree to which its resources are superior to those of the competition. This is the *resource advantage principle*: To create a superior offering, the company must have superior resources relative to the competition. Because a company's resources are need-specific, the choice of target customers is crucial in defining a company's resource advantage over the competition. The uniqueness of customer needs determines the degree to which a company requires specialized resources to fulfill these needs, as well as the degree of the competition for this segment. The more unique the customer needs, the more the company requires specialized resources to serve those customers, and the fewer the viable competitors likely to exist in the market.

From a competitive perspective, the process of identifying a company's target customers is a function of three key factors: customer needs, and the resources of both the company and its competitors involved in serving these needs. The relationship among these three factors is illustrated in Figure 3. A company's goal is to identify customer needs that it has the unique resources to fulfill. These are the optimal target customers because the company can create superior value for these customers and serve them in a way its competitors cannot (the dark-shaded segment in Figure 3). Because of their attractiveness and lack of competition, such markets are often referred to as "blue oceans." In its pursuit of the "blue oceans," a company must avoid the "red oceans," characterized by intense competition because both the company and its competitors have matching resources to fulfill customers' needs (the central segment in Figure 3).

Figure 3: The Resource Advantage Principle

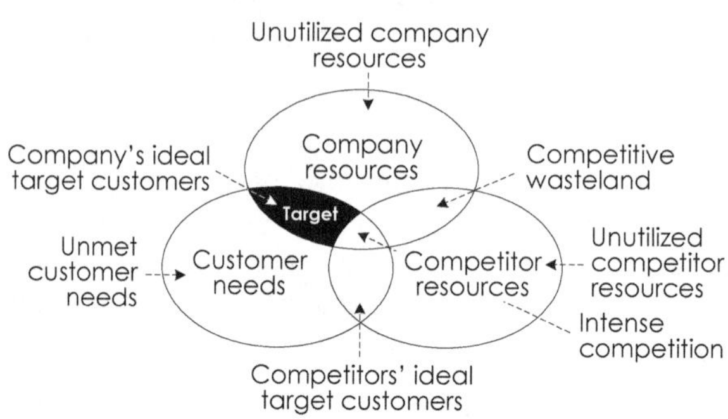

The development of marketing offerings should always be driven by customer needs. Yet, obsession with the competition often leads companies astray, encouraging them to develop offerings that match those of competitors even in the absence of an underlying customer need. Such competitor-driven rather than customer-driven offerings create a competitive wasteland, squandering company's resources by replicating competitors' mistakes while missing real market opportunities.

Because a company's resources do not perfectly overlap with customer needs, some of these resources will remain unutilized when serving a particular segment, and some of the customers' needs will remain unmet by the company's offering. These unutilized needs and resources can be used to provide the company with directions for future development. Thus, unmet customer needs offer the company with an opportunity to develop the necessary resources to create offerings that will fulfill these needs. By the same logic, unutilized company resources call for identifying unmet customer needs and developing offerings to fulfill those needs.

Tactical Targeting

Tactical targeting is similar to strategic targeting in that it also involves identifying target customers. However, unlike strategic targeting, which aims to determine which customers to target and which to ignore, tactical targeting aims to identify an effective and cost-efficient approach to communicate and deliver the offering to already selected target customers. The key aspects of tactical targeting are discussed in more detail below.

The Identification Problem

The decision of which customers to serve and which to ignore is driven by the company's understanding of the needs of these customers and its ability to fulfill these needs better than the competition. Yet, while knowing customer needs is crucial for deciding which customers to target and which to ignore, needs are not readily observable and therefore cannot be acted on to reach these customers. Indeed, knowing only customers' needs without knowing who these customers are, means that a company will have to communicate its offering and make it available to everyone—an approach that is not cost effective, especially when trying to reach niche customer segments. Identifying ways to reach target customers who have been chosen based on the value they are seeking from and bringing to the company is the crux of the identification problem (Figure 4).

Figure 4: The Customer Identification Process

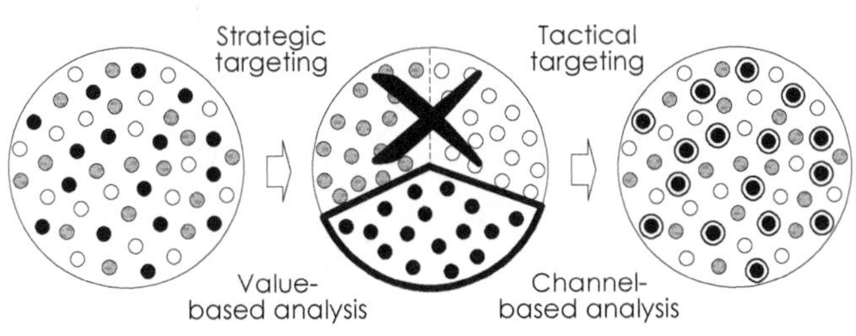

Because targeting aims to optimize the value-creation process, value-based segmentation is almost always the starting point of marketing analysis. To reach the value-based customer segments, companies need to identify a set of readily observable characteristics—also referred to as a *profile*—that describe these segments and use these observable characteristics to communicate and deliver its offerings. The process of linking value-based segments to corresponding observable and actionable profiles is the essence of tactical targeting.

Defining a customer profile involves defining the observable characteristics of a value-based target segment, comprising two types of factors: demographic and behavioral.

- **Demographic factors** outline the key descriptive characteristics of target customers. Commonly used demographics include age, gender, income, level of education, ethnicity, social class, stage in the life cycle, employment status, household size, and geographic location.
- **Behavioral factors** outline the key aspects of customers' behavior. Common behavioral factors include purchase quantity, frequency of repurchase, price sensitivity, promotion sensitivity (e.g., customer response to incentives), loyalty, communication format (e.g., the type of media most frequently utilized by customers), and distribution channel (e.g., the retail format preferred by the customer).

The relationship between strategic and tactical targeting is illustrated in Figure 5. Strategic targeting is value-focused and is a function of the attractiveness of target customers and the compatibility of their needs with the company's resources. The focus on value, although crucial for the success of the company's offering, has the important shortcoming that value is unobservable and, hence, cannot be readily acted on to reach target customers. This shortcoming is addressed by tactical targeting, which involves identifying the demographic and behavioral profile of the strategically selected target customers. Thus, strategic and tactical targeting are two inseparable and complementary aspects of the process of identifying target customers.

Figure 5: Strategic and Tactical Targeting: Linking Customer Value and Profile

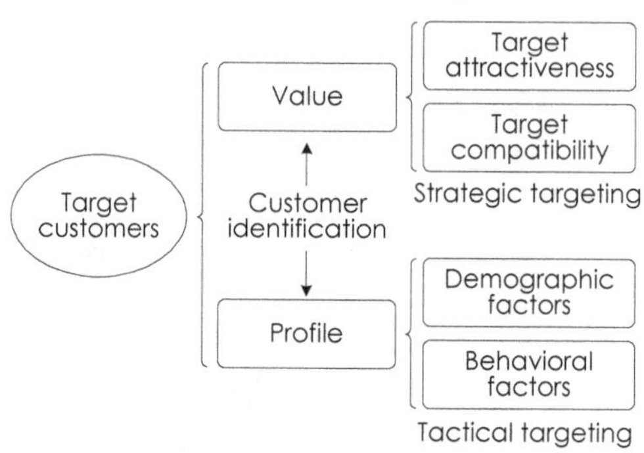

To illustrate, consider a credit card company launching a new credit card featuring a loyalty program that rewards customers for using the card with travel benefits, including airline tickets and hotel stays. The strategically identified target customers include those who need a credit card and would enjoy free airline tickets and/or hotel accommodations (customer value) while using the card frequently and not defaulting on the payments (company value). The problem faced by this company is that customer needs are unobservable, meaning that, a priori, it is difficult to know which consumers might enjoy the travel benefits offered by the card. Likewise, customers' future usage of the credit card and the likelihood of their not defaulting on payments are unobservable. The unobservable nature of the characteristics defining segment attractiveness to the company and segment compatibility with the company's resources makes it difficult for the company to identify these customers in order to effectively communicate and distribute the card.

To solve this problem, the company must link the value-based customer segment with certain observable characteristics describing this segment. Thus, to identify customers with high card usage and a low likelihood of default, the company might consider customers' credit scores and purchase history, which reflect their buying patterns, purchasing power, and likely future behavior, including the probability of repaying the loan. Here, the credit score offers a link between the unobservable (e.g., the likelihood of repaying the loan) and the observable demographic and behavioral factors, enabling the company to focus its promotional efforts on customers who are more likely to create value for the company. Furthermore, to identify customers for whom the company can create value (e.g., those looking for travel rewards), the company might focus on customers who are likely to travel more frequently, read travel magazines and/or watch travel shows, as well as those who tend to seek travel-related information. Thus, by focusing on customers whose profiles are aligned with the value-based target segment, a company can maximize the effectiveness and cost efficiency of its targeting activities.

Targeting Effectiveness and Cost Efficiency

Targeting reflects the company's *intent* to focus on certain customers, which might or might not be the actual outcome of its actions. In this context, the effectiveness and cost efficiency of a company's targeting efforts is determined by the degree to which its actions reach the desired target segment, which in turn depends on the degree to which the identified customer profile fits the desired value characteristics of its target customers. The greater the overlap between the identified customer profiles and the "ideal" target customers, the more effective and cost-efficient the company's targeting strategy.

When identifying the profiles of its target customers, the company walks a fine line between defining the market too broadly and defining it too narrowly. Overly broad targeting is not cost efficient because it calls for the expenditure of significant resources to reach customers that the company has no intention of targeting. In contrast, overly narrow segmentation is ineffective because it will likely cause the company to overlook customers interested in the offering. The goal, therefore, is to find the best link between the need-based target segments and the corresponding profile-based segments.

The "perfect" targeting, in which each target customer is defined in terms of both its value and profile (Figure 6A), is rarely possible. The misalignment of value and profile can result in one of three common types of targeting errors. One possibility is that the profile of target customers is defined too broadly, such that it includes not only the target customers but also many noncustomers (Figure 6B). The problem with this approach—often referred to as *shotgun targeting*—is that it is not cost efficient because the company will end up promoting the offering to customers who are not aligned with its strategic goals. Alternatively, the company might define the profile of its target customers too narrowly, such that it includes only a subset of its target customers (Figure 6C). The problem with this approach—often referred to as *oversegmentation*—is that it is not effective because the company will forgo promoting its offering to some of its strategically chosen customers. Finally, the company might define the profile of its target customers in a way that only marginally overlaps (or does not overlap at all) with its desired target customers (Figure 6D). The problem with this shot-in-the-dark approach is that it is neither effective nor cost efficient because it includes only a subset of its target customers while wasting resources by reaching customers who do not fit its strategic goals.

Figure 6. Targeting Efficiency

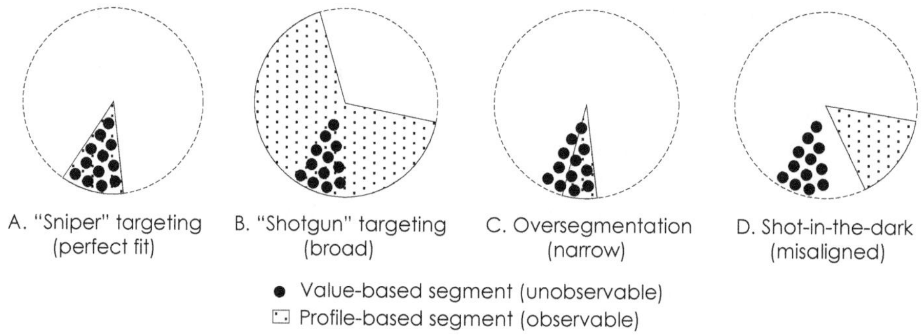

Targeting Multiple Segments

The discussion so far has focused on a scenario in which a firm identifies and targets a single customer segment. Single-segment marketing, however, is the exception rather than the rule. Most offerings exist as part of a product line, with different offerings targeting different customer segments. Indeed, even companies that start with a single offering achieve wider customer adoption over time. As their customer base becomes more diverse, these companies transition from a single offering to a product line with offerings that fit the needs of the diverse customers it serves.

Because the needs of each customer segment are distinct, the basic principle in targeting multiple segments is that the company must develop a strategy and tactics for each segment it aims to pursue (Figure 7). To accomplish this, a company must evaluate its ability to create value for each segment as well as each segment's ability to create value for the company (strategic targeting) and then identify the means to communicate and deliver the offering to these customers in an effective and cost-efficient manner (tactical targeting).

Figure 7. Targeting Multiple Segments

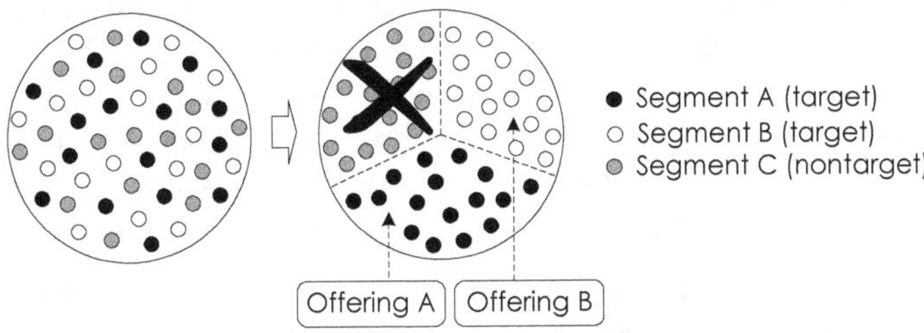

The concept of product line targeting can be better understood when compared with its alternative—one-for-all targeting (also referred to as mass marketing), which describes a scenario in which the same offering is aimed at a diverse set of customers. A classic example of mass marketing is Henry Ford's decision to produce the same car—the Model T—for all customers. The essence of this approach is captured in Henry Ford's famous phrase, "Customers can have any color they want as long as it is black." The alternative strategy, segment-based targeting, involves developing specific offerings for each group of customers with diverse preferences. For example, to compete with Ford's Model T, General Motors offered its customers an extensive array of cars that varied in size, functionality, and color—an approach captured in General Motors President and CEO Alfred Sloan's vision of "a car for every purpose and purse."

A product line recognizes the diversity of customer needs and allows a company to design offerings that meet the needs of customers more effectively than a single offering can. The downside of a product line vis-à-vis a single offering is that it often leads to higher development, communication, and distribution costs. Accordingly, a product line is warranted only when each offering targets a unique customer segment with distinct needs and resources and develops a corresponding strategy and tactics to create a viable value exchange with each segment. The process of developing and managing product lines is discussed in more detail in Chapter 17.

Segmentation

The discussion so far has focused on the logic, the key aspects, and the core principles of targeting, assuming that potential buyers have already been assigned to distinct segments. In reality, however, this is not the case. In order to choose a particular target segment, the market must already be segmented, and each market segment should be defined as such. Accordingly, the focus of this section is on the process and key principles of the process of dividing potential buyers into market segments.

The Essence of Segmentation

Segmentation is a categorization process that groups customers by focusing on those differences that are relevant for targeting and ignoring those differences that are irrelevant. The process of segmentation is based on the notion that the efficiency of a company's marketing activities can be greatly improved by ignoring the nonessential differences among customers and treating customers with similar needs and resources as if they were a single entity. Accordingly, segmentation focuses marketing analysis on the important aspects of customer needs, enabling managers to group customers into larger segments and develop offerings for the entire segment rather than for each individual customer.

Segmentation can involve two opposing processes—differentiation and agglomeration (Figure 8). On one hand, segmentation is a differentiation process that aims to divide all buyers in the market into groups by focusing on the differences in their needs and resources with respect to the company's offering. The process of differentiation is illustrated in the left part of Figure 8, whereby a (mass) market in which customers viewed as being similar in their needs and resources is divided into three (homogeneous) segments such that customers in each segment are similar to one another and at the same time different from those in the other segments. On the other hand, segmentation is an agglomeration process that aims to group individual buyers into segments by focusing on the similarities in their needs and resources with respect to the company's offering. The process of agglomeration is illustrated in the right part of Figure 8, whereby an idiosyncratic market in which customers viewed as having unique needs and resources are grouped into three (homogeneous) segments, such that customers in each segment are similar to one another and at the same time different from those in the other segments. Thus, even though differentiation and agglomeration are opposite processes, they aim to achieve the same goal—facilitate the process of identifying target customers—and yield the same outcome.

Figure 8. Segmentation as a Process of Differentiation and Agglomeration

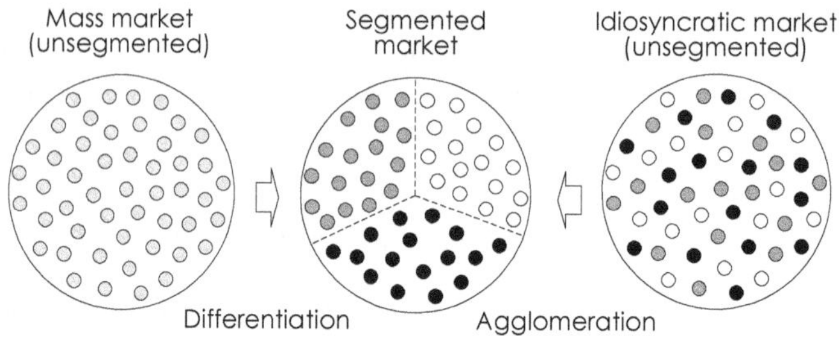

Segmentation enables companies to streamline their activities by developing offerings for groups of customers with similar needs. The key benefit of segmentation is in allowing the company to optimize marketing expenditures by grouping customers who are likely to respond in a similar fashion to the company's offerings. However, because grouping customers inevitably ignores the individual differences within each group, segmentation might decrease the attractiveness of the company's offering by not fully customizing the offering to fit the needs of individual customers. The key drawback of segmentation is that grouping customers into segments might not take into account potentially important differences that exist among customers within each segment. Thus, segmentation can increase the cost efficiency of targeting but also might decrease its effectiveness.

A common misperception is that the selection of target customers starts with dividing customers into segments and deciding which segments to target only after market segments have been identified. This is a myopic view because the main purpose of segmentation is to facilitate targeting, and without taking into account the logic of the company's targeting efforts one is likely to segment the market in a way that is unrelated to the subsequent targeting decision. Although for presentation purposes segmentation typically precedes targeting, from a conceptual standpoint, segmentation and targeting are an iterative process of identifying target customers. Thus, segmentation is targeting-specific, meaning that markets are segmented in a way that facilitates targeting, and targeting is segment-driven, meaning that a segment must already be defined in order to be selected as a target.

Because segmentation aims to facilitate targeting, two types of segmentation processes can be distinguished: *value-based segmentation* for the purposes of strategic targeting and *profile-based segmentation* for the purposes of tactical targeting. These two types of segmentation and the corresponding targeting decisions are illustrated in Figure 9.

Figure 9. Segmentation and Targeting: The Big Picture

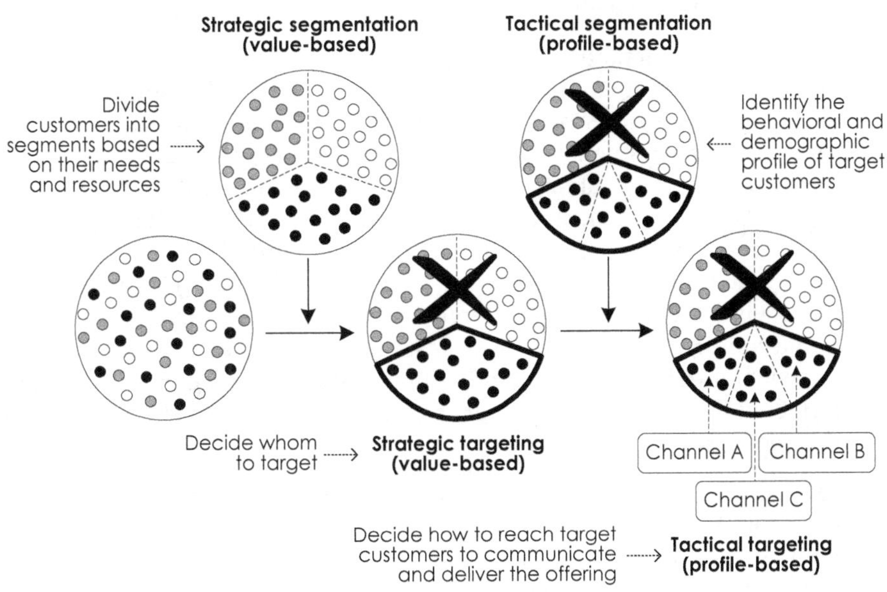

Strategic segmentation groups customers based on the company's ability to create and capture value from these customers, while ignoring the irrelevant differences among customers within the same segment. Strategic segmentation lays the ground for strategic targeting, which involves selecting one (or more) of the identified segments that the company will serve by developing target-specific offering(s). Following strategic targeting, tactical segmentation involves grouping customers who have already been identified as strategic targets into segments based on their profile characteristics—demographics and behavior—in a way that facilitates the company's tactical targeting. Building on the tactical segmentation, tactical targeting identifies the specific channels to be used to reach target customers in order to communicate and deliver the offering.

Key Segmentation Principles

To be effective, the process of grouping customers into market segments must follow four key principles: relevance, similarity, exclusivity, and comprehensiveness. The essence and the rationale underlying these four principles are outlined in more detail below.

- **Relevance**. Because segmentation aims to facilitate targeting, it should group customers based on their likely response to the company's offering. There is virtually an infinite number of criteria that one could use to divide customers into segments. Most of these criteria, however, are unrelated to factors that underlie the company's targeting strategy and, as a result, produce market segments that do not facilitate the development of a meaningful strategy and tactics. Segmenting markets without a particular targeting purpose in mind is most often a waste of a company's resources and a distraction for managers trying to identify viable targeting strategies.
- **Similarity**. Segmentation aims to group customers so that those within each segment are quite similar to one another (i.e., have homogeneous preferences) in the way they are likely to interact with the company's offering. In general, a larger number of segments leads to a greater similarity (homogeneity) among the customers within each segment, such that the resulting segments are more likely to comprise customers with uniform preferences. Note, however, that a more granular segmentation calls for the development of a greater number of customized offerings—an approach justified only in cases when the underlying differences between these segments are essential to the company's ability to create customer value. Therefore, the optimal degree of similarity among the individual customers in a given segment is determined by the company's ability to create value for and capture value from this segment.
- **Exclusivity**. In addition to being similar to one another, customers in each segment should be different (heterogeneous) from those in other segments with respect to the way they interact with the company's offering. Thus, segments should be mutually exclusive, meaning that customers with similar values and profiles should be assigned to the same segment rather than be spread out across segments.

- **Comprehensiveness**. An important market segmentation principle is that segments should be comprehensive, meaning that they should include all potential customers in a given market, such that each customer is assigned to a segment. Accordingly, segmentation should produce segments that are collectively exhaustive, whereby no potential customers are left unassigned to a segment.

The four segmentation principles are illustrated in Figure 10. Here, the first scenario (Figure 10A) illustrates a segmentation that conforms to all four principles: it is relevant with respect to the targeting goals; it involves segments that are homogeneous with respect to underlying preferences; it involves segments that are mutually exclusive, whereby customers with similar preferences belong to the same segment; and it is collectively exhaustive, whereby it comprises all potential buyers in the market. In contrast, the other four scenarios illustrate segmentations that violate each of the four principles. Thus, the second scenario (Figure 10B) illustrates a segmentation that uses an irrelevant criterion, such that the resulting segmentation does not capture the differences in customer needs (indicated by different shadings) relevant for targeting. Likewise, the third scenario (Figure 10C) illustrates a segmentation that violates the similarity principle, whereby customers in one of the segments have heterogeneous preferences. The fourth scenario (Figure 10D) further illustrates a segmentation that does not follow the exclusivity principle, whereby customers with similar preferences are spread across different segments. Finally, the fifth scenario (Figure 10E) illustrates a non-exhaustive segmentation that fails to include some potential customers in one of its segments.

Figure 10. Key Segmentation Principles

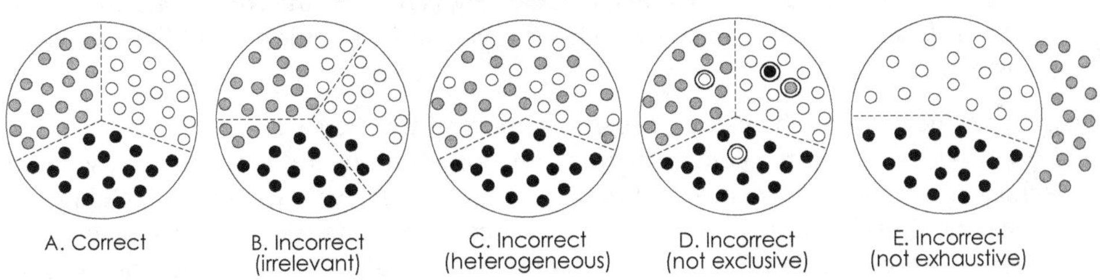

The development of a sound segmentation is crucial for selecting a viable target market that will serve as the cornerstone of the company's business model. Indeed, segmentation and targeting are two complementary aspects of the process of identifying target customers; errors in one of these aspects is likely to trickle down to the other, ultimately resulting in choosing suboptimal target customers and creating a flawed value exchange. In this context, a company's value-creation process starts with the way it evaluates the needs and resources of its target customers, grouping them into segments and selecting which segments to target and which to ignore.

SUMMARY

Targeting is the process of identifying customers for whom the company will optimize its offering. Targeting involves two decisions: selecting which customers to serve and identifying actionable strategies to reach these customers.

Strategic targeting involves identifying which customers (segments) to serve and which to ignore. Because it aims to optimize value for customers, the company, and its collaborators, strategic targeting is typically derived from value-based segmentation rather than from profile-based segmentation. The targeting decision is guided by two key criteria: target attractiveness (customers' potential to create value for the company) and target compatibility (a company's ability to create value for the customers).

Tactical targeting involves developing an effective and cost-efficient plan to communicate and deliver the offering's value to the already selected target customers. Tactical targeting links the (typically unobservable) value-based segments to specific observable and actionable characteristics. Such observable characteristics, also referred to as a *customer profile*, involve demographic (e.g., age, gender, income, and geographical location) and behavioral (e.g., purchase frequency, purchase quantity, and price sensitivity) factors.

To succeed, an offering should create superior value for its target customers and collaborators. To accomplish that, a company needs to identify customers whose needs it can fulfill better than the competition. A company's *competitive advantage* is determined by the degree to which it has the resources to create customer value that is unique and cannot be readily copied by the competition.

Targeting *effectiveness* and *cost efficiency* is defined by the degree to which a company's tactical targeting is consistent with the strategically identified target customers. The greater the overlap between the need-based (strategic) target segments and the corresponding profile-based (tactical) segments, the greater the effectiveness and cost-efficiency of the company's targeting efforts.

Because the needs of each customer segment are distinct, the basic principle in *targeting multiple segments* is that the company must develop a unique strategy for each segment it decides to pursue. To accomplish this, a company must evaluate the underlying customer needs of each targeted segment, its own core competencies and strategic assets, the ways it will create value for its collaborators and deal with its competitors, as well as the impact of the relevant context factors.

Segmentation is a categorization process that groups customers by focusing on those differences that are relevant for targeting and ignoring those differences that are irrelevant. The process of segmentation is based on the notion that the efficiency of a company's marketing activities can be greatly improved by ignoring the nonessential differences among customers and treating customers with similar needs and resources as if they were a single entity. Accordingly, segmentation focuses marketing analysis on the important aspects of customer needs, enabling managers to group customers into larger segments and develop offerings for the entire segment rather than for each individual customer.

Segmentation must follow four *key principles*: it must group customers on characteristics that are relevant to their likely response to the offering, produce (homogeneous) segments comprising customers with similar characteristics, produce segments that are different from one another, and be comprehensive, meaning that they should include all potential customers.

RELEVANT CONCEPTS

Customer Equity: The monetary and strategic value customers are likely to create for the company during their tenure with this company. Customer equity goes beyond the current profitability of a customer to include the entire stream of profits (adjusted for the time value of money) that a company is likely to receive from this customer. A customer can create value for the company in at least three different ways: (1) by directly generating revenues (and profits) for the company through purchase of the company's products and services (direct value), (2) by promoting the company's products and services to other buyers (communication value), and (3) by providing the company with information that can help increase the effectiveness and efficiency of its operations (information value).

Demographics: A set of characteristics used to describe a given population. Demographics commonly used in marketing include factors such as population size and growth, age dispersion, geographic dispersion, ethnic background, income, mobility, education, employment, and household composition.

Firmographics: The key characteristics of an organization, typically used for segmentation purposes. Firmographics include factors such as location, size of company, organizational structure, industry, buying process, growth, revenues, and profitability.

Heterogeneous Market: Market composed of customers who vary (i.e., are heterogeneous) in their response to a company's offering.

Homogeneous Market: Market composed of customers likely to react in a similar manner to the company's offering (e.g., they seek the same benefits, have similar financial resources, can be reached via the same means of communication, and have access to the offering through the same distribution channels).

Lifetime Customer Value: See *customer equity*.

MECE Rule: A popular segmentation heuristic stating that segmentation should yield segments that are both *mutually exclusive* and *collectively exhaustive*. This rule combines two of the four segmentation principles identified earlier in this chapter—exclusivity and comprehensiveness. Thus, the MECE rule indicates that segments should be sufficiently different from one another so that they do not overlap (i.e., mutually exclusive); at the same time, identified segments should include *all* customers in a given market (i.e., collectively exhaustive).

Niche Strategy: Marketing strategy aimed at a distinct and relatively small customer segment.

Occasion-Based Targeting: Targeting strategy that groups customers based on purchase and consumption occasions. Occasion-based targeting is useful in cases in which customer needs vary across purchase occasions, and the same customer is likely to fall into different usage-based segments at different times. For example, when buying wine, a customer's preference might vary as a function of the occasion (for cooking, for daily consumption, for a special occasion, or for a gift). By focusing on usage occasions rather than on the individual characteristics of the customer, occasion-based targeting accounts for the fact that the same customer is likely to display different needs depending on the occasion. Unlike user-based targeting, which assumes that customer needs do not vary across purchase occasions, occasion-based targeting does not make such an assumption, implying that an individual customer (or segment) can have different needs on different purchase occasions.

Psychographics: Relatively stable individual characteristics such as personality, moral values, attitudes, interests, and lifestyle.

User-Based Targeting: Targeting strategy that groups customers based on their relatively stable individual characteristics, which are likely to determine their needs and behavior across different purchase and consumption occasions. User-based targeting focuses on individual customers, assuming that their preferences are constant across usage occasions, whereas occasion-based targeting focuses on usage occasions rather than on individual customers. User-based targeting assumes that customer needs do not vary across purchase occasions, and hence, that an individual's needs can be fulfilled with a single offering. Accordingly, user-based targeting is appropriate in settings in which customers' needs are relatively stable across purchase occasions and can be used as a reliable predictor of their behavior on any particular purchase occasion. To illustrate, the preference for regular versus light (diet) soft drinks is fairly stable across individuals and calls for user-based targeting. User-based targeting can be viewed as a special case (assuming that customer preferences are constant across usage occasions) of the more general approach of need-based targeting.

ADDITIONAL READINGS

Kim, W. Chan and Renée Mauborgne (2005), *Blue Ocean Strategy: How to Create Uncontested Market Space and Make the Competition Irrelevant.* Boston, MA: Harvard Business School Press.

McDonald, Malcolm and Ian Dunbar (2012), *Market Segmentation: How to Do It, How to Profit from It.* Burlington, MA: Elsevier.

Weinstein, Art (2013), *Handbook of Market Segmentation: Strategic Targeting for Business and Technology Firms* (3rd ed.). New York, NY: Haworth Press.

CHAPTER FIVE

CREATING CUSTOMER VALUE: DEVELOPING A VALUE PROPOSITION AND POSITIONING

There is only one boss. The customer. And he can fire everybody in the company from the chairman on down, simply by spending his money somewhere else.

—Sam Walton, founder of Walmart

Creating customer value is a central component of a company's strategy. Because customers are the ultimate source of value for the company and its collaborators, customer value is the key to creating market value. The two key aspects of creating customer value—value proposition and positioning—are the focus of this chapter.

The Big Picture

The development of a customer value proposition and positioning follows the identification of customers that the company will serve with its offering (discussed in more detail in Chapter 4). An offering's value proposition delineates the value—defined by the specific benefits and costs—that target customers will receive from the offering. Building on the value proposition, the positioning identifies the primary benefit(s) of the offering that will serve as the main reason for customers to choose it. The processes of identifying target customers, developing a value proposition, and positioning are illustrated in Figure 1.

Figure 1: Identifying Target Customers, Developing a Value Proposition, and Positioning

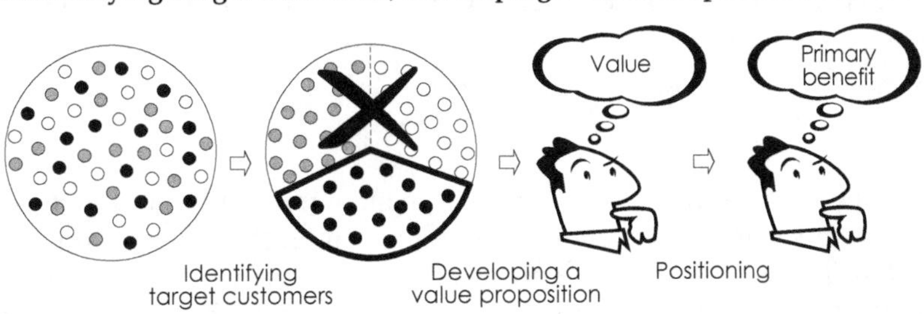

The development of a customer value proposition and positioning is intricately related to the process of identifying target customers. Indeed, even though they are presented in Figure 1 as a progression, in reality these processes are iterative, whereby the development of a value proposition and positioning both determines and follows from the choice of target customers. The development of a value proposition precedes the identification of target customers because the company's ability to create superior customer value is a key targeting criterion. At the same time, the development of a value proposition follows from the selection of target customers because a meaningful value proposition necessitates knowing the needs and preferences of target customers. Recognizing the iterative nature of the processes of identifying target customers and developing a value proposition and positioning, this chapter focuses on the key aspects of developing a value proposition and positioning on the assumption that target customers have already been identified.

Developing a Value Proposition

The customer value proposition defines the value that an offering aims to create for its target customers. The key aspects of the concept of customer value, the value function, and creating a competitive value advantage are outlined below.

Customer Value as a Marketing Concept

The concept of customer value is central to defining the value exchange in any market. Accordingly, understanding the essence of customer value and identifying its key domains is essential for the development of a viable marketing strategy.

The Essence of Customer Value

Customer value reflects the worth of an offering; it is a customer's assessment of the company's offering with respect to its ability to fulfill certain needs. From a company's perceptive, the value-creation process involves defining the key aspects (attributes) of the company's offering that are aligned with customer needs (Figure 2). In this context, an offering's value is determined by the fit between its attributes and the needs of the target customers: The better the offering's attributes fit the needs of its target customers, the greater the value created by this offering.

Figure 2: Value as a Function of Customer Needs and Offering Attributes

Two aspects of value merit attention: it is intangible and idiosyncratic. Because it is a customer's subjective evaluation of the worth (utility) of the company's offering, value is *intangible*; it does not physically exist in the marketplace. Value is not an attribute of a company's offering; it is created when a customer interacts with the company's offering. Furthermore, because value reflects a customer's assessment of the offering, it is *idiosyncratic*, whereby the same offering can have different value for different customers. Thus, an offering that is appealing to one customer might be of little or no value to another customer. For example, a lower priced, lower quality offering is likely to be attractive to price-conscious customers and unattractive to those customers seeking high performance and exclusivity.

The Domains of Customer Value

Depending on the underlying customer needs, an offering can create value across three domains: functional, psychological, and monetary. These three domains of customer value are depicted in Figure 3 and briefly outlined below.

Figure 3: Dimensions of Customer Value

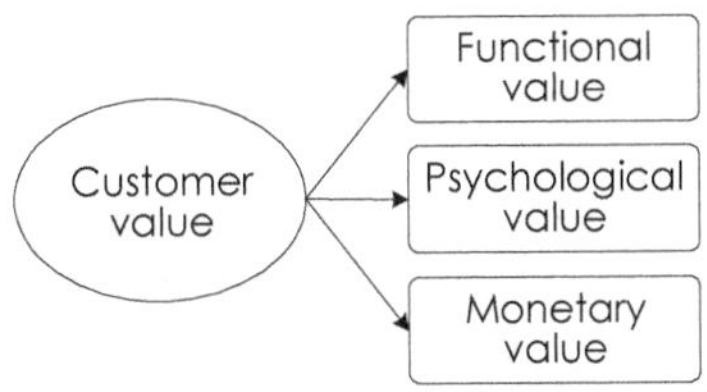

- **Functional value** is defined by the benefits and costs directly related to an offering's performance. Attributes that create functional value include performance, reliability, durability, compatibility, ease of use, design, customization, form, style, and packaging. For offerings that serve primarily utilitarian functions, such as office and industrial equipment, functionality is often the paramount consideration.

- **Psychological value** is defined by the psychological benefits and costs associated with the offering. Psychological value goes beyond the functional benefits of the offering to create psychological benefits for target customers. For example, customers might value the emotional benefits provided by a car, such as the joy of driving a high-performance vehicle as well as the social status and lifestyle conveyed by the car. In categories such as luxury and fashion, where customers seek emotional and self-expressive benefits, the psychological value conveyed by the offering is often of primary importance.

- **Monetary value** is defined by the monetary benefits and costs associated with the offering. Attributes that create monetary value include the offering's price, fees, discounts, and rebates, as well as the various monetary costs associated with using and disposing of the offering. Even though monetary value is typically associated with costs, an offering can also carry monetary benefits, such as cash-back offers, monetary bonuses, cash prizes, financial rewards, and low-interest financing. In commoditized categories with undifferentiated offerings, the monetary aspect of the offerings is often the dominant criterion for choice.

Even though they represent different dimensions of customer value, these domains are not mutually exclusive. An offering can create value in all three domains. Consider Starbucks, the Seattle-based global coffeehouse chain. Every week Starbucks serves millions of customers around the world, providing them with fresh-brewed coffee and in the process delivering value in these three domains. From a functional perspective, Starbucks coffee provides its customers with energy, helping them to wake up, rejuvenate in the afternoon, and stay up late at night. Starbucks delivers psychological benefits by becoming part of the daily routine for customers, giving them a sense of belonging and a means to express their identity by creating their "own" beverages. Finally, from a monetary perspective, Starbucks creates disutility (negative value) associated with the price customers pay at the register, which in turn can be attenuated by the available price promotions and loyalty programs.

The Value Function

A company creates customer value by designing market offerings that can fulfill a particular customer need better than the competition. To create customer value, a manager must ensure that the key aspects (attributes) of the offering are aligned with customer needs—a decision that calls for understanding the value consumers place on different aspects of the company's offering. Therefore, identifying customers' value function—that is, how customers evaluate the performance of the market offerings on different attributes and how they combine these valuations to form an overall assessment of each option—is of utmost importance because it enables the company to identify and prioritize which aspects of the offering must be improved based on their potential to create customer value.

Customer Value as a Function of Offering Attributes

Customers do not evaluate market offerings based on their objective attribute characteristics but based on the expected subjective value (utility) of these attributes. The customer value function reflects the way in which attributes of the offering translate to subjective benefits and costs for target customers.

An offering's ability to create value is determined by three key factors: (1) the *attributes* defining the company's offering, (2) the relative *importance* of these attributes for target customers, and (3) the offering's *performance* on these attributes. For example, when choosing a mobile phone, a customer might consider several attributes, including battery life, operating system, brand reputation, form factor, camera resolution, and price. Furthermore, different attributes might vary in importance for this customer, such that battery life, operating system, and brand reputation are of utmost importance, and price of least importance. Finally, this customer is likely to assess how well each of the available phones performs on the above attributes. Combining these different aspects of the valuation process will yield this customer's assessment of the value of each of the available decision alternatives and drive the ultimate choice. Customers' valuation of a market offering can be represented with the following value equation:

$$V_A = f(w_i, a_i)$$

Here V_A is the value of offering A, i is an index that specifies the particular attribute being evaluated, w_i is the importance of that attribute, and a_i is the offering's performance on that attribute. The index i ranges from 1 (in the case of offerings defined by a single attribute) to the total number of attributes describing a given offering (n). The symbol f means that the value is a function of attribute importance (w_i) and offering performance (a_i), without implying a specific relationship (e.g., a linear function) between these factors. To choose among multiple offerings, consumers typically compare their valuations of each of the available options (e.g., V_A versus V_B versus V_C) and select the one with the highest value.

For simplicity, the value function (f) is commonly assumed to be the sum of the offering's performance on individual attributes a_i, weighted (multiplied) by the relative importance of these attributes w_i. Assuming such a weighted-additive relationship between the different aspects of the offering, the value function can be represented as follows:

$$V_A = w_1 * a_1 + w_2 * a_2 + w_3 * a_3 + \ldots + w_n * a_n$$

Let's say that the consumer in the above example is using a 10-point scale to rate the importance of each attribute of the mobile phone, rating battery life, operating system, and brand reputation as 9; the form factor and camera resolution as 5; and price as 1. Furthermore, let's say that this consumer is using a 10-point scale to rate the performance of each camera on each attribute, rating the battery life of the first phone (A) as 4, the operating system as 8, the brand reputation as 6, the form factor as 5, the camera resolution as 7, and the price as 9. Accordingly, the valuation of camera A can be calculated as: $V_A = 9*4+9*8+9*6+5*5+5*7+1*9 = 231$. Following the same logic, the consumer can evaluate the other options (e.g., V_B and V_C) and choose the one with the highest value.

Despite its popularity, the weighted-additive value function is subject to important limitations that stem from its four key assumptions. Specifically, it assumes that (1) customers have well-articulated valuations of the offerings' performance on different attributes, (2) an increase in an offering's performance on a given attribute will result in a proportional increase in value, (3) the valuation of an offering is symmetric with respect to improving or diminishing its performance, and (4) buyers consider all available information about an offering in a systematic fashion. The research in the area of psychology and behavioral economics, however, has shown that these assumptions often do not hold. In this context, four aspects of the value function merit attention: *reference-point dependence, loss aversion, diminishing marginal value*, and *effort optimization*. These properties of the value function are outlined in more detail below.

Reference-Point Dependence

The reference-point dependence aspect of the value function reflects the fact that consumers often do not have well-articulated preferences and that their evaluations of market offerings depend on the decision context. Specifically, the reference-point dependence principle means that the value of an offering is determined in terms of changes from a reference point, such that its disadvantages are framed as losses and its advantages as gains (Figure 4). To illustrate, when considering the processing power of a computer, customers are likely to evaluate it relative to the power of their current computer, which will serve as a reference point. As a result, the same computer is likely to be evaluated as an improvement (gain) by customers used to a less powerful computer and as a downgrade (loss) by customers used to a more powerful computer.

Figure 4: Reference-Point Dependence

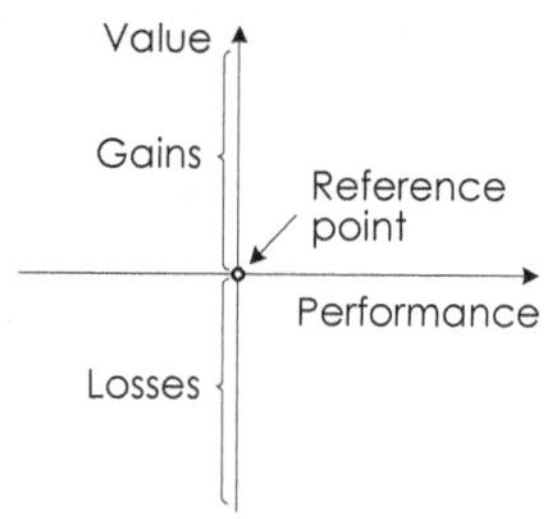

The principle of reference-point dependence is frequently used in pricing, whereby buyers are given two prices—the "regular" price that aims to serve as a reference point and the "sale" price that reflects a discount from the regular price. This practice tends to be more effective when consumers do not have sufficient expertise to objectively assess the value of the offering as well as when actual product quality is not readily observable. In such cases, buyers tend to focus their attention on the difference between the "regular" and the "sale" price and rely on this difference—rather than on the actual benefits provided by the offering—to make a choice. Accordingly, the reference-point dependence principle is an important aspect of the pricing model of many retailers, including JoS. A. Bank, JCPenney, and Kohl's. Likewise, the "new and improved" product development strategy builds on the principle of reference dependence to focus buyers' attention on the marginal improvement of the offering vis-à-vis its predecessor.

Loss Aversion

The loss-aversion aspect of the value function extends the principle of reference-point dependence to assert that people value the positive (gains) and negative (losses) deviations from the reference point in a different fashion, placing more weight on losses than gains. This asymmetric valuation pattern is reflected in the fact that the value function is steeper for losses than gains, such that the subjective experience of losses are exaggerated relative to that of corresponding gains.

The effect of loss aversion can readily be seen if one compares the differences in the subjective valuation of a change in the performance of the offering (reflected on the horizontal axis in Figure 5) that is of the same magnitude in terms of its absolute value but occurs in opposite directions—an improvement in one case and a detraction in the other. The subjective experience and evaluation of this change varies depending on the nature of the change (advancement vs. detraction), such that losses loom larger than corresponding gains. Thus, the loss-aversion principle implies that people place higher value on something they need to give up compared with something they stand to gain.

Figure 5: Loss Aversion

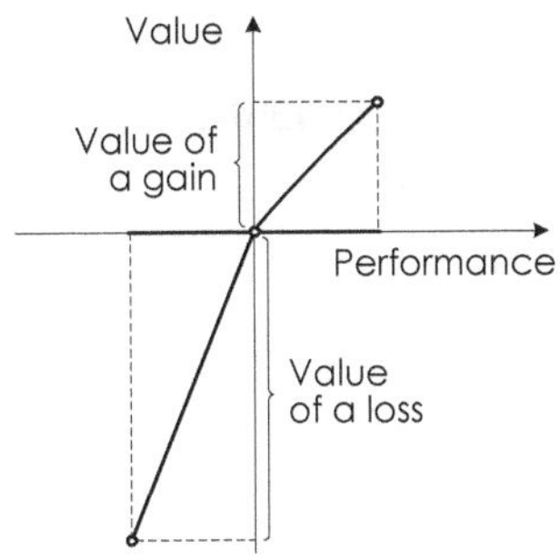

Consider, for example, buyers' reactions to fluctuations in the stock market: A loss of $1,000 hurts proportionally more than the satisfaction derived from a gain of $1,000. In the same vein, customers are likely to vary in their reactions to adding and deleting product features, whereby the disutility of having to give up a feature is likely to be greater than the utility of gaining the same feature. Loss aversion is also one of the building blocks of the no-questions-asked return policy of many retailers. Once customers take possession of the offering their reference point changes, such that the status quo of having the offering becomes the reference point for the subsequent decision regarding the disposition of this offering. As a result, returning the offering is no longer considered as a non-gain (i.e., the inverse equivalent of a gain) but as a loss, decreasing the likelihood that the buyer will return the offering. The shift in the reference point following the purchase process leads to a decrease in the initial probability of a purchase resulting in a return.

Diminishing Marginal Value

The principle of diminishing marginal value implies that the utility from improving an offering's performance on the same dimension does not increase in a monotonic fashion, and that after a certain point improving the offering's performance will produce marginally diminishing increases in the subjective valuation of the offering. The diminishing marginal value principle states that the value function is not linear, whereby increasing an offering's performance produces equivalent increases in customer utility. Rather, value function is concave, such that improving the offering's performance will have greater impact on its subjective value at a lower level of performance; as the offering's overall performance improves, further improvements will have progressively decreasing impact.

The effect of diminishing marginal value can readily be seen if one compares the differences in the subjective valuations of the same changes in the offering's performance (reflected on the horizontal axis in Figure 6) that occur at different levels of performance. The diminishing marginal value principle implies that an increase in an offering's performance on a given attribute will yield greater value when the initial level of this attribute's performance is low rather than when it is high. Once an offering reaches a certain level of performance on a given attribute, further improvements in performance on this attribute tend to be perceived as relatively less valuable. In lay terms, the more customers have of something, the less an improvement means to them.

Figure 6: Diminishing Marginal Value

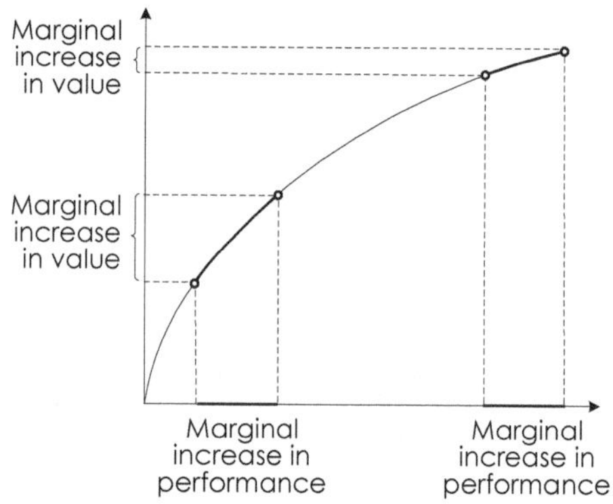

Consider, for example, the effect of improving the processing power of a computer on the utility a buyer derives from this improvement: When the processing power is relatively low, even small increases in processing power have a relatively large impact. As the processing power becomes relatively high, the same increase in power that used to produce a large increase in perceived performance now has much less impact. A similar effect can be observed with other products, such as the number of blades in a razor: The increase from one to two blades was perceived as a great enhancement, but as the overall number of blades increased from two to three, four, then five, the marginal increase in the perceived value from adding another blade was not as large as in the beginning.

Effort Optimization

The three properties of the value function discussed so far—reference-point dependence, loss aversion, and diminishing marginal value—describe how consumers assess the utility of the individual attributes of the offering without explicitly addressing the issue of how consumers combine these attributes to form an overall valuation of the choice alternatives and decide among the available choice options. In this context, a particular aspect of the value function that merits attention is how consumers use the attribute valuations to make a choice.

When considering the available choice alternatives, buyers pursue two conflicting goals: On one hand, they are trying to make an accurate decision by choosing the option that best fits their needs and, on the other hand, they are trying to minimize the mental effort involved in the decision. The goal of minimizing decision effort entices buyers to follow shortcuts, or *heuristics*, that aim to circumvent cognitive effort, albeit at the expense of choice accuracy. The likelihood of using heuristics is greater in the case of relatively less important decisions, when buyers are often willing to sacrifice accuracy in order to simplify choice.

One popular decision heuristic—referred to as satisficing—involves selecting the first option that meets the buyers' criteria without necessarily considering all of the available options. Satisficing is perhaps the least effortful and at the same time the least accurate heuristic. Thus, buyers relying on the satisficing heuristic might end up choosing different options depending on the order in which they evaluate the options. In addition to satisficing, buyers might also simplify their decision by reducing the number of attributes on which they evaluate the available options. Thus, buyers might evaluate only the most important attributes, without taking into account the performance of the options on all attributes (referred to as the equal-weight heuristic). In an extreme case, buyers might consider only the most important attribute describing the choice options and select the option with the highest value on that attribute (referred to as the lexicographic heuristic). Alternatively, buyers might use a heuristic that implies a cut-off rule, thereby excluding options that do not meet a certain threshold value on key attributes. The goal of this heuristic (also referred to as an elimination-by-aspects heuristic) is to make the decision set more manageable by trimming options that are unlikely to be chosen.

Decision heuristics vary in the degree to which high levels of an offering on one dimension can compensate for low levels on another. Thus, the satisficing and elimination-by-aspects heuristics are noncompensatory in nature, meaning that a low level on one attribute cannot be offset by a high level on another attribute, whereas the equal-weight and the lexicographic heuristics and the weighted-additive model are compensatory, meaning that an option can be chosen despite extremely low values on some attributes, as long as its deficiencies can be compensated for by strong performance on other attributes.

Developing a Competitive Advantage

An offering's ability to create value for target customers is necessary but not sufficient to ensure its market success. In addition to fulfilling customer needs, an offering should be able to fulfill these needs better than the competition. Therefore, an offering's ability to create customer value must be considered in a competitive context and take into account the offering's competitive advantage (Figure 7).

Figure 7. Creating Superior Customer Value

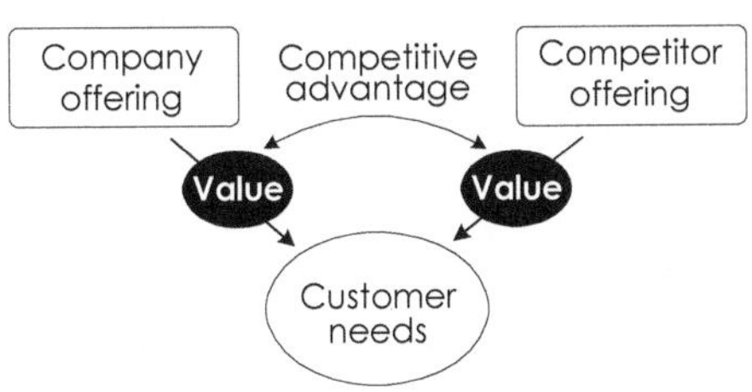

Competition is not just about differentiation; it is about differentiation that creates greater customer value. Because competitive advantage is determined by an offering's ability to create superior customer value, only attributes that are relevant to customer needs can create a competitive advantage. Differentiating on attributes that are irrelevant and do not add value for customers does not lead to a competitive advantage. In fact, differentiation on irrelevant attributes might even decrease the perceived value of the offering if customers believe that the irrelevant attributes come at the expense of other more important benefits.

In an ideal world, a company's offering should aim to dominate the competitive offering on all attributes. In reality, however, this is rarely the case. Because companies vary in resources, their offerings vary in the benefits they deliver to target customers. In this context, an offering's competitive advantage is defined by two factors: points of difference and points of parity. *Points of difference* involve attributes that are important for target customers and on which the company's offering is perceived to be different from that of its competitors. Specifically, there are two types of differences: *competitive advantage*, which reflects important attributes on which an offering dominates the competition, and *competitive disadvantage*, which describes attributes on which an offering is inferior to the competition. *Points of parity*, on the other hand, refer to attributes on which an offering's performance matches that of the competition.

The concepts of competitive differentiation, points of parity, and points of difference are illustrated in Figure 8, which reflects customer evaluations of the attribute performance of the offerings in a given market. Here, the horizontal axis identifies the attributes that have the potential to create value for target customers, and the vertical axis reflects customers' valuation of the benefits derived from the corresponding attributes of the offering. To account for the fact that some benefits are more important than others, individual attributes are usually ordered in terms of their importance, starting with the most important one. In this context, attributes on which the company's offering can create superior customer value relative to competitive offerings define its competitive advantage, attributes on which it is inferior define its competitive disadvantage, and attributes on which offerings are equivalent define the points of competitive parity.

Figure 8: Competitive Value Map

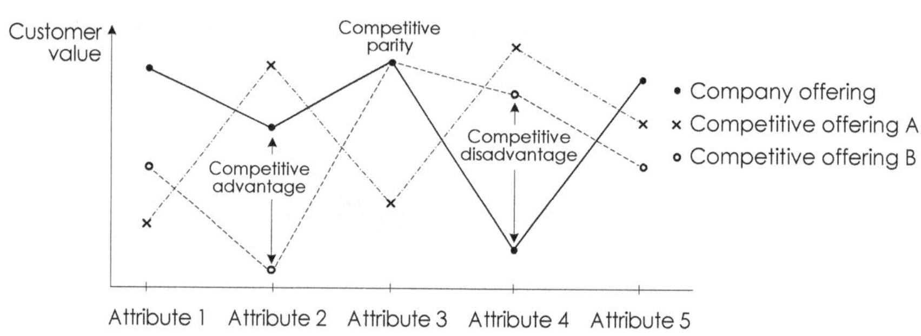

Note that competitive differentiation is not about actual differences among competitive offerings; it is about differences that are noticeable and perceived as relevant by target customers. Minor differences in market offerings that are not noticed by target customers or are deemed to be irrelevant do not constitute a competitive advantage. For example, if target customers cannot tell the difference in the performance of a 250 and a 260 horsepower car or if they find this difference meaningless, these offerings will be considered at competitive parity. By the same logic, an offering might be viewed as having a competitive advantage even when its attributes are identical to that of competitive offerings, as long as the offerings are differentiated in the mind of the customer. For example, two offerings might be at parity in their objective characteristics, but the stronger brand name associated with one of these offerings might make customers believe that this offering is, in fact, superior, giving it a competitive edge.

Strategies for Creating Superior Customer Value

The above discussion implies that to succeed an offering should aim to maximize its advantage on the attributes that are most important to target customers, while maintaining parity on the less relevant attributes. This raises the question of identifying actionable strategies a manager can use to create a competitive advantage. The three core strategies to achieve competitive advantage stem from the customer value equation $V_A = f(w_i, a_i)$ discussed earlier in this chapter. Recall that customer value is defined as a function of the importance of each of the relevant attributes (w_i) and the offering's perceived performance on each of these attributes (a_i). Accordingly, a manager can adopt one or more of the following three strategies for increasing the offering's value and creating a competitive advantage:

- **Improve the offering's performance on a given attribute.** In the context of the customer-value equation, this involves improving a_i, with i identifying the specific attribute to be improved. For example, to make a software program more attractive to customers who care most about performance, a company might consider improving its speed.
- **Add a new attribute on which the offering has an advantage.** In the context of the customer-value equation, this involves increasing the number of attributes (i) on which customers evaluate the offering. For example, a software company might differentiate its offering from the competition by introducing a novel feature that is perceived as valuable by target customers.
- **Increase the perceived importance of an attribute on which the offering has an advantage.** An alternative approach to make an offering more attractive is to change the perceived importance of some of its attributes in a way that bolsters an attribute on which it is superior to competitive offerings. For example, a company with software that is relatively slow but is compatible with most other existing software products might promote the importance of compatibility. In the context of the customer-value equation, this involves improving w_i, where i is compatibility. Note that unlike the first two strate-

gies, which involve improving the company's offerings, here the company aims to change buyers' beliefs about the relative importance of the different attributes defining the offering.

The above three strategies outline the key approaches a manager can take to enhance the value of an offering. When choosing which particular strategy to pursue, a manager must consider three factors: which strategy is likely to have the greatest increase in customer value, which strategy is likely to have the greatest value (e.g., lowest cost) for the company, and which strategy is the most difficult to copy by the competition. Selecting the strategy that optimizes these three factors is likely to contribute to the offering's market success.

Positioning the Offering

Positioning builds on the offering's value proposition to define the key reason for customers to choose the offering. The essence of positioning and its key components – frame of reference and primary benefit—are the focus of this section.

Positioning as a Marketing Concept

Positioning reflects the company's view of how its offering should be thought of by customers; it is the process of creating a distinct image of the company's offering in a customer's mind. For example, Volvo positions its cars as the safest vehicles on the road, Toyota emphasizes reliability, and BMW focuses on the driving experience.

The concept of positioning can be better understood when compared with the concept of the value proposition. Unlike the value proposition, which captures *all* the benefits and costs of an offering, positioning focuses customers' attention only on the *most important aspect(s)* of the offering's value proposition. Positioning aims to present the advantages of the offering in a way that accentuates its primary benefit(s) and provides customers with a compelling reason to choose the company's offering.

Because positioning typically highlights the most important benefit of the offering, it often can be summarized in a single phrase that is subsequently used to develop a tagline in the company's communications. For example, Domino's focus on speed led to the tagline *Fresh, hot pizza delivered in 30 minutes or less, guaranteed.* Papa John's focus on quality resulted in the tagline *Better Ingredients. Better Pizza.* Tide's focus on performance generated the tagline *If it's got to be clean...it's got to be Tide.* Avis's focus on service resulted in the tagline *We try harder.* Visa's focus on worldwide acceptance spawned the tagline *It's everywhere you want to be.*

The development of a positioning strategy involves two key decisions: (1) defining the frame of reference that customers should use when thinking about the company's offering and (2) identifying the offering's primary benefit. These two decisions are discussed in more detail below.

Defining the Frame of Reference

Customer valuation of market offerings is influenced by the reference points used to assess the attributes of the individual offerings. In this context, defining a frame of reference aims to provide customers with a benchmark that will underscore the value of the offering. Such benchmarks help customers categorize the offering in their minds and define the benefits and costs associated with the offering. Based on the choice of a reference point, five types of frames of reference can be distinguished.

- **Need-based framing** directly links the benefits of the offering to a particular customer need. For example, Coca-Cola's (1929) positioning as *"the pause that refreshes"* appealed directly to customers' need for a refreshment. Disneyland's (1955) positioning as *The Happiest Place on Earth*, Miller Lite's positioning *Great Taste . . . Less Filling!* and Walmart's positioning *Save Money. Live Better* are other examples of need-based framing.

- **User-based framing** defines the offering by associating it to a particular type of buyer. For example, brands such as Rolls-Royce, Louis Vuitton, and Patek Philippe are often associated with the upper social class and used to convey the image of high status and exclusivity. Honda's (1963) campaign *You Meet The Nicest People on a Honda* and Pepsi's (1963) campaign *Pepsi Generation* are other examples of user-based framing.

- **Category-based framing** defines the offering by relating it to an already established product category. For example, Coca-Cola's (1906) positioning as *The great national temperance beverage* defined Coke through its category membership and BMW's positioning as *The ultimate driving machine* defines its offerings relative to the car (driving machines) category.

- **Competitive framing** defines the offering by explicitly contrasting it to competitors' offerings and typically highlighting those aspects of the offering that differentiate it from the competition. The referent offering can be explicitly identified, or it can be broadly described without identifying a particular brand. DiGiorno's positioning *It's not delivery. It's DiGiorno,* and 7-Up's positioning as the *Un-cola* are examples of a competitive framing.

- **Product-line framing** defines the offering by comparing it to other offerings in the company's product line. Product-line framing highlights the differences between the generations of the same offering, and typically involves contrasting the benefits of the newly released product with those of the product it aims to replace. For example, Procter & Gamble used the tagline *Five Is Better than Three* to differentiate its five-blade Gillette Fusion razor from its three-blade predecessor, Mach3; and Microsoft highlighted the advantages of its Windows 7 operating system by comparing it to Vista, its predecessor.

The above five frames of reference can be grouped into the more general categories of noncomparative and comparative frames. *Noncomparative* framing directly relates the value of the offering to the reference point without explicitly contrasting it to other offerings. Need-based, user-based, and category-based frames of reference tend to be noncomparative. *Comparative* framing, on the other hand, defines the offering by contrasting it to other offerings. Competitive framing and product-line framing typically involve comparative frames of reference.

As a general rule, competitive positioning is employed by niche offerings trying to gain share from the market leader. Competitive positioning is rarely used by the market leader because by comparing its offering with one with a smaller share, the market leader often ends up implicitly promoting the referent offering. For example, Microsoft's Bing search engine was introduced by (favorably) comparing itself to the market leader, Google, aiming to attract some of its customers. In contrast, Google's positioning does not involve a comparison with other search engines as it stands to gain relatively little from such comparisons. Note that this rule applies only to companies that directly compete with one another; it does not hold for companies targeting different customer segments. For example, a larger share mass-market brand could benefit by comparing itself with a smaller share upscale brand (e.g., Volkswagen comparing itself to Porsche).

Identifying the Primary Benefit

Because positioning involves prioritizing an offering's existing benefits and costs, the same offering can often be positioned in multiple ways. For example, TiVo can be positioned as a device that allows viewers to pause live television, as a one-step recording device, as a device to fast forward commercials, as a device offering instant replay, or as a device that allows viewers to record one channel while watching another. Vitamin Water can be positioned as a source of nutrition, as an energy drink, as a thirst quencher, or simply as a source of hydration.

The key to positioning is making tradeoffs—deciding not to promote certain benefits to bring the key benefit(s) into focus. Thus, positioning involves prioritizing the benefits of the offering, a process referred to as benefit laddering. Based on the domain of the primary benefit, three positioning strategies can be identified:

- **Positioning on functional benefits** aims to create functional value by emphasizing a particular aspect of an offering's performance. For example, Porsche emphasizes performance, Maytag emphasizes reliability, and Visa emphasizes its worldwide acceptance.
- **Positioning on psychological benefits** emphasizes the psychological value associated with the offering. For instance, offerings such as Montblanc, Rolls-Royce, and Dom Pérignon are positioned to instill feelings of luxury, exclusivity, and prestige. An offering's positioning may also be influenced by the company's positioning as a leader in product innovation, as in the case of Apple, Google, and Samsung, or by its image as a socially responsible organization, as in the case of Ben and Jerry's, Newman's Own, and Ecolab. An offering may also be positioned by emphasizing its risk-minimizing benefits,

such as reducing uncertainty and gaining peace of mind—a strategy exemplified by Allstate insurance's tagline *You're in good hands with Allstate.*

- **Positioning on monetary benefits** emphasizes the monetary value associated with the offering. To illustrate, Southwest Airlines, Walmart, and Priceline.com emphasize low price as a key aspect of their value propositions, and Discover credit card emphasizes its cash-back feature as *America's number one cash rewards program.*

In addition to choosing which benefits to promote, the manager must also decide how many benefits to feature in its positioning. In this context, there are three common positioning strategies: single-benefit positioning, multi-benefit positioning, and holistic positioning.

- **Single-benefit positioning** involves emphasizing the value delivered by the one (primary) attribute the company believes will most likely provide customers with a compelling reason to choose its offering. Single-attribute positioning does not mean that the offering is inferior on its secondary attributes; it simply highlights the importance of a single attribute in order to establish a distinct message in the minds of customers (Figure 9). To illustrate, the driving experience is one of many aspects of BMW's value proposition, which also includes attributes such as comfort, fuel economy, design, quality, reliability, and safety. Yet BMW has consciously decided to emphasize performance above and beyond the other attributes to create a distinct image in the minds of its target customers. The rationale for this approach is the belief by many buyers that a specialized offering that does only one thing must do it very well, whereas an offering that does many things is unlikely to excel in any of them. Furthermore, superiority on the most important attribute is considered a valid reason for choice, helping buyers to justify their choices to others as well as to themselves.

Figure 9: Single-Benefit Positioning

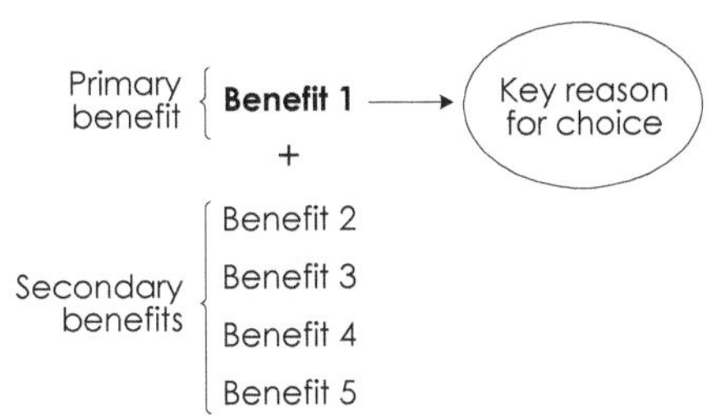

- **Multi-benefit positioning** emphasizes the benefits delivered by the offering on two or more attributes (Figure 10). A classic dual-benefit positioning is the one utilized by Procter & Gamble's Ivory Soap: *99 44/100% pure; it floats.* A more recent example of a multi-benefit positioning involves Apple's iPad, promoted as a *Magical and Revolutionary Device at an Unbelievable Price*. The advantage of multi-benefit positioning over single-benefit positioning is that it captures multiple aspects of the offering's value proposition. On the downside, multi-benefit positioning runs the risk of diluting the offering's image in the mind of the customer and failing to establish a compelling reason for choice. In general, multi-benefit positioning is not as common as single-benefit positioning and is typically limited to two attributes.

Figure 10: Dual-Benefit Positioning

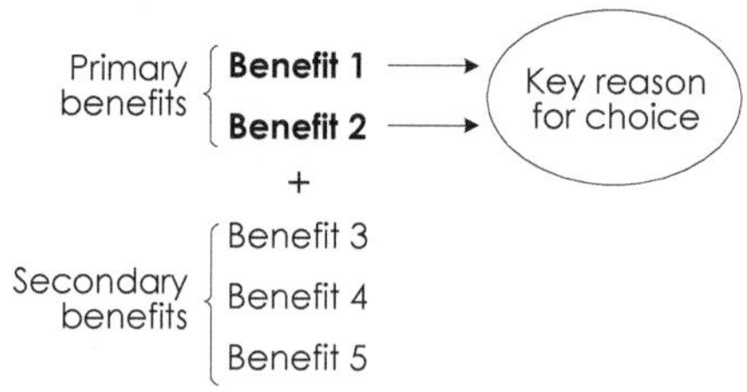

- **Holistic positioning** emphasizes overall performance without highlighting individual benefits, enticing customers to choose the offering based on its performance as a whole rather than on particular benefits (Figure 11). For example, Gillette's positioning as *The best a man can get* aims to create a perception of superior overall performance. Colgate Total, as implied by its name, claims to offer the best overall package of category benefits. Similarly, Amoco's positioning as *America's number one premium gasoline*, Tylenol's positioning as *The brand most hospitals trust*, and Hertz's positioning as the *#1 car rental company in the world* emphasize market leadership to signal superior overall performance.

Figure 11: Holistic Positioning

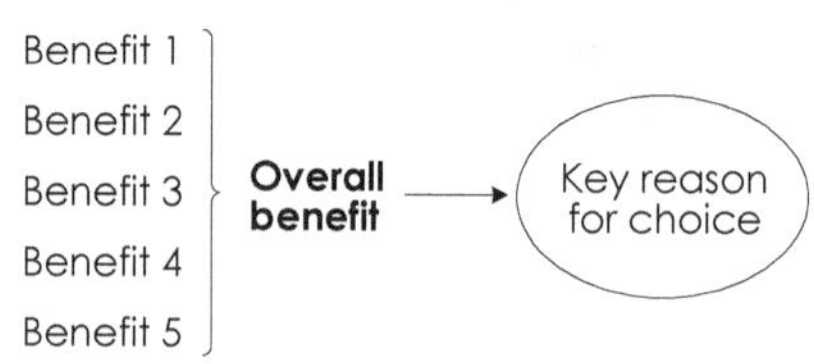

An offering's positioning strategy is outlined in a positioning statement that identifies the offering's target customers and its value proposition for these customers. The key principles of writing a positioning statement are discussed in more detail in Chapter 20.

SUMMARY

Because customers ultimately create value for the company and its collaborators, managing customer value is essential for a company's success. The two key aspects of managing customer value involve developing a value proposition and developing a positioning strategy.

The *value proposition* reflects all benefits and costs associated with a particular offering. Because value is a function of customers' needs, an offering's ability to create value is customer-specific: An offering that creates value for some customers might fail to do so for a different customer segment. The success of an offering is determined by the degree to which it can fulfill customer needs better than the competition on each of the three value dimensions: functional, monetary, and psychological.

The customer *value function* reflects the way in which attributes of the offering translate to subjective benefits and costs for target customers. For simplicity, the value function is often assumed to be the sum of the offering's performance on individual attributes, weighted (multiplied) by the relative importance of these attributes. The weighted-additive value function is based on the assumptions that (1) customers have well-articulated valuations of the offerings' performance on different attributes, (2) an increase in an offering's performance on a given attribute will result in a proportional increase in value, (3) the valuation of an offering is symmetric with respect to improving or diminishing its performance, and (4) buyers consider all available information about an offering in a systematic fashion. These assumptions often need to be corrected for the effects of four decision factors: *reference-point dependence, loss aversion, diminishing marginal value,* and *effort optimization.*

An offering's *competitive advantage* is defined by two factors: points of difference and points of parity. Points of difference (competitive advantage and competitive disadvantage) involve attributes that are important for target customers and on which the company's offering is perceived to be different from that of its competitors. Points of parity, on the other hand, refer to attributes on which an offering's performance matches that of the competition. Competitive advantage is defined by differences that are noticeable and perceived as relevant by target customers. Minor differences in market offerings that are not noticed by customers or are deemed to be irrelevant do not constitute a competitive advantage. To create and/or strengthen its competitive advantage a company can adopt the following strategies: (1) improve the offering's performance on a given attribute, (2) add a new attribute on which the offering has an advantage, and/or (3) increase the perceived importance of an attribute on which the offering has an advantage.

Positioning focuses customers' attention on the most important aspect(s) of the offering's value proposition. Positioning involves two key decisions: identifying the frame of reference and defining the primary benefit.

The *frame of reference* provides customers with a benchmark for assessing the value of the offering. Based on the choice of a reference point, five types of frames of reference can be distinguished: (1) need-based framing, which directly links the benefits of the offering to a particular customer need, (2) user-based framing, which defines the offering by associating it with a particular type of buyer, (3) category-based framing, which defines the offering by relating it to an already established product category, (4) competitive framing, which defines the offering by explicitly contrasting it with competitors' offerings, and (5) product-line framing, which defines the offering by comparing it with other offerings in the company's product line. Depending on the frame of reference, two positioning strategies can be differentiated: noncomparative positioning, which relates the offering's benefits directly to customers' needs, and comparative positioning, which contrasts the offering's benefits to those of a competitive offering.

The *primary benefit* reflects the main reason for customers to choose the offering and typically involves a functional, psychological, or monetary benefit. Based on the type and/or the number of primary benefits, there are three common positioning strategies: single-benefit positioning, multi-benefit positioning, and holistic positioning.

RELEVANT CONCEPTS: THE VALUE FUNCTION

The value function reflects the way people translate product features into subjective benefits (utility). Some of the key properties of the value function—reference-point dependence, loss aversion, diminishing marginal value, and effort optimization—were discussed in more detail earlier in this chapter. A popular representation of the value function capturing the first three properties—reference-point dependence, loss aversion, and diminishing marginal value—is shown in Figure 12.

Figure 12. The Value Function[1]

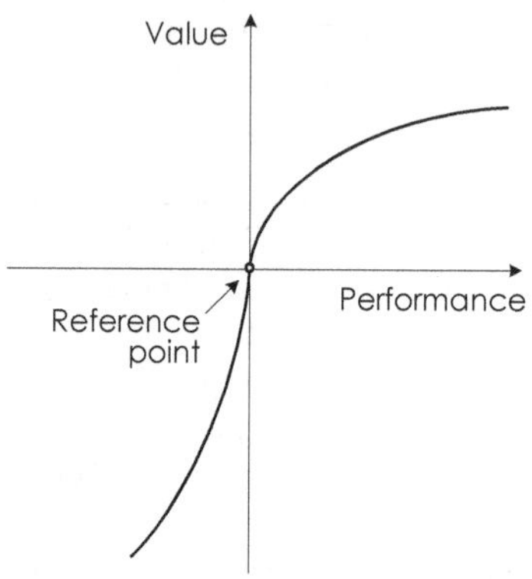

Here, the value function is represented by an S-shaped curve in a two-dimensional space in which the horizontal axis represents the actual performance and the vertical axis represents the subjective value (utility) from that performance. The origin of the two axes defines the buyer's reference point and is also the point that separates gains from losses (on the vertical axis) and offering improvements from detractions (on the horizontal axis) on the value curve. The three properties of the value function—reference-point dependence, loss aversion, and diminishing marginal value—are reflected in the fact that the value curve is concave for gains, convex and steeper for losses, and originates from the reference point used to evaluate the offering.

RELEVANT CONCEPTS: POSITIONING MAPS

Positioning maps reflect buyers' perception of an offering's performance relative to that of the competition. Positioning maps are derived from customer evaluations of various aspects of the offerings available in a given market. Positioning maps can have any number of dimensions, although two-dimensional maps are the most common because they are the easiest to interpret (Figure 13).

Figure 13. Positioning Map

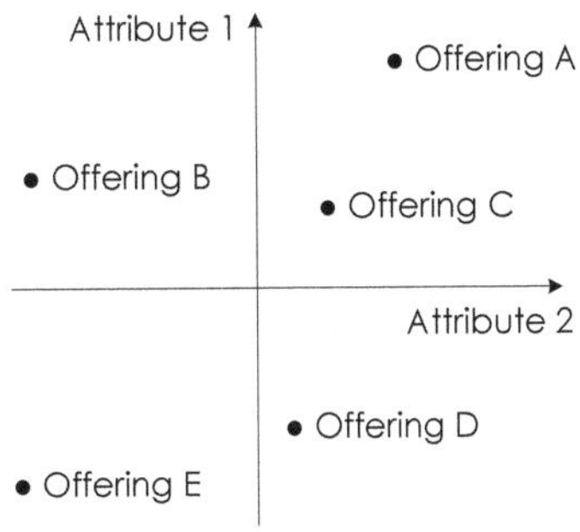

To illustrate, in the case of headache remedies, a positioning map can illustrate the relative performance of different drugs on factors such as effectiveness and duration, such that the most effective and longest lasting drugs will occupy the upper right corner of the chart and the least effective and shortest duration drugs will occupy the lower left corner.

Positioning maps can be derived by asking respondents to rate an option's performance on a set of predefined attributes and then aggregating these attribute-based evaluations into a few (usually two) more general factors. Alternatively, positioning maps can use customers' ratings of the similarities among the available offerings to derive the underlying dimensions and plot the offerings on a two-dimensional space. In addition to plotting the available offerings, positioning maps can also display consumers' ideal points, which reflect their ideal combinations of different aspects of the offering.

ADDITIONAL READINGS

Barwise, Patrick and Sean Meehan (2004), *Simply Better: Winning and Keeping Customers by Delivering What Matters Most.* Boston, MA: Harvard Business School Press.

Kahneman, Daniel (2011), *Thinking, Fast and Slow.* New York, NY: Farrar, Straus and Giroux.

Ries, Al and Jack Trout (2001), *Positioning: The Battle for Your Mind* (3rd ed.). New York, NY: McGraw-Hill.

NOTE

1 Adapted from Kahneman, Daniel and Amos Tversky (1979), "Prospect Theory: An Analysis of Decision under Risk," *Econometrica*, 47 (March), 263–91.

CHAPTER SIX

CREATING COMPANY VALUE: MANAGING REVENUES, COSTS, AND PROFITS

If one does not know to which port one is sailing, no wind is favorable.
—Seneca, Roman philosopher

A company is a business entity established for the purpose of creating value for its stakeholders. Accordingly, managing company value is the fundamental aspect of a company's strategy, defining its existence as a business enterprise. The key aspects of managing company value are the focus of this chapter.

Understanding Company Value

A company creates value for its stakeholders by creating value for its customers and collaborators in a way that enables the company to capture value to achieve its goals. To create value for its stakeholders, the company must define the benefits it aims to receive from the offering and relate these benefits to its ultimate goals. In this context, creating company value can be viewed as a process of capturing value derived from the market exchange in which the company creates value for its customers and collaborators.

Company value is defined relative to the company's goal and comprises all relevant benefits and costs associated with the offering. In this context, an offering can create value for the company in three different domains: monetary, functional, and psychological. These three domains define the overall benefit a company receives from a given offering and are discussed in more detail below.

- **Monetary value** involves the monetary benefits of the offering. Monetary value is directly linked to a company's desired financial performance and typically involves factors such as net income, profit margins, sales revenue, earnings per share, and return on investment. Monetary value is the most common type of value sought for offerings managed by for-profit companies.

- **Functional value** reflects the functional benefits and costs of the offering. An offering can create functional value for the company by facilitating other offerings in the company's portfolio. For example, an entry-level car sold at cost can help the manufacturer gain market share among younger customers when they decide to trade up. A free software program can provide a company with a technological platform for developing high-margin offerings. Functional goals do not need to be related to profits. For example, creating value for society by improving different aspects of social welfare is a common goal for many nonprofit organizations.
- **Psychological value** stems from outcomes of psychological importance for company employees and stakeholders. For example, a company's socially responsible actions such as preserving the environment and supporting various social causes can help build the corporate brand and culture. In the same vein, offerings that demonstrate a company's leadership in a particular area, such as research and development, can also create value for the company by helping to attract valuable employees and promote brand loyalty.

These three types of value correspond to the two types of company goals—monetary and strategic—whereby the monetary value corresponds to the company's financial goals and the functional and psychological value reflect the offering's ability to fulfill a company's strategic goals. The relationship among the three dimensions of company value and the company's goals is illustrated in Figure 1.

Figure 1. The Three Dimensions of Company Value

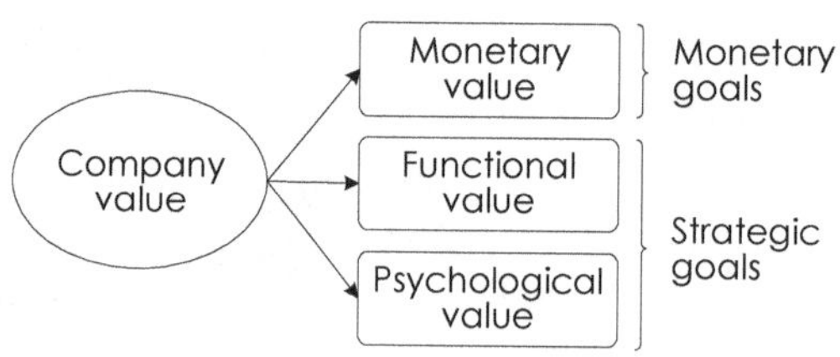

Because maximizing monetary value is the primary goal for most companies, most offerings must either directly or indirectly be linked to profitability. Accordingly, the rest of this chapter focuses on understanding the key factors influencing profitability, as well as on identifying strategies for effectively managing profit growth.

Managing Profit Growth

To design successful profit-growth strategies, a manager must understand the key drivers of a company's bottom line, prioritize their impact, and focus on changes that will have the greatest impact on profits. The key profit drivers can be presented in the form of a decision tree that delineates the individual factors contributing to the company's bottom line. A typical profit-growth decision tree is illustrated in Figure 2 and discussed in more detail below.

Figure 2. The Key Profit Drivers

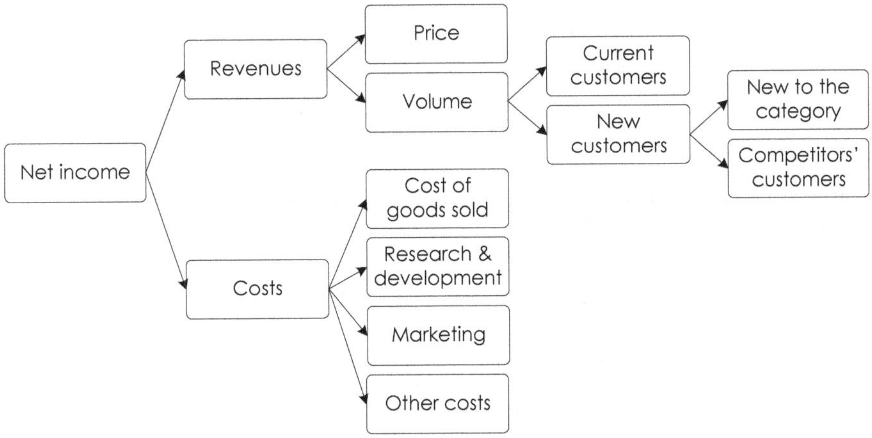

On the most general level, a company's net income is defined by the difference in revenues and costs. Therefore, to grow income a company must increase revenues and/or reduce costs. Revenue growth (also referred to as top-line growth), in turn, can be achieved by increasing sales volume and/or changing the unit price. At the same time, costs can be reduced by lowering various types of expenses, including cost of goods sold, research-and-development costs, marketing costs, and other costs such as general and administrative expenses and the cost of capital.

While both increasing sales revenues and decreasing costs can have a significant impact on profit growth, growing revenues rather than cutting costs is more likely to produce sustainable growth over time. Similarly, even though price optimization can have a significant impact on profits, increasing sales volume rather than modifying price is usually the key source of sustainable profitability. In this context, growing sales volume is often viewed as the main source of profit growth, subject to optimizing the offering's price and the costs.

To increase sales volume, a company can either focus on its current customers by increasing the quantity and frequency of purchases, or it can focus on acquiring customers that it does not currently serve. Furthermore, growing the sales volume from new customers can follow two strategies: attracting customers who are new to the particular product category and thus growing the size of the entire market, and attracting customers who already buy competitors' offerings and "stealing" them from the competition.

The most effective strategy to grow profits depends on a company's goals, resources, and the specific market conditions. In some cases, profitability can best be achieved by increasing sales volume, for example, by generating incremental volume from current customers. In other scenarios, profit growth might also involve lowering costs, for example, by streamlining operations or reducing marketing expenses. Different strategies for achieving profit growth are outlined in more detail in the following sections.

Managing Profit Growth by Increasing Sales Revenues

Increasing sales revenues is the prevalent approach to achieving long-term profitability. Sales growth can be achieved using internal resources—an approach referred to as "organic" growth—or by acquiring or merging with another company. The focus of this section is on organic growth, which is arguably the most common sales growth strategy. In this context, there are two main approaches for increasing sales revenues: growing sales volume and optimizing price. These two strategies are discussed in more detail in the following sections.

Increasing Sales Revenues by Growing Sales Volume

On the most general level, there are three basic strategies for increasing sales volume: market growth, steal share, and market penetration. *Market-growth* strategy (also referred to as primary-demand strategy) involves increasing sales volume by attracting new-to-the-category customers who currently are not using either the company's or competitors' offerings. In contrast, the *steal-share* strategy involves growing sales volume by attracting customers who are already category users and are buying competitors' offerings. Finally, the *market-penetration* strategy involves increasing sales volume by increasing the quantity purchased by the company's own customers rather than explicitly trying to "steal" competitors' customers or attract new buyers to the product category. Thus, the market-growth and steal-share strategies reflect a company's efforts to manage customer adoption, and the market-penetration strategy reflects a company's efforts to manage customer usage of the company's offerings. These three strategies are illustrated in Figure 3 and discussed in more detail in Chapter 14.

Figure 3. Strategies for Growing Sales Volume

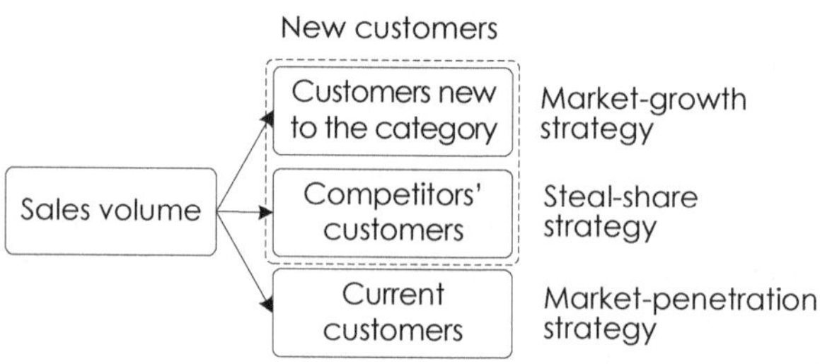

To grow sales volume, a company must create value for its target customers. This can be achieved by pursuing four core strategies that aim to improve the awareness, availability, attractiveness, and/or affordability of the offering. Thus, a company might aim to grow sales volume by increasing *awareness* of the offering by communicating its benefits to target customers. A company might also grow sales volume by increasing the *availability* of the offering by expanding manufacturing capacity, enhancing distribution coverage, strengthening retailer support, and minimizing stock-outs. Alternatively, a company might grow volume by increasing the *attractiveness* of its offering by improving product functionality (e.g., by improving the quality of the raw materials and/or by using superior technologies), by realigning product benefits with customer needs and/or improving service quality (e.g., by insourcing), and by increasing the value of the brand. Finally, sales volume can be increased by improving the *affordability* of the offering by lowering price (e.g., giving up margins to gain share), offering incentives, and decreasing the other costs associated with the offering. These four strategies are discussed in more detail in Chapter 15.

Increasing Sales Revenues by Optimizing Price

Setting prices is a vital component of managing sales revenues. The impact of pricing on sales revenues depends on the way customers react to changes in price. On the one hand, raising prices increases profit margins, which has a positive impact on profits. On the other hand, raising prices tends to decrease sales volume due to the lower customer value associated with a higher price. Thus, sales revenues can be increased by raising prices in cases when the positive impact of increasing profit margins is greater than the negative impact of the corresponding decrease in sales volume. Alternatively, sales revenues can be increased by lowering price in cases when the positive impact of the increase in sales volume is greater than the negative impact of the corresponding decrease in profit margins.

The impact of price on sales volume is a function of customers' price elasticity, which reflects the degree to which a change in price leads to a change in quantity sold. The lower the price elasticity, the more likely it is that raising the price can increase sales revenues (see Chapter 10 for more details). Thus, in cases where price elasticity is low and the decrease in sales volume caused by a higher price can be offset by an increase in revenues attributed to the higher price, raising prices can lead to greater sales revenues. Alternatively, when price elasticity is high and lost revenues from a price cut can be offset by an increase in sales volume, lowering price can lead to higher sales revenues.

Two issues in managing price merit attention. First, the term *price* is used fairly broadly to reflect not only the list price of an offering but also various monetary incentives that typically accompany the list price. These incentives include price reductions, coupons, rebates (in the case of customer transactions), and trade discounts such as volume discounts and allowances (in the case of collaborator transactions). Consequently, managing sales revenues requires optimizing not only an offering's price but also its price incentives. A more detailed discussion of price and incentives management is offered in Chapters 10 and 11.

Furthermore, because a manufacturer's offerings are in most cases sold by a third party (wholesalers, retailers, distributors, and dealers), its sales revenues are determined not so much by the retail price that customers pay as by the (wholesale) price the company charges its channel partners. Therefore, managing price involves managing not just the final customer price but also managing the prices throughout the retail channel. A more detailed discussion of the company's relationship with its channel partners is offered in Chapters 7 and 13.

Managing Profit Growth by Lowering Costs

An alternative strategy to growing profits involves lowering costs rather than increasing sales revenues. A company's costs can be classified into four categories: cost of goods sold, research-and-development costs, marketing costs, and miscellaneous other costs such as general and administrative costs and cost of capital. These four strategies for lowering costs are discussed in more detail below.

- **Lowering the cost of goods sold**. The term *cost of goods sold* describes expenses directly related to creating the goods or services being sold and can have both a variable (e.g., the cost of raw materials and the cost of turning raw materials into goods) and a fixed component (e.g., the depreciation of equipment). There are two basic ways to lower the cost of goods sold. The first is to *lower the costs of inputs*—such as raw materials, labor, and inbound logistics—used in developing the company's offering. Lowering the costs of inputs can be achieved by outsourcing, switching suppliers, and adopting alternative technologies that use more cost-effective inputs. The second approach to managing the cost of goods sold is to *lower the costs of the processes* that transform the inputs into the end product, such as optimizing operations and adopting alternative technologies that use more cost-effective processes.

- **Lowering research-and-development costs.** Research and development typically involves fixed costs necessary for designing the company's offering and, in many industries, accounts for a significant portion of the overall costs. Strategies for decreasing research-and-development costs involve adopting technologies that shorten the product development cycle, minimize equipment costs, and manage labor costs.

- **Lowering marketing costs**. Depending on the company's business model, marketing costs can account for a significant portion of the overall costs associated with the offering. Marketing costs involve several different types of expenses. The *cost of incentives* involves consumer-focused promotions such as price reductions, coupons, rebates, contests, sweepstakes, and premiums. *Communication costs* comprise advertising expenditures (television, radio, print, online, outdoor, point-of-purchase, and event advertising), public relations expenditures (press coverage, product placement, and social media), and personal selling (sales force). *Distribution costs* reflect the margins received by distributors, cost of the sales force,[1] and trade incentives such as trade allowances, volume discounts, and co-op advertising allowances. *Miscellaneous marketing costs* reflect the costs of factors such as marketing research and marketing overhead.

- **Lowering miscellaneous other costs**. In addition to decreasing the cost of goods sold, research-and-development expenditures, and marketing expenses, overall costs can be lowered by decreasing all other costs such as administrative costs, legal costs, and cost of capital.

Common strategies for lowering the above four types of costs involve achieving economies of scale, learning, and scope. *Economies of scale* that stem from greater manufacturing and sales volume lead to a decrease in per-unit costs. The rela- relationship between costs and production volume is not monotonic: As the output volume increases, marginal costs tend to decrease initially until they reach the point at which they begin to increase, leading to diseconomies of scale. A conceptually related source of lowering costs involves economies from moving up the *learning curve*. In this case, the savings stem from the increased productivity from the experience accumulated over time. Finally, in addition to economies of scale and learning, costs savings can result from *economies of scope*—that is, from synergies among different offerings. Economies of scope are conceptually similar to economies of scale in that an increase in size typically leads to lower costs. Unlike economies of scale, however, where cost savings stem from increasing the scale of production for a single offering, economies of scope refer to cost savings resulting from synergies among different offerings in a company's portfolio.

SUMMARY

Company value is defined relative to the company's goal and comprises all relevant benefits and costs associated with the offering. An offering can create value for the company in three different domains: monetary, functional, and psychological. Because maximizing monetary value is the primary goal for most companies, the success of most offerings is either directly or indirectly linked to profitability.

Achieving sustainable profit growth is the ultimate goal for most companies. Managing profit growth can be achieved by increasing sales revenues and/or reducing costs. Increasing sales revenues can be achieved by managing price and/or by increasing sales volume, which in turn can be achieved by stealing share from competitors, bringing new customers to the category, and increasing sales to existing customers. Managing costs involves decreasing costs of goods sold, research-and-development costs, marketing costs, as well as miscellaneous other costs.

Increasing *sales revenues* is the prevalent approach to achieving long-term profitability. Increasing sales revenues can be achieved through two basic strategies: growing sales volume and optimizing price.

Strategies for growing *sales volume* include (1) growing the entire market by attracting new-to-the-category customers who currently are not using either the company's or competitors' offerings, (2) stealing share by attracting customers who currently are using competitors' offerings, and (3) market penetration by increasing the quantity purchased by the company's own customers. Market-growth and steal-share strategies reflect a company's efforts to manage customer adoption, and the market-penetration strategy reflects a company's efforts to manage customer usage of the company's offerings.

The impact of *varying the price* on sales revenues depends on the way customers react to changes in price. Sales revenues can be increased by raising prices in cases when the positive impact of increasing profit margins is greater than the negative impact of the corresponding decrease in sales volume. Alternatively, sales revenues can be increased by lowering prices in cases when the positive impact of the increase in sales volume is greater than the negative impact of the corresponding decrease in profit margins.

In addition to increasing revenues, profit growth can be achieved by *lowering costs*, including the cost of goods sold, research-and-development costs, marketing costs, and miscellaneous other costs such as general and administrative costs and cost of capital. Common strategies for lowering the above four types of costs involve achieving economies of scale, learning, and scope.

RELEVANT CONCEPTS: ECONOMIC VALUE ANALYSIS

The existence of three different dimensions that create company value raises the question of how to compare the benefits and costs created on these dimensions. Specifically, in the case of for-profit companies, the question often is how to translate strategic value into monetary value. To answer this question, a manager must assess the monetary value of the functional and psychological benefits of the offering—a process commonly referred to as *economic value analysis*. Accordingly, economic value analysis involves translating the nonmonetary benefits of an offering into financial terms (Figure 4).

Figure 4. Economic Value Analysis

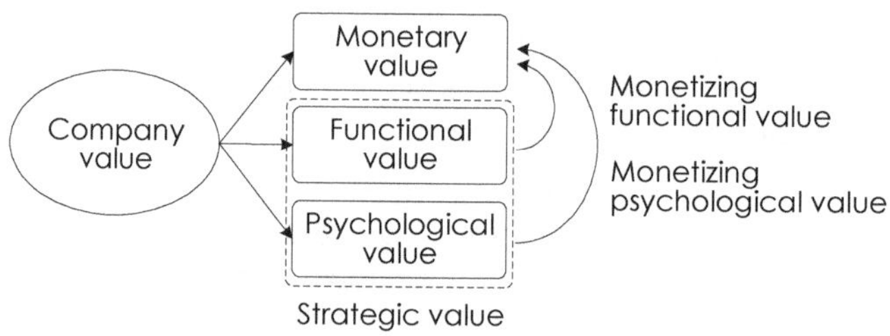

Economic value analysis is predicated on the idea that the strategic benefits of an offering, such as its functional and psychological value to the company, can be quantified and monetized based on the long-term financial impact these benefits are likely to have on the entire company. Because it estimates the long-term monetary impact of nonmonetary factors, economic value analysis is related to the notion of the total cost of ownership. Similar to economic value analysis, the total cost of ownership monetizes the nonmonetary aspects of the offering. Unlike economic value analysis, however, the total cost of ownership takes into account only the functional (and not psychological) benefits and often focuses only on the cost side of the value created by the offering. In this context, the concept of total cost of ownership is somewhat narrower in scope compared to the economic value analysis.

RELEVANT CONCEPTS: THE INCOME (PROFIT-AND-LOSS) STATEMENT

The income statement (also referred to as the *profit and loss statement*) is a financial document showing a company's income and expenses during a given period. It typically identifies revenues, costs, operating expenses, operating income, and earnings (Figure 5).

Figure 5: The Income (Profit-and-Loss) Statement

Gross Revenues	
Sales revenues	$ 18,000
Returns and allowances	(3,000)
Total (Gross) Revenues	15,000
Cost of Goods Sold	
Product costs	(4,500)
Services costs	(1,500)
Total Cost of Goods Sold	(6,000)
Gross Profit	9,000
Gross Margin	60%
Operating Expenses	
Sales and marketing	5,000
General and administrative	1,000
Research and development	1,500
Total Operating Expenses	7,500
Operating Income	1,500
Operating Margin	10%
Other Revenues (Expenses)	
Interest expense	(250)
Depreciation and amortization	(100)
Income tax expense	(400)
Total Other Revenues (Expenses)	(750)
Net Income (Earnings)	750
Net (Profit) Margin	5%

Gross (Profit) Margin: The ratio of gross (total) profit to gross (total) revenue (sometimes also used as a synonym for gross profit). Gross margin analysis is a useful tool because it implicitly includes unit selling prices of products or services, unit costs, and unit volume. Note, however, the difference between gross margin and contribution margin: Contribution margin includes all variable costs; in contrast, gross margin includes some, but often not all, variable costs, a number of which can be part of the operating margin.

$$\text{Gross margin} = \frac{\text{Gross profit}}{\text{Gross revenue}} = \frac{\text{Gross revenue} - \text{Cost of goods sold}}{\text{Gross revenue}}$$

Gross Profit: The difference between gross (total) revenue and total cost of goods sold. Gross profit can also be calculated on a per-unit basis as the difference between unit selling price and unit cost of goods sold. For example, if a company sells 100 units, each priced at $1 and each costing the company $.30 to manufacture, then the unit gross profit is $.70, the total gross profit is $70, and the unit and total gross margins are 70%.

$$\text{Gross profit}_{\text{Total}} = \text{Revenue}_{\text{Total}} - \text{Cost of goods sold}_{\text{Total}}$$

$$\text{Gross profit}_{\text{Unit}} = \text{Price}_{\text{Unit}} - \text{Cost of goods sold}_{\text{Unit}}$$

Gross Revenue: Total receipts from a company's business activities.

Net Earnings: See *net income.*

Net Income: Gross revenue minus all costs and expenses (cost of goods sold, operating expenses, depreciation, interest, and taxes) during a given period of time.

$$\text{Net income} = \text{Gross revenue} - \text{Total costs}$$

Net Margin: The ratio of net income to gross (total) revenue.

$$\text{Net margin} = \frac{\text{Net income}}{\text{Gross revenue}}$$

Operating Expenses: The primary costs, other than cost of goods sold, incurred to generate revenues (e.g., sales, marketing, research and development, and general and administrative expenses).

Operating Income: Gross profit minus operating expenses. Operating income reflects the firm's profitability from current operations without regard to the interest charges accruing from the firm's capital structure.

$$\text{Operating income} = \text{Gross profit} - \text{Operating expenses}$$

Operating Margin: The ratio of operating income to gross (total) revenue.

$$\text{Operating margin} = \frac{\text{Operating income}}{\text{Gross revenue}}$$

RELEVANT CONCEPTS: MARGIN ANALYSIS

Contribution Margin ($): When expressed in monetary terms ($), contribution margin typically refers to the difference between total revenue and total variable costs. Contribution margin can also be calculated on a per-unit basis as the difference between the unit selling price and the unit variable cost. The per-unit margin, expressed in monetary terms ($), is also referred to as contribution (i.e., the dollar amount that each unit sold "contributes" to the payment of fixed costs).

$$\text{Contribution margin}_{\text{Total}}(\$) = \text{Revenue}_{\text{Total}} - \text{Variable costs}_{\text{Total}}$$

$$\text{Contribution margin}_{\text{Unit}}(\$) = \text{Price}_{\text{Unit}} - \text{Variable costs}_{\text{Unit}}$$

Contribution Margin (%): When expressed in percentages (%), contribution margin typically refers to the ratio of the difference between total revenue and total variable costs to total revenue. Contribution margin can also be expressed as the ratio of unit contribution to unit selling price.

$$\text{Contribution margin (\%)} = \frac{\text{Revenue}_{\text{Total}} - \text{Variable cost}_{\text{Total}}}{\text{Revenue}_{\text{Total}}} = \frac{\text{Price}_{\text{Unit}} - \text{Variable cost}_{\text{Unit}}}{\text{Price}_{\text{Unit}}}$$

Fixed Costs: Expenses that do not fluctuate with output volume within a relevant period. Typical examples of fixed costs include research-and-development expenses, mass-media advertising expenses, rent, interest on debt, insurance, plant-and-equipment expenses, and salary of permanent full-time workers. Even though their absolute size remains unchanged regardless of output volume, fixed costs become progressively smaller per unit of output as volume increases, a decrease that results from the larger number of output units over which fixed costs are allocated. See also *variable costs.*

Margin: The difference between two factors, typically expressed either in monetary terms or percentages. There are two types of margins: (1) contribution margins, which reflect the relationship between variable and fixed costs and (2) income margins, which reflect the relationships between a company's gross (total) profit, income, and gross (total) revenue.

Marginal Cost: The cost of producing one extra unit.

Trade Margin: The difference between unit selling price and unit cost at each level of a marketing channel. Trade margins can be expressed in monetary terms or as a percentage. A useful approach to analyzing margins involves mapping the distribution channel structure to identify margins for each channel member (Figure 5). Note that margins are most often calculated based on sales revenue (sales price) rather than based on cost (purchase price).

Figure 6: Calculating Distribution Channel Margins

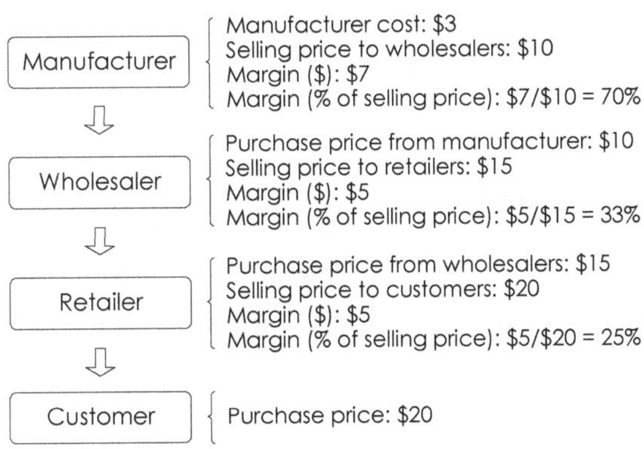

Variable Costs: Expenses that fluctuate in direct proportion to the output volume of units produced. For example, the cost of raw materials and expenses incurred by consumer incentives (e.g., coupons, price discounts, rebates, and premiums) are commonly viewed as variable costs. Other expenses, such as channel incentives (e.g., promotional allowances) and sales force compensation, can be classified as either fixed or variable costs depending on their structure (e.g., fixed salary vs. performance-based compensation). See also *fixed costs.*

RELEVANT CONCEPTS: BREAK-EVEN ANALYSES

Break-even analysis aims to identify the point at which the benefits and costs associated with a particular action are equal, and beyond which profit occurs. The most common types of break-even analyses include break-even of a fixed-cost investment, break-even of a price cut, break-even of a variable-cost increase, and break-even analysis of cannibalization (discussed in Chapter 17).

Break-even analysis of a fixed-cost investment identifies the unit or dollar sales volume at which the company is able to recoup a particular investment, such as research-and-development expenses, product improvement costs, and/or the costs of an advertising campaign. The break-even volume of a fixed-cost investment (BEV_{FC}) is the ratio of the size of the fixed-cost investment to the unit margin.

$$BEV_{FC} = \frac{\text{Fixed-cost investment}}{\text{Unit margin}}$$

To illustrate, consider an offering priced at \$100 with variable costs of \$50 and fixed costs of \$50M. In this case, BEV_{FC}= \$50M/(\$100 – \$50)= 1,000,000. Thus, for a \$50M fixed-cost investment to break even, sales volume should reach 1,000,000 items.

Break-even analysis of a price cut estimates the increase in sales volume needed for a price cut to have a neutral impact on profitability. To break even, lost profits resulting from a lower margin after a price cut must be equal to the additional profits generated by the incremental sales volume from the lower price. Specifically, the break-even rate (BER_{PC}) at which sales should increase so that a price cut has a neutral impact on profitability can be calculated as follows:[2]

$$BER_{PC} = \frac{\text{Margin}_{\text{OldPrice}}}{\text{Margin}_{\text{NewPrice}}}$$

To illustrate, consider the impact of a price cut from \$100 to \$75 for a product with a variable cost of \$50. In this case, $\text{Margin}_{\text{OldPrice}}$ = \$100 – \$50 = \$50 and $\text{Margin}_{\text{NewPrice}}$ = \$75 – \$50 = \$25. Therefore, BER_{PC} = \$50/\$25 = 2. Thus, for the price cut to break even, sales volume should double at the lower price.

Break-even analysis of a variable-cost increase identifies the sales volume at which a company neither makes a profit nor incurs a loss after increasing variable costs. From a conceptual standpoint, the analysis is identical to that of the price cut, whereby the break-even rate of an increase in variable costs (BER_{VCI}) is:[3]

$$BER_{VCI} = \frac{\text{Margin}_{\text{OldVC}}}{\text{Margin}_{\text{NewVC}}}$$

To illustrate, consider the impact of an increase in variable costs from \$50 to \$60 for a product priced at \$100. In this case, $\text{Margin}_{\text{OldVC}}$ = \$100 – \$50 = \$50 and $\text{Margin}_{\text{NewVC}}$ = \$100 – \$60 = \$40. Therefore, the break-even volume of a variable cost increase BER_{VCI} = \$50/\$40 = 1.25. Thus, for the variable-cost increase to break even, the ratio of the new to old sales should be 1.25, meaning that sales volume should increase by a factor of .25, or by 25%.

RELEVANT CONCEPTS: KEY MARKETING METRICS

Compound Annual Growth Rate (CAGR): The year-to-year growth rate of an investment during a specified period.

Internal Rate of Return (IRR): The annualized effective compounded return rate that can be earned on the invested capital (i.e., the yield on the investment).

Market Share: An offering's share of the total sales of all offerings within the product category in which the brand competes. Market share is determined by dividing an offering's sales volume by the total category sales volume. Sales can be defined in terms of revenues or on a unit basis (e.g., number of items sold or number of customers served).

$$\text{Market share} = \frac{\text{An offering's sales in a given market}}{\text{Total sales in a given market}}$$

Market Size: Monetary value of an existing or potential market, typically measured on an annual basis. Market size is also used in reference to the number of customers in a particular market.

Return on Investment (ROI): Net income as a percentage of the investment required for generating this income.

$$\text{ROI} = \frac{\text{Gain from an investment} - \text{Cost of investment}}{\text{Cost of investment}}$$

Return on Marketing Investment (ROMI): A measure of the efficiency of a company's marketing expenditures. Most often calculated in terms of incremental net income, sales revenues, market share, or contribution margin. ROMI can also be calculated with respect to the overall marketing expenditures or to a specific marketing mix variable (e.g., branding, incentives, or communication).

$$\text{ROMI} = \frac{\text{Incremental net income generated by the marketing investment}}{\text{Cost of the marketing investment}}$$

Return on Sales (ROS): Net income as a percentage of sales revenues.

$$\text{ROS} = \frac{\text{Net income}}{\text{Sales revenue}}$$

ADDITIONAL READINGS

Best, Roger J. (2012), *Market-Based Management: Strategies for Growing Customer Value and Profitability* (6th ed.). Upper Saddle River, NJ: Prentice Hall.

Henderson, Bruce, D. (1974), "The Experience Curve Reviewed: Why Does It Work?" in *Perspectives on Strategy: From the Boston Consulting Group* (1998), Carl W. Stern and George Stalk Jr., Eds. New York, NY: John Wiley & Sons.

Kotler, Philip, Dipak C. Jain, and Suvit Maesincee (2002), *Marketing Moves: A New Approach to Profits, Growth, and Renewal.* Boston, MA: Harvard Business School Press.

NOTES

1 Note that the sales force might serve a dual function—communicating and distributing the offering.

2 To have a neutral or positive impact on the company's bottom line, the additional profits generated by the incremental volume resulting from a lower price must be equal to or greater than the lost profits that result from a lower margin.

$$Profit_{NewPrice} \geq Profit_{OldPrice}$$

Given that profit is a function of unit volume and unit margin, the above equation can be modified as follows:

$$Volume_{NewPrice} \cdot Margin_{NewPrice} \geq Volume_{OldPrice} \cdot Margin_{OldPrice}$$

Hence, the increase in sales volume that needs to be achieved for a price cut to break even is:

$$BEV_{PC} = \frac{Volume_{NewPrice}}{Volume_{OldPrice}} = \frac{Margin_{OldPrice}}{Margin_{NewPrice}}$$

3 The basic principle of calculating the break-even point of an increase in an offering's variable costs is similar to that of estimating the break-even point of a price cut. The key difference is that a decrease in the margin generated by the new offering is a result of an increase in the offering's costs rather than a decrease in revenues.

CHAPTER SEVEN

CREATING COLLABORATOR VALUE: MANAGING BUSINESS MARKETS

Coming together is a beginning. Keeping together is progress. Working together is success.
—Henry Ford, American industrialist

Collaborators are entities that work with the company to create value for target customers. Because most collaborators are business entities, collaboration typically involves business-to-business relationships aimed at creating customer value. The key aspects of the process of creating value through collaboration are the focus of this chapter.

Collaboration as a Business Process

As a business process, collaboration aims to improve a company's ability to create value for its target customers in a way that helps achieve its own strategic goals. The essence of collaboration, its advantages and drawbacks, levels of collaboration, and alternatives to collaboration are discussed in more detail below.

The Essence of Collaboration

Collaboration involves entering into a relationship with an external entity and delegating to it a subset of the company's activities. Value creation through collaboration reflects a fundamental shift away from the traditional business paradigm in which a company alone creates customer value to a new paradigm in which the value is jointly created by the company and its collaborators. The concept of a fully integrated company with its own supply, manufacturing, and distribution has been replaced with that of outsourcing, which delegates many business functions to external entities. This shift toward collaborative business enterprise stems from the belief that greater effectiveness and cost efficiency can be achieved from greater expertise and scale of operations. Accordingly, collaboration brings together different entities—suppliers, manufacturers, distributors (dealers, wholesalers, and retailers), research-and-development companies, service providers, external sales force, advertising agencies, and marketing research companies—to create a sustainable value exchange.

Because it captures the relationships between business entities, collaboration is often viewed strictly as a business-to-business process unrelated to the company's consumer-focused activities. This is because business and consumer markets are very different on a variety of dimensions, including the type of customers served, the type of products and services offered, the selling process, and the nature of the relationship between the buyer and the seller. Yet, despite their differences, a company's business-focused and consumer-focused activities are closely related because they represent different aspects of an overarching value-creation process that determines the ultimate success of both business-to-business and business-to-consumer activities.

The key marketing principle—creating superior value for target customers in a way that benefits the company and its collaborators—is also the key principle that guides all forms of collaboration. Therefore, the relationship between a company and its collaborators should always be considered in the context of creating value for target customers. In this context, it can be argued that there are few, if any, "pure" business-to-business relationships that can be considered independently from their ability to create customer value. Most business-focused relationships are in reality business-to-business-to-customer collaborations, meaning that the business-to-business component can meaningfully exist only as part of the overall value-creation process.

To illustrate, consider the typical vertical collaboration between a manufacturer and a retailer. The success of this collaboration is determined to a large degree by the ability of the manufacturer to create value not only for the retailer but also for the end customer. If the manufacturer's offerings fail to create value for the customer, the retailer, in turn, will find it difficult to sell the company's offerings to these customers, which ultimately will hinder the collaboration between the manufacturer and the retailer. To succeed in the business-to-business aspect of collaboration, the manufacturer must envision the entire value-creation chain, including the end customer, and design its offering to create value for both its collaborators and end customers. The same logic holds for entities involved in horizontal collaboration, such as research and development, product design, and manufacturing. The sustainability of this type of collaboration is also a function of the degree to which actions of the companies involved create value for target customers. Indeed, because target customers are the key source of revenues that are shared by collaborators, failure to create value for these customers will have a negative effect on the shared revenues, which, in turn, will threaten the sustainability of the collaboration.

Because collaboration is a value-creation process, it spans the processes of designing, communicating, and delivering value to target customers. Accordingly, collaboration can occur in three domains: (1) value-design collaboration—including product and service development, brand building, price setting, and incentive design; (2) value-communication collaboration—including advertising, public relations, and social media; and (3) value-delivery collaboration—including the actual delivery of a company's products and services. Note that even though they can serve different functions in the value-creation process, collaborating entities can be involved in all three aspects of designing, communicating, and delivering value.

For example, in addition to delivering the company's offerings to target customers, distribution channels can play an important role in customizing the product, augmenting the service, setting the price, and managing incentives, as well as in communicating the offering's benefits by means of in-store advertisements, displays, and direct mail. In the same vein, in addition to communicating the value of an offering, advertising agencies can facilitate its branding, optimize its pricing, and design and distribute targeted incentives.

Advantages and Drawbacks of Collaboration

Like most business relationships, collaboration has its advantages and drawbacks. Specifically, collaboration offers several important *benefits* for participating entities: effectiveness, cost efficiency, flexibility, and speed.

- **Effectiveness**. Collaboration enables companies to specialize in a particular aspect of the value-delivery process (e.g., research and development, manufacturing, and distribution). Because collaboration enables each party to take advantage of the other's expertise, it can provide both entities with a competitive advantage.
- **Cost efficiency**. In addition to facilitating the effectiveness of the value-creation process, collaboration can also make it more cost efficient because by specializing in a given function, each collaborator can achieve greater economies of scale and experience. Specialization might also encourage a company to invest in cost-efficient solutions (e.g., an inventory-management system) that it would not invest in if it lacked a scale of operations.
- **Flexibility**. Relative to developing the necessary in-house expertise, collaboration requires a lesser commitment of resources and, hence, offers much greater flexibility in terms of switching technologies, entering new markets, and exiting existing ones. For example, the development of a new distribution channel requires substantial resources and hence calls for a long-term commitment, whereas using an already existing distribution channel (e.g., renting rather than buying the shelf space) allows a company's commitment to a project to be much more flexible.
- **Speed**. Collaboration enables a company to achieve the desired results much faster than building in-house expertise. For example, a manufacturer can gain access to target markets virtually overnight using an existing distribution chain, whereas launching its own distribution channel would take considerably longer.

Despite its numerous benefits, collaboration has several important *drawbacks* that include loss of control, loss of competencies, and empowering the competition.

- **Loss of control**. Delegating certain aspects of a company's activities to an external entity often leads to loss of control over the value-creation process. For example, outsourcing manufacturing operations frequently hinders the company's ability to monitor production processes and product quality.

Outsourcing also diminishes the company's ability to monitor the financial aspects of the value-creation process.

- **Loss of competencies**. Outsourcing key activities tends to weaken a company's core competencies. For example, outsourcing research-and-development activities over time tends to diminish a company's ability to drive innovation.
- **Empowering the competition**. Outsourcing key activities also might enable collaborating entities to develop a set of strategic competencies, thus becoming a company's potential competitor.

Like with most business decisions, entering into a collaborative relationship involves weighing the relevant benefits and costs. When the benefits from collaboration outweigh the corresponding costs for each of the relevant parties, the collaboration tends to be sustainable. In contrast, when collaboration fails to create superior value for collaborators, they might pursue alternative options such as replacing collaborators or insourcing and dissolving the collaboration.

Levels of Collaboration

A company's relationship with its collaborators can vary in the extent to which it is formalized. Based on the nature of the relationships among collaborating entities, collaboration can be either explicit or implicit.

- **Explicit collaboration** involves contractual relationships, such as long-term contractual agreements, joint ventures, and franchise agreements. The key advantage of explicit collaboration is that it fosters a formal relationship among collaborating entities, which ultimately leads to greater effectiveness and cost efficiency. At the same time, explicit collaboration has certain drawbacks, such as lower flexibility, greater switching costs, and the strategic risk of creating a potential competitor by sharing proprietary information (e.g., pricing policies, profit margins, and cost structure).
- **Implicit collaboration** typically does not involve contractual relationships and is much more flexible than explicit collaboration. This flexibility, however, comes at the cost of an inability to predict the behavior of various channel members. Another shortcoming of implicit coordination is the lower level of commitment, resulting in unwillingness to invest resources to customize the channel for a particular manufacturer. Implicit coordination is also likely to lead to lower cost efficiency (vis-à-vis explicit collaboration) resulting from a lower degree of coordination (e.g., due to lack of systems integration).

Alternatives to Collaboration

A common alternative to collaboration involves insourcing the activities performed by collaborators by creating a new, company-controlled entity, or by acquiring (or merging with) an existing entity. Depending on the relative position of the entities in the value-creation process, there are two types of integration: vertical and horizontal.

- **Vertical integration** typically involves the acquisition of an entity occupying a different level in the value-delivery chain. Depending on the relative position of the entities, there are two common types of vertical integration: forward and backward. Extending ownership upstream (toward suppliers) is referred to as backward integration, whereas extending ownership of activities downstream (toward buyers) is referred to as forward integration. For example, a manufacturer acquiring a retailer to establish its own distribution system is a form of forward integration, and a retailer acquiring a wholesaler or a manufacturer is a form of backward integration.

  Vertical integration tends to be favored by companies seeking to control the key aspects of the value-delivery process. For example, ExxonMobil engages in worldwide oil and gas exploration, production, supply, and transportation. Starbucks directly manages all aspects of its business, including sourcing, roasting, distributing, and serving the coffee. American Express directly markets to customers, issues its cards, processes the payments through its own network, and directly acquires the merchant relationships.

- **Horizontal integration** involves acquiring a business entity at the same level of the value-delivery chain. For example, a retailer acquiring another retailer or a manufacturer merging with another manufacturer constitutes horizontal integration. Horizontal integration might occur among entities with similar core competencies—a common scenario for companies seeking economies of scale through consolidation, and for those seeking economies of scope through diversification.

  Horizontal integration tends to be favored by companies for a variety of reasons, including gaining access to new markets, acquiring the rights to proprietary technology or research, reducing the competition in strategically important markets, and gaining power over the other entities in the value-delivery chain.

Managing Collaborator Relationships

Despite a company's efforts to optimize the value of its offerings for collaborators, company and collaborator goals often are not perfectly aligned. As a result, collaborator relationships can face tensions resulting from the different goal-optimization strategies pursued by collaborating entities. Such tensions are often facilitated by the power imbalance of the collaborating entities and frequently lead to explicit conflicts.

Collaborator Power

Collaborator power refers to the ability of a given company to exert influence over another entity. This influence often leads to an imbalance in the value exchange in favor of the more powerful entity and to market outcomes such as higher prices, margins, discounts, and allowances; preferential access to scarce resources; and premier shelf space and product-delivery schedules.

Power in collaborator relationships is a function of a number of factors, including the differentiation of collaborator offerings, collaborator size, strategic importance of the collaboration for each entity, and their switching costs.

- **Offering differentiation**. Companies with differentiated offerings in high demand are likely to have more power over their collaborators than companies with commoditized offerings. For example, companies with strong brands such as Coca-Cola, Adidas, and Samsung have more power dealing with their distribution partners than companies with lesser known brands.
- **Collaborator size**. Consolidated entities—both manufacturers and distributors—are likely to have more power over fragmented ones. For example, large consumer packaged goods manufacturers such as Procter & Gamble, PepsiCo, Kraft Foods Group, Unilever, and Nestlé often receive preferential treatment (better shelf space, lower volume discounts, and lower promotional allowances) from retailers compared to smaller manufacturers. Similarly, relative to smaller retail stores, retail giants Walmart, Carrefour, and Aldi often receive various monetary and nonmonetary benefits from manufacturers, including preferential volume discounts, greater promotional allowances, and customized product-delivery schedules.
- **Strategic importance**. An entity tends to have more power when it accounts for a significant portion of its collaborators' profits. For example, Walmart is in a position of power when negotiating with small manufacturers because their individual net contribution to Walmart's net income is low, whereas for many of them Walmart accounts for a substantial part of profits.
- **Switching costs**. An entity is likely to have more power when the switching costs of its collaborators are high and its own switching costs are low. Such switching costs might stem from a variety of factors, including a high level of systems integration between a company and its collaborator(s), long-term contractual obligations, and the learning curve associated with collaborating with a new entity.

Collaborator Conflicts

As with most business relationships, collaboration is not without conflicts. Tensions among collaborators are often caused by the differences in their profit-optimization strategies. Based on the nature of the collaborator relationship, there are two types of collaborator conflicts: vertical and horizontal.

Conflicts in Vertical Collaboration

Vertical conflicts typically depict tensions among entities occupying different levels in the value-delivery chain. The most common type of vertical conflict is that between a manufacturer and a retailer. Depending on the nature of the tension, there are two types of channel conflicts: vertical and horizontal. These two types of conflict are illustrated in Figure 1 and are described in more detail below.

Figure 1. Conflicts in Vertical Collaboration

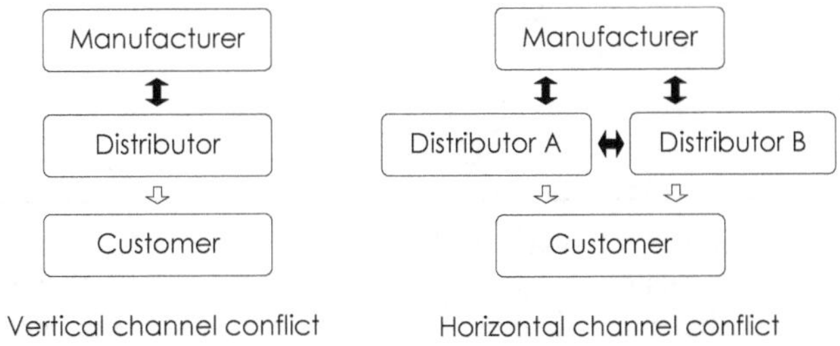

- **Vertical channel conflict** depicts tensions between entities in a single distribution channel (e.g., a manufacturer and a retailer). For example, vertical conflict might involve tensions regarding the size and composition of the manufacturer's product line carried by the retailer. The conflict here stems from the gap between a manufacturer's desire that a retailer carry its entire product line and a retailer's desire to carry only the most profitable, noncompeting offerings from individual manufacturers. Vertical conflict can also occur when collaborating entities exercise their power in the relationship to achieve their strategic goals (e.g., the supplier of a component in high demand raises the price, negatively affecting the manufacturer's profit margins).
- **Horizontal channel conflict** involves tensions among entities in multiple distribution channels (e.g., a manufacturer and two retailers). Horizontal conflicts occur when a manufacturer targets the same customers utilizing multiple distribution channels with different cost structures and profit margins. Consider a manufacturer that makes a product available through a high-margin, full-service retail store as well as through a high-volume, low-margin retailer. This manufacturer is likely to create channel conflict when the two retailers start selling the same product at different price points to the same customers.

Conflicts in Horizontal Collaboration

Horizontal conflicts typically depict tensions between entities occupying the same level in the value-delivery chain (Figure 2). For example, horizontal conflicts might occur between a manufacturer and a research-and-development company collaborating to develop a new product, between two entities collaborating to manufacture the product, and between a manufacturer and a service provider collaborating to offer post-purchase customer service.

Figure 2. Conflicts in Horizontal Collaboration

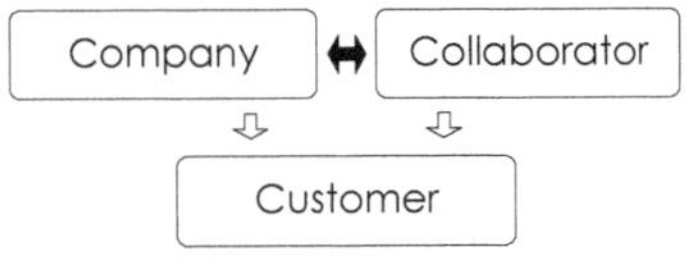

The tension between collaborating entities in this case can be caused by issues such as profit sharing, access to proprietary technologies, ownership of jointly developed intellectual property, and the sharing of core competencies and strategic assets. These tensions are often exacerbated when entities collaborating in one domain are competing in another.

SUMMARY

Collaborators are entities that work with the company to design, communicate, and deliver value to target customers. Common forms of collaboration involve suppliers, manufacturers, distributors (dealers, wholesalers and retailers), research-and-development companies, service providers, external sales force, advertising agencies, and marketing research companies. Depending on the relative position of the collaborating entities in the value-delivery process, collaborators can be classified as either vertical—those located along the value-delivery chain (supplier–manufacturer–distributor–customer)—or horizontal—those usually occupying the same level of the value-delivery chain.

Collaborator value is a function of the degree to which an offering enables collaborators to reach their goals. The benefits of collaboration include greater effectiveness, cost efficiency, flexibility, and time to market; the drawbacks include a loss of control, loss of competencies, and the possibility of strengthening the competition.

Despite a company's efforts to optimize the value of its offering(s) for collaborators, frequently the company's and collaborators' goals are not perfectly aligned. As a result, collaborator relationships often face tensions resulting from different goal-optimization strategies pursued by collaborating entities. Such tensions are often facilitated by the imbalance in power of the collaborating entities and often lead to explicit conflicts.

Collaborator power refers to the ability of a given company to exert influence over another entity. This influence often leads to an imbalance in the value exchange in favor of the more powerful entity and is frequently displayed in market behaviors such as higher prices, margins, discounts, and allowances; preferential access to scarce resources; and premier shelf space and product-delivery schedules.

Collaborator conflict describes tensions among collaborators, often caused by the differences in their goal-optimization strategies. Distribution channels face two common types of conflicts: vertical conflicts, which involve different levels of the same channel (a manufacturer and a retailer), and horizontal conflicts, which involve entities within the same channel level (two retailers).

ADDITIONAL READINGS

Anderson, James C., Nirmalya Kumar, and James A. Narus (2007), *Value Merchants: Demonstrating and Documenting Superior Value in Business Markets*. Cambridge, MA: Harvard Business Review Press.

Palmatier, Robert, Louis W. Stern, Adel I. El-Ansary, and Erin Anderson (2014), *Marketing Channel Strategy* (8th ed.). Upper Saddle River, NJ: Prentice Hall.

Young, S. David and Stephen F. O'Byrne (2000), *EVA and Value-Based Management: A Practical Guide to Implementation*. New York, NY: McGraw-Hill.

Part Three

Marketing Tactics

INTRODUCTION

Strategy without tactics is the slowest route to victory.
Tactics without strategy is the noise before defeat.

—Sun Tzu, Chinese military strategist

Marketing tactics define the way in which an offering's strategy, defined by its target market and value proposition, is reflected in the design of the offering. The key aspects of the offering's tactics, defined by the seven marketing mix variables—product, service, brand, price, incentives, communication, and distribution—are the focus of Part Three.

- **Product** and **service** depict the functional characteristics of an offering. The key decisions involved in creating and managing the product and service aspects of an offering are discussed in Chapter 8.
- **Brand** serves to identify the company's offering, differentiate it from the competition, and create value that goes beyond its product and service attributes. The main aspects of creating and managing brand are the focus of Chapter 9.
- **Price** reflects the monetary aspect of the offering; it refers to the amount of money the company charges for an offering's benefits. The essential elements of pricing are outlined in Chapter 10.
- **Incentives** offer solutions, typically short term, aimed at enhancing the value of the offering by providing additional benefits and/or reducing costs. Managing incentives is discussed in Chapter 11.
- **Communication** aims to inform target customers about the availability of the offering and highlight its key aspects. The essential decisions involved in managing communication are discussed in Chapter 12.
- **Distribution** depicts the channels through which the offering is delivered to target customers. Managing distribution is the focus of Chapter 13.

The key to designing a successful offering is to ensure that it can deliver value to the relevant market entities—target customers, the company, and its collaborators. A systematic approach to developing and managing offerings that logically follows from the articulated strategy is outlined in the following chapters.

CHAPTER EIGHT

MANAGING PRODUCTS AND SERVICES

Quality in a product or service is not what the supplier puts in.
It is what the customer gets out and is willing to pay for.

—Peter Drucker, founder of modern management theory

Product and service management aims to optimize the value that a company's products and services deliver to target customers and do so in a way that benefits the company and its collaborators. The key product and service decisions are the focus of this chapter.

Overview

The product and service aspects of an offering capture its key functional characteristics. *Products* typically change ownership during purchase; once created, they can be physically separated from the manufacturer and distributed to end users via multiple channels. Based on their consumption pattern, products are often classified as either durable or nondurable. Durable goods—cars, household appliances, and machinery—are consumed over multiple occasions and over an extended period. In contrast, nondurable goods—food, disposable items, and cosmetics—are typically consumed on a single occasion or over a short period.

Services are in many respects similar to products, with two main exceptions: change of ownership and inseparability. Unlike products, which typically change ownership during purchase (from the seller to the buyer), services do not usually involve a change in ownership; instead, the customer acquires the right to use the offering within a given time frame. Furthermore, unlike products, which can be physically separated from the manufacturer, services are usually delivered and consumed at the same time.

Because services are created and delivered at the same time, they are difficult to standardize, and their quality varies depending on the interaction between the service provider and the customer. To illustrate, a customer might receive different levels of service from the same service provider at different times and in different locations, and the same service provider might have different interactions with different customers depending on customers' behavior. The inseparability of creating and delivering value also makes services perishable in the sense that they cannot be inventoried—an important consideration in industries such as airlines, hotels, and call centers, where companies with a fixed service capacity face fluctuating customer demand.

Based on the level of uncertainty associated with their benefits, product and service attributes can be classified into one of three categories: search, experience, and credence.[1]

- **Search** products and services are associated with the least amount of uncertainty and are typically identifiable through inspection before purchase.
- **Experience** products and services carry greater uncertainty and are revealed only through consumption.
- **Credence** products and services have the greatest amount of uncertainty and their quality is not truly revealed even after consumption.

For example, in the case of toothpaste, size is a search attribute, taste is an experience attribute, and cavity prevention is a credence attribute. In general, search attributes are more common for tangible offerings, whereas credence attributes are more typical for intangible offerings. Because services have more intangible properties relative to products, they are heavy on experience and credence attributes; in contrast, search attributes are more typical for products than services.

Product and Service Management as a Value-Creation Process

When designing products and services, a manager's goal is to create value for target customers in a way that benefits the company and its collaborators. To achieve this goal, a manager must consider five key factors—target customers, the company's goals and resources, its collaborators, competitors, and the context in which the company operates—and design products and services that deliver market value. The Five Cs are the key decision factors that must be considered in order to design products and services that can create value for target customers, the company, and its collaborators (Figure 1).

Figure 1. Product and Service Management as a Value-Creation Process

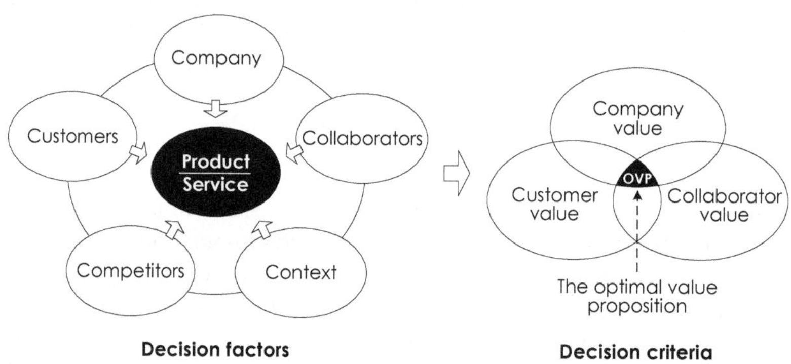

The five decision factors—customers, company, collaborators, competitors, and context (the 5-C framework)—are of strategic importance when designing the product and service aspects of offerings. Because the primary function of an offering is to create value for its target customers, customers' needs play a key role in the development of the company's products and services. A company's products and services also depend on the company's collaborators. For example, a company might seek to optimize the channel's inventory costs by creating space-efficient packaging and/or by extending the shelf life of perishable products. Because most consumer decisions involve a choice among competitive offerings, these offerings often serve as benchmarks for designing new products and services. A company's products and services are also a reflection of its goals and resources because they determine the capability of the company's products to fulfill customer needs. Finally, product and service design is also influenced by the economic, business, technological, sociocultural, regulatory, and physical *context*, including the technological specifications imposed by various government and nongovernment agencies, import/export regulations, and compatibility standards.

In addition to being a function of the Five Cs, product and service design is also influenced by the other elements of the offering's marketing mix: its brand, price, incentives, communication, and distribution. Thus, an offering's products and services should be consistent with its brand, such that high-performance brands are represented by superior products and services and vice versa. Products and services are also contingent on price, such that higher priced offerings typically call for higher quality offerings. Products and services also depend on the offering's communications and should be designed in a way that facilitates informing customers about the key aspects of the offering. Finally, products and services are often designed to optimize their distribution—for example, by facilitating their transportation, storage, and on-shelf display.

Product and Service Decisions

Creating and managing products and services involves a series of specific decisions concerning factors such as performance, consistency, reliability, durability, compatibility, ease of use, technological design, degree of customization, form, style, and packaging. These factors are described in more detail below.

- **Performance**. Products vary in their performance on different attributes. For example, cars vary in engine power, acceleration, comfort, safety, and fuel efficiency; computers vary in processing power, battery life, display size, and connectivity; snacks vary in taste, nutritional value, and calorie content. The key principle when deciding on the level of performance of a given offering is optimizing its value for the relevant market entities: target customers, the company, and its collaborators. In cases when a given offering is part of a product line, its performance also needs to be coordinated with the other offerings included in this product line (see Chapter 17 for more details).

- **Consistency**. An important aspect of designing an offering is ensuring that in-kind products and services are identical and consistent with specifications. Because variability is a key characteristic of services, consistency is of vital importance in service delivery and is one of the main contributors to the success of companies such as McDonald's, Starbucks, and Ritz-Carlton. A popular approach to managing product consistency is the Six Sigma method described in more detail at the end of this chapter.

- **Reliability**. Reliability refers to the probability that the product or service will operate according to its specifications and will not malfunction for the duration of its projected life cycle. Reliability is often used as a differentiating point to create a unique positioning for a company's offering. For example, FedEx promises "absolutely, positively overnight" next-day delivery service, the discount brokerage TD Ameritrade guarantees that certain trades will be executed within five seconds, and Verizon claims to be the most reliable wireless network in the United States with a call-completion rate of more than 99.9%.

- **Durability**. Another important consideration in product design involves the expected length of the offering's life cycle. Because durability is an important consideration in buyers' decision processes, products that are perceived to be more durable tend to be preferred by customers. At the same time, while durable products help companies attract new customers and build loyalty among existing customers, durability tends to have a negative impact on the frequency of repeat purchases because users are often reluctant to replace fully functioning products with new ones. As a result, manufacturers have to design superior models that will encourage customers to upgrade. This process of designing new products in a way that makes prior generations inferior is often referred to as planned obsolescence (see Chapter 16 for more details).

- **Compatibility**. Compatibility refers to the degree to which an offering is consistent with certain already existing standards and complementary products. Compatibility can be used strategically by companies to create barriers to entry by ensuring that offerings are uniquely compatible with customers' existing systems and processes. Product compatibility is also an effective strategy in networked environments, where users are forced to adhere to a certain standard. To illustrate, the popularity of Microsoft Office products is to a great degree a function of the need for compatibility when sharing information. Compatibility is also a key consideration in multipart pricing, where a company charges a relatively low price for the first part of the offering and higher prices for the complementary parts (e.g., razors and blades). In this case, unique (patented) compatibility is essential so that only parts manufactured by the same company can work together (e.g., only Gillette-manufactured blades should fit a Gillette razor).

- **Ease of use**. An important aspect of many products and services is their ease of use. There is a common misconception that greater functionality, such as a greater number of features, inevitably leads to greater satisfaction. In reality, however, this is not the case: Adding functionality in cases when customers lack the knowledge necessary to utilize it can backfire. To illustrate, in an attempt to incorporate the latest technology in its newly redesigned 7-series, in 2003 BMW introduced iDrive, an over-engineered computer system used to control most secondary functions of a car, including the audio system, climate, and navigation. Designed to manage more than 700 functions with a single knob, the iDrive had a steep learning curve and quickly became the most controversial feature of the 7-series.

- **Technological design**. Depending on the novelty of the offering, two technology-development methods can be identified: product innovation and product variation. The product-innovation approach involves technology-based innovations and innovative use of existing technology to design new offerings. Unlike the product-innovation strategy, which leads to substantive functional differences among offerings, the product-variation approach leads to offerings characterized by relatively minor variations in their functionality, such as adding different colors, flavors, tastes, sizes, designs, or packaging variations.

- **Degree of customization**. When designing its offerings, a company needs to decide on the degree to which these offerings will be customized for target customers. At one extreme, a company might decide to pursue a mass-production strategy, offering the same products and services to all customers. At the other extreme, the company might pursue a one-to-one customization in which the company's products and services are customized for each individual customer. A compromise between the mass-production approach and the one-to-one customization approach is segment-based customization. By developing offerings for groups of customers with similar needs, segment-based customization allows companies to develop fewer offerings while ensuring that these offerings fit customer needs. To illustrate, Dell offers more than 100 options from which customers can choose to customize their computers; Porsche offers nearly 1,000 customization options for its flagship 911 Carrera; and Nike offers more than 10,000 different design and color sport-shoe customization options through its website nikeid.com.

- **Form**. Product design typically involves decisions concerning the physical aspects of the offering, such as its size and shape. Design plays an important role in manufacturing, transporting, storing, inventorying, and consuming the product. Because customers vary in the amounts they consume, packaged goods are often available in a variety of sizes and shapes. For example, Johnson & Johnson's pain relief medicine, Tylenol, is available in more than fifty different SKU forms: regular, extra strength, and children's dosages; normal and extended relief; tablets, caplets, gelcaps, geltabs, and liquid—all in a variety of sizes.

- **Style**. The look and feel is particularly important for products that have a primarily hedonic and self-expressive function, such as luxury cars, designer furniture, and fashion apparel, and could be somewhat less relevant for utilitarian products, such as manufacturing equipment. Because product styling can create value above and beyond the functional characteristics of the product, it is used by companies to differentiate their offerings from the competition. For example, Apple revolutionized the personal computer industry by designing computers that were not only powerful and fast but also aesthetically pleasing. Method Products, a home and personal cleaning products company, has managed to successfully differentiate its products through innovative, futuristic styling of the containers.
- **Packaging**. Packaging serves several key functions: *protecting* the product during transportation and storage; physically *containing* liquid, powder, and granular goods; *agglomerating* small items into larger packages; *preventing* tampering, counterfeit, and theft; providing *convenience* in transportation, handling, storing, display, sale, and consumption; offering *information* on how to transport, store, use, and dispose of the product; and *promoting* the product to potential buyers by providing them with reasons to choose it. Packaging can also be used to create value above and beyond the value created by the product itself. To illustrate, Tiffany's signature blue box highlights the exclusivity of the offering and at the same time strengthens its brand image and helps differentiate it from the competition.

In addition to deciding on the characteristics of the individual products and services, companies often must decide how to differentiate them from the other offerings in their product lines, as well as how to manage products and services throughout their life cycles. A more detailed discussion of managing the product and service life cycle and product-line management is offered in chapters 16 and 17.

SUMMARY

Product and service management aims to optimize the company's offering so that it delivers superior value to target customers, the company, and its collaborators. Products typically change ownership during purchase; once created, they can be physically separated from the manufacturer and distributed to end users via multiple channels. In contrast, services imply a right of use (rather than ownership) and are typically delivered and consumed at the same time.

Managing products and services is influenced by two types of factors: *strategic*, which include the offering's customers, the company, collaborators, competition, and context, and *tactical*, which depend on the other marketing mix variables: brand, price, incentives, communication, and distribution.

Product and service management involves deciding on factors such as performance, consistency, reliability, durability, compatibility, ease of use, technological design, degree of customization, form, style, and packaging. In addition to deciding on the characteristics of the individual products and services, companies often have to decide on how to differentiate them from the other offerings in their product lines.

RELEVANT CONCEPTS

Consumer Packaged Goods (CPG): A term used to describe consumer products packaged in portable containers: food, beverages, health and beauty aids, tobacco, and cleaning supplies.

Six Sigma: A methodology for managing process variations that cause defects, introduced by Motorola and later adopted by General Electric. (Sigma refers to the Greek letter σ, commonly used in statistics as a measure of the degree of variance in a given population.) The *Six Sigma* approach builds on the idea that for an offering to be consistent with specifications, the difference between the actual and the desired outcomes should not exceed six standard deviations. In this context, a widely accepted definition of a *Six Sigma* process is one that reduces defect levels below 3.4 defective items per million outcomes. Over time, the term *Six Sigma* has evolved beyond its literal definition as a specific metric and is often used in reference to a more general methodology of improving business processes that focuses on understanding customer needs and aligning the business processes to fulfill these needs with minimal variation.

Stock Keeping Unit (SKU): A unique identifier assigned to each distinct product or service.

ADDITIONAL READINGS

Berry, Leonard and A. Parasuraman (2004), *Marketing Services Competing through Quality.* New York, NY: Free Press.

Gremler, Dwayne D., Mary Jo Bitner, and Valarie A. Zeithaml (2012), *Services Marketing: Integrating Customer Focus across the Firm* (6th ed.). Boston, MA: McGraw-Hill/Irwin.

Lehmann, Donald R. and Russell S. Winer (2006), *Product Management* (4th ed.). Boston, MA: McGraw-Hill/Irwin.

NOTE

1 Nelson, Phillip (1970), "Information and Consumer Behavior," *Journal of Political Economy,* 78 (March–April), 311–329.

CHAPTER NINE

MANAGING BRANDS

Any fool can put on a deal, but it takes genius, faith, and perseverance to create a brand.
—David Ogilvy, founder of Ogilvy & Mather advertising agency

Brands benefit customers by creating value that goes beyond the product and service characteristics of the offering. Because of their fundamental role in creating market value, brands are among the most valuable strategic assets of a company. The key aspects of creating and managing brands are the focus of this chapter.

Overview

The increased commoditization in many categories has shifted the focus of differentiation from products and services to brands. Brands help differentiate the offering in two main ways: by creating a unique brand identity and by associating the brand with a meaning that resonates with its potential buyers.

- **Brand identity** includes the identifying characteristics of the brand, such as brand name, logo, symbol, character, slogan, jingle, product design, and packaging. Brand identity elements should be unique, memorable, likeable, and consistent with the other brand elements and with the meaning of the brand. Brand elements should also be flexible to adapt to changes in the market environment (to accommodate shifts in consumer preferences) and the company's product-line strategy (to be extendable to other product categories). Furthermore, the company should be able to protect the uniqueness of its brand elements against infringement by competitors.

- **Brand meaning** reflects the brand-related perceptions and beliefs held by the buyers; it reflects buyers' understanding of the value proposition associated with a particular brand. The meaning of the brand has a tripartite impact on customers' perceptions of value. First, it can signal the quality of the products and services associated with the brand. For example, brands such as Tide, Tylenol, and Michelin are commonly associated with quality products. Second, brands can signal the price image of the offering, indicating the monetary savings that are likely to be associated with the brand. For example, Walmart, Costco, and Aldi brands are often associated with low prices.

Finally, brands can create additional emotional (satisfaction from using and owning the brand), social (group acceptance resulting from ownership of a particular brand), and self-expressive benefits (use of the brand as a means to express one's identity). For example, Rolls-Royce, Louis Vuitton, and Tiffany's signify social status, and Harley-Davidson, Oakley, and Abercrombie & Fitch are associated with unique self-expressive values.

The primary function of brand identity is to identify the company's offering and differentiate it from the competition by creating value that goes beyond the product and service characteristics of the offering. To illustrate, the identity of BMW is captured by elements such as its distinct name and logo, whereas its meaning—*the ultimate driving machine*—reflects the mental associations that target customers make with the brand. A brand's identity can exist independently from its target customers; in contrast, a brand's meaning exists primarily in the minds of the buyers.

Branding as a Value-Creation Process

Brands aim to create value that goes beyond the functional benefits of the offering. To achieve this goal, a manager must consider five key factors—target customers, the company, its collaborators, competitors, and the context in which the company operates—and develop a brand that creates market value. The Five Cs are the key decision factors that must be considered in order to design brands that can create value for target customers, the company, and its collaborators (Figure 1).

Figure 1. Branding as a Value-Creation Process

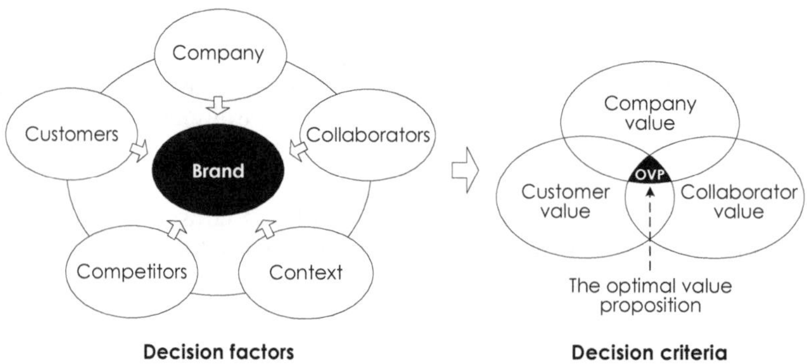

The Five Cs—customers, company, collaborators, competitors, and context—define the strategy involved in building strong brands. Because creating value for its target customers is a primary function of any brand, customer needs are the cornerstone for building successful brands. An offering's brand is also influenced by the company's resources, such that a company with an established reputation and expertise in a particular domain can use this reputation to build its brand. An offering's brand can be influenced by its collaborators, frequently leading to the development of cobranding strategies (e.g., Microsoft and Intel, Coca-Cola and Splenda, and Citibank and MasterCard). An offering's brand is also a function of the competition because it affects the brand's ability to create unique and shared associations (often referred to as points of difference and points of parity). Finally, an offering's branding is influenced by the various economic, business, technological, sociocultural, regulatory, and physical aspects of the environment in which it operates. For example, because they have become synonymous with a particular category and are commonly used as a generic term, Aspirin, Thermos, and Escalator have lost their legal trademark-protected brand status.

In addition to being influenced by the Five Cs, branding decisions are also a function of the other aspects of the marketing mix, including product and service characteristics, price, incentives, communication, and distribution. Thus, the more commoditized a company's product or service is and the less observable its benefits are, the greater the importance of brands in differentiating the offering. An offering's brand must also be consistent with its price and incentives: low prices and frequent discounts can hurt the image of an upscale brand, just as high prices can hurt the image of a value brand. In the same vein, brand-focused communications tend to strengthen the brand, whereas price- and incentive-focused communications typically have the opposite effect, eroding the brand image.[1] Finally, an offering's brand is a function of its distribution channels, which often serve as a means for brand building (e.g., Disney World theme parks and Apple and Niketown retail stores function as channels delivering Disney, Apple, and Nike brands).

Brand Hierarchy

An important branding decision involves determining whether different offerings in a company's product line should be positioned as individual brands or should share the same brand name. In this context, brand hierarchy (or brand architecture) reflects the relationship among different brands in a company's portfolio. There are two core approaches to managing multiple brands: individual branding and umbrella branding.

- **Individual branding** involves creating a separate brand for each product or product line. To illustrate, Tide, Cheer, Bold, and Era are individual brands of laundry detergents created by Procter & Gamble. Chevrolet, Buick, Cadillac, and GMC are individual brands of General Motors. Campbell Soup Company uses Campbell's for soups, Pepperidge Farm for baked goods, and V8 for juices. Sears uses Kenmore for appliances, Craftsman for tools, and DieHard for batteries. Diageo manages dozens of alcoholic beverage brands including Smirnoff, Ketel One, Tanqueray, Johnnie Walker, J&B, José Cuervo, Captain Morgan, Baileys, Hennessy, Guinness, Dom Pérignon, and Moët & Chandon.
- **Umbrella branding** involves using a single brand for all of a company's products. For example, General Electric, Heinz, Virgin, and Costco (Kirkland Signature) use a single brand for nearly all of their products. Umbrella brand-

ing often involves sub-branding, in which the umbrella brand is combined with a lower tier brand. For instance, Courtyard by Marriott, Residence Inn by Marriott, Fairfield Inn by Marriott, and SpringHill Suites by Marriott exemplify using sub-brands in the context of umbrella branding. Similarly, Porsche uses sub-branding for the different offerings in its product line: Carrera, Boxster, Cayenne, and Cayman. A more subtle form of sub-branding involves using brand names with the same origin: Nescafé, Nesquik, Nestea, and Nespresso are used by Nestlé to brand different beverages.

Companies with multiple product lines might also employ hybrid branding that involves a variety of individual, umbrella-branding, and sub-branding strategies. To illustrate, Chevrolet and Cadillac are individual brands of General Motors; at the same time, each one serves as an umbrella brand for its sub-brands (Camaro, Impala, Corvette, Malibu, Monte Carlo, and Blazer are Chevrolet sub-brands, and CTS, STS, XLR, and Escalade are Cadillac sub-brands).

A key advantage of an individual-brand strategy is that it enables a company to serve diverse customer segments in diverse product categories without diluting the image of its brands. Individual brands also tend to have greater brand equity because they are independent from the parent brand and can be the subject of acquisitions. On the downside, building new brands without the support of an existing brand takes a substantial amount of time, money, and managerial resources.

A key advantage of umbrella branding is that it leverages the equity of an existing brand, benefiting from the instant recognition of the core brand while avoiding the costs associated with building a new brand. Using umbrella branding in product-line extensions can strengthen the parent brand by raising its image, especially in the case of adding a high-end offering. Umbrella branding can also strengthen the existing brand by increasing its visibility to target customers. A drawback to using umbrella branding is that poor performance by any product carrying the brand name can easily hurt the reputation of the parent brand. For example, in 1986 General Motors introduced a Chevrolet-based compact car branded as Cadillac Cimarron and, by doing so, weakened the image of its upscale Cadillac brand.

Brand Dynamics

Once created, brands evolve throughout time. There are two common types of brand changes: *brand repositioning*, which involves changes to the identity and meaning of a company's brand, and *brand extensions*, which involve broadening the set of underlying offerings to which the brand is applied. These two types of brand dynamics are discussed in the following sections.

Brand Repositioning

Brand repositioning involves changing an essential aspect of the brand, most often to increase its relevance to target customers. Common reasons to reposition a brand include: (1) to respond to a change in target customers, (2) to reach a new target market, (3) to counteract a change in a competitor's branding strategy, and (4) to respond to legal challenges. These reasons are illustrated in more detail below.

- **React to the changing needs of target customers.** One of the most common reasons for repositioning a brand is to ensure that it remains relevant to the changing needs of its target customers. For example, to reflect the changing values and lifestyles of women, General Mills has consistently refined the image of Betty Crocker, a fictitious character designed to offer cooking advice to consumers. Throughout the years, she has had nearly a dozen different "looks," morphing from the stern, gray-haired, older woman in 1936 to today's olive-skinned, dark-haired Betty. Similarly, to increase its appeal to younger customers, Procter & Gamble repositioned its half-century-old beauty brand, Oil of Olay. The key changes introduced in 2000 included abbreviating the name to Olay (to avoid associations equating oil to "greasy"), streamlining its logo, replacing the woman's image (which resembled a nun) on the label with a younger one, and cleaning up the packaging design.

- **Reach a new target market.** Companies often reposition their brands when entering new markets to allow the brand image to reflect the specifics of that market and better resonate with the needs and values of target customers. For example, Philip Morris' Marlboro brand was originally introduced in 1924 as a women's cigarette, tagged "Mild as May"; in 1954 it was repositioned using the rugged cowboy image of the Marlboro Man, which was more likely to appeal to male smokers. Procter & Gamble's cleaning product Mr. Clean was introduced as Mr. Proper in Germany, Flash in the United Kingdom, Monsieur Propre in France, Mastro Lindo in Italy, Don Limpio in Spain (from *limpiar*—"to clean"), and Maestro Limpio in Mexico.

- **React to a change in a competitor's positioning.** Because companies strive to create superior customer value relative to that of other offerings in the marketplace, a change in the positioning of a competitor's offering often induces the company to reposition its brand to preserve and enhance its competitive advantage. To illustrate, the popularity of the Energizer Bunny in the United States forced Duracell to discontinue the use of its brand mascot—the Duracell Bunny—that is now used only outside of North America.

- **Respond to legal challenges.** In 1991 Kentucky Fried Chicken abbreviated its name to KFC to avoid paying license fees to the state of Kentucky, which trademarked the name in 1990. A decade and a half later, after reaching an agreement with the State of Kentucky in 2006, KFC began to reintroduce its original name, rebranding itself once again as Kentucky Fried Chicken.

Brand Extensions

Brand extension refers to the strategy of using the same brand name in a different context, such as a different product category or a different price tier. For example,

Starbucks, which has become synonymous with coffee, extended its brand to include ice cream sold in grocery stores. Montblanc—which over a century built a reputation for producing the finest quality pens—extended its brand to include items such as luxury watches, sunglasses, cufflinks, wallets, briefcases, and even fragrances. In the same vein, Oakley extended its brand from eyewear to unrelated domains, such as apparel, footwear, bags, and watches.

The primary reason for extending an existing brand is to leverage its equity by applying it to a new offering. The popularity of brand extensions stems from the fact that building new brands is a costly and time-consuming task. As a result, when entering a new product category, companies often choose to leverage the equity of their existing brands rather than invest in creating new ones. Based on their relationship with the core offering, brand extensions can be vertical or horizontal.

Vertical Brand Extensions

Vertical brand extensions stretch the brand to a product or service in a different price tier. Depending on the direction in which the original offering is being extended, two types of vertical brand extensions can be distinguished: upscale extensions in which the brand is applied to an offering in a higher price tier, and downscale extensions, in which the brand is applied to an offering in a lower price tier (Figure 2).

Figure 2. Vertical Brand Extensions

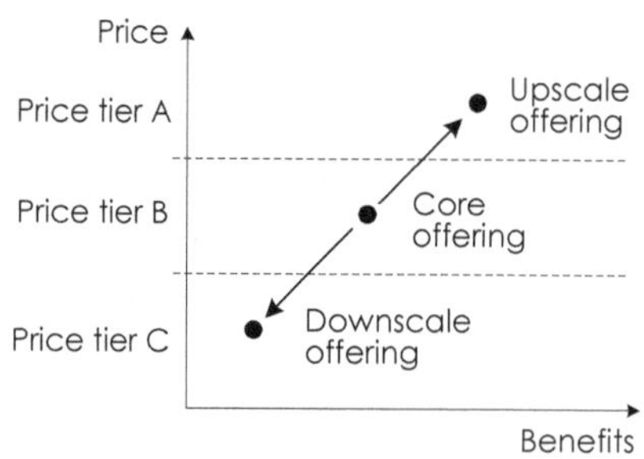

Examples of *upscale brand extensions* include Gallo's entry into the premium wine segment with Gallo Family Vineyards Estate Series, Volkswagen's attempt to enter the luxury car market with the Volkswagen Phaeton in 2004, and Levi Strauss' attempt to enter the designer suit category in the 1980s. Because the image of the core brand generally hurts rather than helps the upscale extension, upscale brand extensions are not very common and companies often choose to launch a separate brand rather than extend an existing one. To illustrate, consider the decisions of Toyota and Volkswagen to enter the luxury car market. Both companies decided to extend their product line to upscale offerings but chose different branding strategies. Believing that its existing brand name could not convey the luxury image required to successfully compete with the Mercedes S-class and BMW 7-series, Toyota launched a new brand—Lexus—rather than try to extend its existing brand. In contrast, Volkswagen launched its upscale extension branded as Volkswagen Phaeton, prominently featuring the VW logo on the front and the back of the car. The aftermath is that Toyota succeeded in establishing Lexus as a premiere luxury brand, whereas Volkswagen failed to convince potential buyers that it could be a luxury brand.

Examples of *downscale brand extensions* include the Mercedes A-series, Porsche's Boxster, and Armani Exchange. Because they leverage the image of the core brand, downscale extensions tend to be more successful than upscale ones. The key shortcoming for downscale brand extensions is the potential dilution of the brand's image. To illustrate, the brand image of Lotus Cars (English manufacturer of sport cars) was negatively influenced by the introduction of Lotus Elise—a downscale extension featuring a Toyota-sourced engine that has been used in several Toyota models, including Celica and Corolla.

Horizontal Brand Extensions

Horizontal brand extensions involve applying the brand to a different product category, typically within the same price tier (Figure 3). For example, Ralph Lauren successfully extended its Polo brand from clothing to home furnishings such as bedding and towels, Timberland extended its brand from boots to outerwear and travel gear, and Porsche extended its brand from sport cars to sedans and sport utility vehicles.

Figure 3. Horizontal Brand Extensions

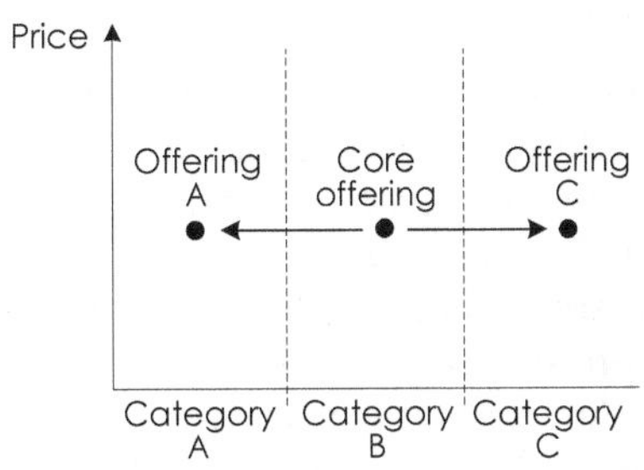

A potential downside of horizontal brand extensions is brand dilution, which is likely to occur when a brand is extended to diverse product categories that are inconsistent with its essence. For example, Heinz All-Natural Cleaning Vinegar—the company's first nonfood product launched in 2003—failed, in part, because consumers were confused by the Heinz-branded vinegar-based cleaning aid. In the same vein, Costco's strategy to use a single brand—Kirkland Signature—for all of its store-branded products, from food and wine to cleaning supplies, appliances, and clothes, curbs its ability to attach a specific meaning to its brand.

Brand Equity

The term brand equity refers to the financial value of the brand; it determines the premium that should be placed on a company's valuation because of brand ownership. The key aspects of conceptualizing and measuring brand equity are discussed in the following sections.

Brand Equity and Brand Power

A key driver of brand equity is the brand's power. Brand power reflects the brand's ability to differentiate the offering from the competition and create customer value through meaningful associations. Unlike brand equity, which reflects the value of the brand to the company, brand power reflects the value a brand creates in the minds of customers.

Brand equity is a function of brand power as well as the company's utilization of the power of its brand, reflected in its user base, sales volume, and pricing. A stronger brand does not automatically translate into greater brand equity. For example, although the Armani, Moët & Chandon, Audi, and Lexus brands are considered stronger than the Gap, McDonald's, Volkswagen, and Toyota brands, respectively (as measured by the greater price premium they command over identical unbranded products), the equity of the latter set of brands is estimated to be higher than that of the former: For example, the brand equity of Toyota is estimated to be higher than the brand equity of Lexus, even though Lexus commands a greater price premium compared to Toyota.[2]

Brand power can be defined as the differential impact of brand knowledge on consumer response to an offering's marketing efforts.[3] This means that a brand has greater power when customers react more favorably to an offering because they are aware of the brand name. To illustrate, one of the benefits of brand power is the price premium customers are willing to pay for the branded product compared to the identical unbranded product. In addition to the price premium, other dimensions of brand power include greater customer loyalty; enhanced perception of product performance; greater licensing, merchandising, and brand extension opportunities; less vulnerability to service inconsistencies and marketing crises; more elastic response to price decreases and more inelastic response to price increases; greater communication effectiveness; and increased channel power. Because powerful brands can influence all aspects of an offering, building strong brands is of crucial importance to sustainable growth.

Measuring Brand Equity

Knowing the monetary value of a company's brands is essential for company valuation, such as in the case of mergers and acquisitions, sale of assets, licensing, financing, and estimating benefits from or damages to the brand. Despite the importance of brand equity, there is no commonly agreed-on methodology for its calculation; instead, there are several alternative methods, each placing emphasis on different aspects of brand equity. The three most common approaches to measuring brand equity are outlined below.

- **Cost-based approach** involves calculating brand equity based on the costs involved (e.g., marketing research, advertising, and legal costs) if the brand needs to be created from scratch at the time of valuation.

- **Market-based approach** involves calculating brand equity based on the difference in the cash flows generated from the branded product and a functionally equivalent but nonbranded product, adjusted for the costs of creating the brand. The market-based approach can be summarized as follows:

$$\text{Brand equity} = \text{Sales revenues}_{\text{Brand}} - \text{Sales revenues}_{\text{Generic}} - \text{Branding costs}$$

- **Financial approach** involves calculating brand equity based on the net present value of the cash flows derived from the brand's future earnings. This approach typically involves three key steps: (1) estimating the company's future cash flows, (2) estimating the contribution of the brand to these cash flows, and (3) adjusting these cash flows using a risk factor that reflects the volatility of the earnings attributed to the brand. The financial approach can be summarized as follows:

$$\text{Brand equity} = \text{NPV of future cash flows} \cdot \text{Brand contribution factor} \cdot \text{Risk factor}$$

  The financial approach to estimating brand equity can be illustrated using Interbrand's methodology, which is the basis for *Business Week's* annual ranking of the top 100 brands. Interbrand's method involves three steps. The first step consists of estimating the percentage of the overall revenues that can be attributed to the brand. Based on reports from analysts at JPMorgan Chase, Citigroup, and Morgan Stanley, Interbrand projects five years of earnings and sales for the products and services associated with the brand. Interbrand then deducts the estimated earnings that can be attributed to tangible assets, on the assumption that the income generated beyond that point is the result of intangible assets. The next step involves stripping out the nonbrand intangibles, such as patents, trademarks, technological know-how, and management strength to determine the portion of the company's income generated by intangible assets that can be attributed to the brand. The final step involves assessing the risk profile of these projected earnings based on a variety of factors, such as market leadership, stability, market growth, global reach, trend, support (investment in the brand), and protection. The discount rate resulting from this risk analysis is applied to brand-related earnings to produce the net present value of the brand.

The validity of the above brand equity models is closely tied to the validity of their assumptions, such that small changes in the underlying assumptions can lead to significant changes in brand valuations. Therefore, using alternative valuation methods that employ different assumptions can greatly improve the accuracy and consistency of the resulting brand equity estimates.

SUMMARY

A brand is a marketing tool created for the purpose of differentiating a company's offering from the competition and creating value for customers, the company, and its collaborators. A brand has two key aspects: (1) brand identity, which includes identifying characteristics, such as name, sign, symbol, character, and design, and (2) brand meaning, which reflects a set of offering-related associations in the mind of the buyer. Brand identity aims to *identify* the company's offering and *differentiate* it from the competition. In contrast, brand meaning aims to *create value* (for customers, the company, and its collaborators) that goes beyond the product and service characteristics of the offering.

Managing brands involves two types of decisions: (1) *strategic decisions*, which are a function of the offering's target market, defined by its customers, company, collaborators, competition, and context, and (2) *tactical decisions*, which are a function of the other marketing mix variables: product, service, price, incentives, communication, and distribution.

Two important branding decisions involve managing the brand hierarchy and managing the brand dynamics. *Brand hierarchy* reflects the relationships among different brands in a company's portfolio. The two popular approaches to managing multiple brands are individual branding and umbrella branding. Brand dynamics reflect the evolution of the brand over time. The two common types of brand dynamics are *brand repositioning*—which involves changes to an existing brand, most often to make the brand more relevant to its target customers—and *brand extension*—which involves broadening the set of underlying product categories to which the brand is applied without necessarily changing the core brand.

Brand equity is the net present value of the financial benefits derived from the brand. Brand equity is a function of brand power, as well as a number of additional factors reflecting the company's utilization of the strength of its brand. *Brand power* reflects the brand's ability to differentiate the offering from the competition and create customer value through meaningful associations. Unlike brand equity, which reflects the value of the brand to the company, brand power reflects the value the brand creates for customers. The three most popular approaches to measuring brand equity are cost-based (the cost of recreating the brand), market-based (the difference in the cost-adjusted cash flows of a branded and nonbranded product), and financial (the net present value of the cash flows of the offering's future earnings that are attributed to the brand). Using alternative valuation methods that employ different assumptions can greatly improve the accuracy and consistency of the resulting brand equity estimates.

RELEVANT CONCEPTS

Brand Audit: A comprehensive analysis of a brand, most often to determine the sources of brand equity.

Brand Essence: The fundamental nature of the brand, also referred to as "brand promise." Brand essence distills the meaning of the brand into one key aspect—the positioning of the brand. One way to think about brand essence is to think of the "ness" of the brand, such as "BMW-ness," "Apple-ness," and "Microsoft-ness."

Branded House: Term used in reference to the branding strategy in which a company's brand is used on all of the offerings in its brand portfolio. Companies using this strategy include General Electric, Ford, Heinz, and Virgin. See also *house of brands*.

Cobranding: Branding strategy that involves combining two or more brands, typically from different product categories. Examples of cobranding include United Airlines–JPMorgan Chase–Visa credit cards, Lexus "Coach edition" sport utility vehicles, and HP–iPod MP3 players. A form of cobranding involves ingredient branding in which an ingredient or component of a product has its own brand identity, such as Teflon surface protector, Gore-Tex fabrics, NutraSweet and Splenda sweeteners, and Intel microprocessors.

Copyright: A legal term describing rights given to creators for their literary and artistic works. The types of works covered by copyright include literary works such as novels, poems, plays, reference works, newspapers, and computer programs; databases; films, musical compositions, and choreography; artistic works, such as paintings, drawings, photographs, and sculpture; architecture; and advertisements, maps, and technical drawings.

Fighting Brand: A downscale (lower priced) brand introduced to shield a major brand from low-priced competitors.

Generification: Colloquialized use of brand names (e.g., in reference to the products they are associated with). The use of a brand name as a generic term can lead to the loss of a company's right to the exclusive use of that brand name. To illustrate, Trampoline, Brazier, Escalator, Thermos, Yo-Yo, and Aspirin lost their trademark-protected status because of popular use; Xerox, Rollerblade, Velcro, and Google are considered to be at risk of following them.

Global Brand: A brand with a comprehensive international distribution system, such as Coca-Cola, Pepsi, and Sony.

Goodwill: Accounting term referring to a company's intangible assets, including the monetary value of the company's brand(s). Goodwill is recorded on a company's books when it acquires another company and pays a premium over the listed book value of its assets.

House of Brands: Term used in reference to a branding strategy in which a company holds a portfolio of individual and typically unrelated brands. Companies using this strategy include Procter & Gamble, Unilever, and Diageo. See also *branded house*.

Industrial Property: A type of intellectual property that involves (1) *inventions* (patents), (2) *industrial designs*, and (3) *identity marks* such as trademarks, service marks, commercial names, and designations, including indications of source and appellations of origin. An invention is a product or process that provides a new way of doing something or offers new solutions to technical problems; a patent is an exclusive right granted for an invention. An industrial design is the aesthetic aspect of a product and might consist of three-dimensional features such as shape or surface, or two-dimensional features such as patterns, lines, or color. Industrial design is primarily of an aesthetic nature and does not protect any technical aspects of the product to which it is applied. Identity marks such as trademarks, service marks, commercial names, and designations are designed to identify an offering or a company and protect it from the competition. A trademark (or service mark in the case of services) is a distinctive sign that identifies certain goods or services as those produced or provided by a specific entity. A geographical indication is a sign used on goods that have a specific geographical origin and possess qualities or a reputation that stem from the place of origin. Geographical indications can be used for a wide variety of agricultural products, such as "Tuscany" for olive oil produced in the Tuscany region of Italy, or "Roquefort" for cheese produced in the Roquefort area of France.

Intellectual Property: The legal entitlement attached to the expressed form of an idea, or to some other intangible subject matter. Intellectual property is divided into two categories: (1) *industrial property*, which encompasses inventions, industrial designs, and identity marks such as trademarks, service marks, commercial names, and designations, including indications of source and appellations of origin, and (2) *copyright*, which includes literary and artistic works, such as novels, poems and plays, films, musical works; artistic works, such as drawings, paintings, photographs and sculptures; and architectural designs.

National Brand: A brand available nationwide.

Private Label: Branding strategy in which an offering is branded by the retailer (Kirkland Signature, Costco's private brand; Kenmore, Sears' brand for home appliances; White Cloud, Walmart's private label for laundry detergents). Private labels (also referred to as store brands) are often contrasted with national brands, which are branded by the manufacturer or a third party rather than by the retailer (Coca-Cola, IBM, and Nike). Typically, private labels tend to be less expensive than national brands, although there are many exceptions, such as private labels offered by upscale retailers (Nordstrom, Marks & Spencer).

Regional Brand: A brand available only in a particular geographic region.

Store Brand: See *private label.*

ADDITIONAL READINGS

Aaker, David A. (1996), *Building Strong Brands*. New York, NY: Free Press.

Keller, Kevin Lane (2012), *Strategic Brand Management: Building, Measuring, and Managing Brand Equity* (4th ed.). Upper Saddle River, NJ: Prentice Hall.

Kumar, Nirmalya and Jan-Benedict E. M. Steenkamp (2007), *Private Label Strategy: How to Meet the Store Brand Challenge*. Boston, MA: Harvard Business School Press.

Tybout, Alice M. and Tim Calkins (2005), *Kellogg on Branding*. Hoboken, NJ: John Wiley & Sons.

NOTES

[1] With the exception of companies such as Walmart, Home Depot, and Priceline.com, where low prices are directly related to the essence of the brand.

[2] *Business Week* (2013), "The 100 Top Brands," October 1.

[3] Keller, Kevin Lane (2012), *Strategic Brand Management: Building, Measuring, and Managing Brand Equity* (4th ed.). Upper Saddle River, NJ: Prentice Hall.

CHAPTER TEN

MANAGING PRICE

Price is what you pay. Value is what you get.

—Warren Buffett, American investor and philanthropist

Pricing directly influences the value that the offering creates for target customers, the company, and its collaborators. Moreover, from a company's perspective, price is the only marketing tactic that captures revenue for the company; all other tactics are costs. The main aspects of price management are the focus of this chapter.

Overview

Despite the fundamental role pricing plays in designing and managing a company's offerings, there is little consensus on what constitutes the optimal pricing strategy. Over time, three popular approaches to pricing have emerged: cost-based pricing, competitive pricing, and demand pricing.

- **Cost-based pricing** involves setting prices using the company's costs as a benchmark. For example, in *cost-plus pricing*, an offering's final price is determined by adding a fixed markup to the cost of the offering.
- **Competitive pricing** calls for using competitors' prices as benchmarks. A popular version of this approach, referred to as *competitive-parity pricing*, involves setting the offering's price in a way that puts it at parity with that of competitors.
- **Demand pricing** calls for setting prices based on customers' willingness to pay for the benefits afforded by the company's offering.

Each of these three approaches is in some sense correct because each of the three factors needs to be taken into consideration when setting price. Yet, all three methods miss the point that the pricing decision is not made in isolation but is an integral component of the offering's strategy and tactics. Setting the price is a decision about value, not just price. The "optimal" price is a price that, in combination with the other marketing tactics—product, service, brand, incentives, communication, and distribution—delivers superior market value.

Pricing as a Value-Creation Process

The "ideal" price must optimize the value of the offering for target customers, the company, and its collaborators. When setting prices, a manager must consider five key factors—target customers, the company's goals and resources, its collaborators, competitors, and the context in which the company operates—and identify the price that creates the optimal value proposition. The Five Cs are the key decision factors that must be considered in order to design products and services that can create value for target customers, the company, and its collaborators (Figure 1).

Figure 1. Pricing as a Value-Creation Process

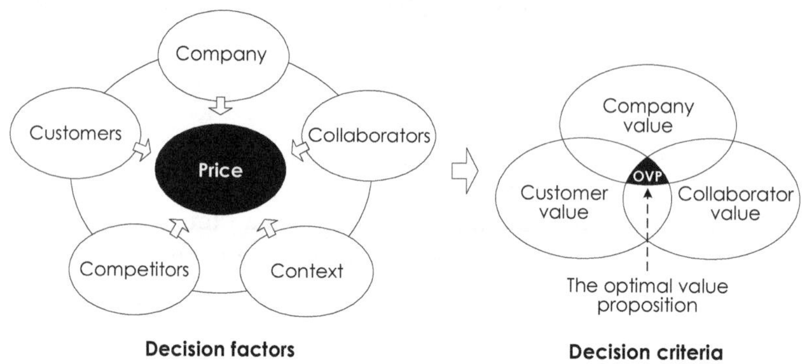

The Five Cs—customers, company, collaborators, competitors, and context—are the key decision factors that need to be considered in setting and managing prices. Thus, price is a function of customers' willingness to pay for the offering's benefits, such that greater willingness to pay typically translates into higher prices. Pricing is also a function of the company's goals and cost structure, whereby aggressive sales goals, and/or lower cost structure often result in lower prices. Pricing is also influenced by the company's collaborators (e.g., channel partners), such that more powerful channels (e.g., Walmart, Costco, and Carrefour) require lower prices. Because most purchase decisions involve choosing between competing offerings, an offering's price is also influenced by competitors' prices. Pricing also is a function of various economic, business, technological, sociocultural, regulatory, and physical factors of the environment in which the company operates.

In addition to being a function of the Five Cs, price is also influenced by the other marketing mix variables: product and service characteristics, brand, incentives, communication, and distribution. Thus, attractive and unique products and services command higher prices compared to less differentiated offerings. Price is also a function of the offering's brand, such that strong brands command substantial price premiums over weaker brands and unbranded offerings. Pricing also depends on the available incentives (e.g., promotional allowances, price discounts, and coupons), which determine the final amount buyers pay for an offering. Price can also be influenced by a company's communication and can be set in a way that facilitates communication (e.g., $1 meal at McDonald's). An offering's price is also a function of its distribution, such that channels with a lower cost structure tend to offer lower prices.

Customer-Based Pricing

Setting the optimal price is driven by a variety of considerations, including the company's strategic goals, customers' price sensitivity, and the psychological aspects of customers' response to the offering's price. The role of these factors in setting the optimal price is discussed in more detail in the following sections.

Skim and Penetration Pricing

Because sales volume is a function of price, the company has to determine the price level at which it is most likely to achieve its goals. When launching a new offering, a company can employ one of two core pricing strategies: skim pricing and penetration pricing.

- **Skim pricing** involves setting a high price to "skim the cream" off the top of the market, represented by customers who seek the benefits delivered by the offering and are willing to pay a relatively high price for it. By setting high prices, skim pricing maximizes profit margins, usually at the expense of market share. Skim pricing is more appropriate in cases where (1) demand is relatively inelastic and lowering the price is not likely to substantially increase sales volume, (2) there is little or no competition for the target segment, (3) cost is not a direct function of volume and significant cost savings are not achieved as cumulative volume increases, (4) being the market pioneer is unlikely to result in a sustainable competitive advantage, and (5) the company lacks the capital required for large-scale production.

- **Penetration pricing** involves setting relatively low prices in an attempt to gain higher sales volume, albeit at lower margins. Penetration pricing is more appropriate in cases where (1) demand is relatively elastic, such that lowering the price is likely to substantially increase sales volume, (2) the target segment becomes increasingly competitive, (3) cost is a function of volume and, as a result, significant cost savings are expected as cumulative volume increases, and (4) being the market pioneer can lead to a sustainable competitive advantage

Price Sensitivity

Typically, sales volume is inversely related to price: Lowering the price results in an increase in the sales volume, and vice versa. The degree to which changing the price influences sales volume is a function of customers' price sensitivity. Lowering the price in order to increase volume is most effective in cases where demand is elastic, meaning that a small change in price leads to a large change in sales volume. In contrast, in cases where demand is inelastic, profits might often be increased by raising the price since the decrease in sales volume resulting from the change in price is likely to be relatively small.

The price-quantity relationship is specific to each offering and is quantified in terms of an offering's price elasticity. Price elasticity represents the percentage change in quantity sold ($\Delta Q\%$) relative to the percentage change in price ($\Delta P\%$) for a given product or service. Because the quantity demanded decreases when the price increases, this ratio is negative; however, for practical purposes, the absolute value of the ratio is used, and price elasticity is often reported as a positive number.

$$E_p = \frac{\Delta Q\%}{\Delta P\%} = \frac{\Delta Q \cdot P}{\Delta P \cdot Q}$$

To illustrate, a price elasticity of –2 means that a 5% price increase will result in a 10% decrease in the quantity sold. In cases where (the absolute value of) price elasticity is greater than 1, demand is said to be elastic in the sense that a change in price causes a larger change in quantity demanded. In contrast, when (the absolute value of) price elasticity is less than 1, demand is said to be inelastic, meaning that a change in price results in a smaller change in quantity demanded. When (the absolute value of) price elasticity is equal to 1, demand is said to be unitary, meaning that a change in price results in an equal change in quantity demanded.

Because price elasticity reflects proportional changes, it does not depend on the units in which the price and quantity are expressed. Note also that because price elasticity is a function of the initial values, the same absolute changes in price can lead to different price elasticity values at different price points. For example, the volume decline resulting from lowering the price by five cents might be 5% when the initial price is $5.00 but only 1% when the initial price is $1.00.

Psychological Pricing

Consumers do not always evaluate prices objectively; instead, their reaction to an offering's price depends on a variety of psychological factors. The five most common psychological pricing effects—reference-price effects, price-quantity effects, price-tier effects, price-ending effects, and product-line effects—are outlined below.

- **Reference-price effects**. To assess the price of a given offering, people typically evaluate it relative to other prices, which serve as reference points. These reference prices can be either internal, such as a remembered price from a prior purchase occasion, or external, such as the readily available price of a competitive offering. By strategically choosing the reference price, a company can frame the price of its offering in a way that makes it more attractive to potential buyers, for example, by comparing it to a more expensive competitive offering (see Chapter 5 for a discussion of reference points).
- **Price-quantity effects**. People are more sensitive to changes in price than to changes in quantity. To illustrate, the sales volume of a ten-pack of hot dogs priced at $2.49 is likely to decline to a greater extent following a $.50 price increase (a ten-pack for $2.99) than following a two-item reduction in unit volume (an eight-pack for $2.49), even though on a per-item basis, the eight-pack is more expensive than the ten-pack.

- **Price-tier effects**. People encode prices in tiers, such that an item priced at \$1.99 is typically encoded in the "\$1+" price tier, whereas an item priced at \$2.00 is typically classified in the "\$2+" price tier. This tiered price encoding leads to the somewhat paradoxical perception that the difference between items priced at \$1.99 and \$2.00 is one dollar rather than one cent.
- **Price-ending effects**. Customers' perception of prices is also a function of price endings. For example, prices ending in "9" often create the perception of a discount, whereas prices ending in "0" might create the perception of quality.
- **Product-line effects**. Because many offerings are available as part of a company's product line, their relative prices can influence the demand for these offerings. To illustrate, restaurants often price wine they are trying to dispose of as the second cheapest in its assortment because many customers who are not willing to spend much on wine are often embarrassed to select the least expensive one.

Competitive Pricing

Price wars are very common in today's competitive markets. Price wars might involve price reductions offered directly from manufacturers to end users (price discounts, volume discounts, and coupons), as well as price cuts and incentives offered by manufacturers to channel partners (wholesale discounts and various promotional allowances). For example, a significant increase in a manufacturer's promotional allowances might prompt retailers to lower prices, thus provoking a price war.

Understanding Price Wars

Price wars often start when a company is willing to sacrifice margins to gain sales volume. Price wars usually begin with an action that results in a price cut on the customers' end. Price cuts, the forerunner of price wars, are popular among managers because they are easy to implement and typically produce fast results, especially when a company's goal is to increase sales volume. Not every price cut, however, leads to a price war. The likelihood of price wars is a function of the following factors:

- **Offering differentiation**. Price wars are more likely when offerings are undifferentiated and can be easily substituted.
- **Cost structure**. Companies are more likely to engage in price wars when significant economies of scale can be achieved by increasing volume.
- **Market growth**. Price wars are more likely to occur when markets are stagnant, and to grow sales a company has to steal share from its direct competitors.
- **Customer loyalty**. Companies are more likely to engage in price wars in markets in which customers are price sensitive and their switching costs are low.

Price wars are easy to initiate but costly to win. Winning a price war often comes at the expense of a significant loss of profits, making it more of a Pyrrhic victory than a true success. Price wars are detrimental to a company's profitability for several reasons:

- **Fixed-cost effect**. Price reductions have an exponential impact on profitability. To illustrate, in the absence of an increase in sales volume, reducing the price of an offering with a 10% profit margin by 1% will result in a 10% decrease in operating income.
- **Competitive reaction**. Because in most cases competitors can easily match price reductions, they are rarely sustainable. Firms with similar cost structures can quickly lower their prices in response to a competitor's action.
- **Increased price sensitivity**. Price wars often result in a shift in customers' future price expectations, such that the lowered prices become the reference points against which future prices are judged.
- **Brand devaluation**. Emphasis on price tends to erode brand power. This effect is exacerbated by the heavy price-focused communication campaigns that tend to accompany most price wars (because a company needs to promote the low price so that it can generate sufficient incremental volume to offset the lost profits resulting from the decrease in price).

Price wars rarely enable companies to achieve their strategic goals, and in most cases the only beneficiaries of a price war are the company's customers. In general, the best strategy for a company to win a potential price war is to avoid it.

Circumventing Price Wars

Even companies not seeking a price war are often confronted with a scenario in which a competitor initiates a price cut. The gut reaction of most managers in such cases is to respond with a matching price cut. This, however, is often a premature and suboptimal reaction. Only after evaluating the antecedents and likely consequences of the price cut can a company identify the optimal response strategy. A relatively simple approach for developing a strategic response to a competitor's price cut is outlined below.

- **Verify the threat of a price war**. Price wars are often caused by miscommunication of pricing information or misinterpretation of a competitor's goals. Thus, when competitive prices are not readily available (e.g., in contract bidding), a company might incorrectly believe that a particular competitor has significantly lowered its price. It is also possible that a competitor's price decrease is driven by internal factors, such as clearing the inventory (e.g., prior to introducing a new model), rather than by an intention to initiate a price war.
- **Evaluate the likely impact of the competitor's actions**. Identify customers most likely to be affected by competitors' price cuts and estimate their value to the company as well as their likely response to the price cut. In certain

cases, a company might choose to abandon markets that have no strategic importance and in which customer loyalty is low.

- **Develop segment-specific strategies to address the competitive threat.** There are three basic strategies to respond to the threat of a price war: not taking an action, repositioning an existing offering, and adding new offerings (see Chapter 14 for more details).
  - *Not taking an action.* The decision to ignore a competitor's price cut reflects a company's belief that the price cut will not have a significant impact on the company's market position, that the price cut is not sustainable and will dissipate by itself, or that serving the customer segment targeted by the price cut is no longer viable for the company.
  - *Repositioning the existing offering by lowering the price or increasing the benefits.* This reduction in price can be accomplished either on a permanent basis by lowering the actual price or as a temporary solution by offering price incentives.
  - *Adding a new offering.* A common response to low-priced competitors involves launching a downscale extension, commonly referred to as a fighting brand. Using a fighting brand enables the company to compete for price-sensitive customers without discounting its premium offering (see Chapter 17 for more details).

SUMMARY

The key to determining the optimal price is to consider its implications on an offering's value for customers, collaborators, and the company in a broad context that involves all other aspects of the company's strategy and tactics. Setting the price is really a decision about value, not just price. Thus, the optimal price is one that, in combination with the other marketing mix variables (product, service, brand, incentives, communication, and distribution), delivers superior value to target customers, the company, and collaborators.

Successful pricing strategies take into account that people do not always perceive pricing information objectively; instead, price perception is often a function of a variety of psychological effects such as reference-price effects, price-quantity effects, price-tier effects, price-ending effects, and product-line effects.

Competing on price often results in price wars, which typically start when companies are willing to sacrifice margins to gain market share. Price wars are likely to occur in the following cases: when offerings are undifferentiated, when capacity utilization is low, when significant economies of scale can be achieved by increasing volume, when markets are mature and a company has to steal share from its direct competitors to grow sales, and when customers' price sensitivity is high and switching costs are low. An effective approach for developing a strategic response to a competitor's price cut calls for verifying the validity of the threat of a price war, prioritizing customers who are most likely to be affected by the competitors' price cut based on their value to the company and price sensitivity, and developing segment-specific strategies to address the competitive threat.

RELEVANT CONCEPTS

Captive Pricing: See *complementary pricing.*

Complementary Pricing: Pricing strategy applicable to uniquely compatible, multipart offerings, whereby a company charges a relatively low introductory price for the first part of the offering and higher prices for the other parts. Classic examples include razors and blades, printers and cartridges, and cell phones and cell phone service. The unique compatibility is crucial to the success of complementary pricing: Only the printer manufacturer should be able to sell cartridges that fit its printers.

Cost-Plus Pricing: A pricing method in which the final price is determined by adding a fixed markup to the cost of the product. It is easy to calculate and is commonly used in industries where profit margins are relatively stable. Its key drawback is that it does not take into account customer demand and competitive pricing.

Cross-Price Elasticity: The percentage change in quantity sold of a given offering caused by a percentage change in the price of another offering.

Deceptive Pricing: The practice of presenting an offering's price to the buyer in a way that is deliberately misleading. Deceptive pricing is illegal in the United States.

Everyday Low Pricing (EDLP): Pricing strategy in which a retailer maintains low prices without frequent price promotions. See also *high–low pricing.*

Experience Curve Pricing: Pricing strategy based on an anticipated lower cost structure, resulting from scale economies and experience curve effects.

High-Low Pricing: Pricing strategy in which a retailer's prices fluctuate over time, typically a result of heavy reliance on sales promotions. See also *everyday low pricing.*

Horizontal Price Fixing: A practice in which competitors explicitly or implicitly collaborate to set prices. Price fixing is illegal in the United States.

Image Pricing: See *price signaling.*

Loss Leader: Pricing strategy that involves setting a low price for an offering (often at or below cost) in an attempt to increase the sales of other products and services. For example, a retailer might set a low price for a popular item in an attempt to build store traffic, thus increasing the sales of other, more profitable items.

Predatory Pricing: A strategy that involves selling below cost with the intent of driving competitors out of business. In most cases, predatory pricing is illegal in the United States.

Prestige Pricing: Pricing strategy whereby the price is set at a relatively high level for the purpose of creating an exclusive image of the offering.

Price Discrimination: A strategy that involves charging different buyers different prices for goods of equal grade and quality.

Price Fixing: A practice in which companies conspire to set prices for a given product or service. Price fixing is illegal in the United States.

Price Segmentation: See *price discrimination*.

Price Signaling: (1) Pricing strategy that aims to capitalize on price–quality inferences (higher priced products are also likely to be higher quality). Primarily used when the actual product benefits are not readily observable (also known as prestige pricing); (2) Indirect communication (direct price collusion is prohibited by law) between companies aimed at indicating their intentions with respect to their pricing strategy.

Product-Line Pricing: Pricing strategy in which the price of each individual offering is determined as a function of the offering's place in the relevant product line.

Second Market Discounting: Pricing strategy in which a company charges lower prices in more competitive markets, such as when exporting to developing countries.

Two-Part Pricing: See *complementary pricing*.

Vertical Price Fixing: The practice whereby channel partners (a manufacturer and a retailer) explicitly or implicitly collaborate to set prices. Price fixing is illegal in the United States.

Yield-Management Pricing: Pricing strategy whereby the price is set to maximize revenue for a fixed capacity within a given time frame (frequently used by airlines and hotels).

ADDITIONAL READINGS

Baker, Ronald J. (2010), *Implementing Value Pricing: A Radical Business Model for Professional Firms*. Hoboken, NJ: John Wiley & Sons.

Baker, Walter L., Michael V. Marn, and Craig C. Zawada (2010), *The Price Advantage* (2nd ed.). Hoboken, NJ: John Wiley & Sons.

Nagle, Thomas T., John E. Hogan, and Joseph Zale (2010), *The Strategy and Tactics of Pricing: A Guide to Growing More Profitably* (5th ed.). Upper Saddle River, NJ: Pearson/Prentice Hall.

CHAPTER ELEVEN

MANAGING INCENTIVES

But wait, there's more!

—Ron Popeil, inventor and infomercial salesman

Incentives offer solutions, typically short-term, aimed at enhancing the value of the offering by providing additional benefits or reducing costs. Because they typically lead to an increase in sales volume, incentives are often referred to as sales promotions. The key aspects of managing incentives are the focus of this chapter.

Overview

Most incentives fall into one of three categories: incentives given to customers (coupons, loyalty programs, sweepstakes, contests, and premiums); incentives given to the company's collaborators, most often channel partners (price cuts, volume discounts, allowances, and co-op advertising); and incentives given to the company's employees (bonuses, rewards, and contests). Furthermore, incentives can be either monetary, such as volume discounts, price reductions, coupons, and rebates, or nonmonetary, such as premiums, contests, and rewards. Unlike monetary incentives, which typically aim to reduce an offering's costs, nonmonetary incentives typically aim to enhance the offering's benefits. The most popular incentives, organized by their focus (customers, collaborators, and company) and type (price and nonprice), are given in Table 1.

Table 1. Incentive Types

	Monetary incentives	Nonmonetary incentives
Customer incentives	Coupons, rebates, price reductions, volume discounts	Premiums, rewards, sweepstakes
Collaborator incentives	Advertising, slotting, stocking, display, and market-development allowances; spiffs; volume discounts; volume rebates; off-invoice incentives	Contests, bonus merchandise, buy-back guarantees, sales support and training
Company incentives	Performance bonuses, monetary prizes, spiffs	Contests, recognition awards, free goods, vacation and travel incentives

Deciding on the optimal mix of these various incentives can be facilitated using a systematic approach, outlined in more detail in the following sections.

Managing Incentives as a Value-Creation Process

Incentives enhance the value of the offering by increasing its benefits and/or reducing its costs. When designing incentives, a manager must consider the Five Cs—target customers, the company's goals and resources, its collaborators, competitors, and the context in which the company operates—and develop incentives that deliver market value. The Five Cs are the key decision factors that must be considered in order to design products and services that can create value for target customers, the company, and its collaborators (Figure 1).

Figure 1. Managing Incentives as a Value-Creation Process

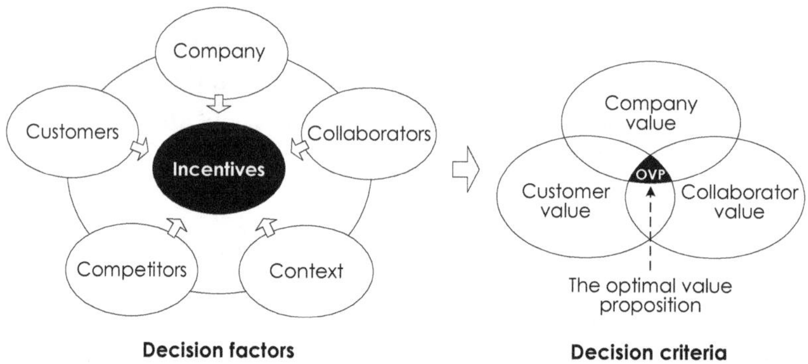

The Five Cs—customers, company, collaborators, competitors, and context—are the key decision factors that merit consideration in managing incentives. Thus, incentives are a function of customers' needs and are more common for discretionary purchases and among price-conscious consumers. The use of incentives is also driven by a company's desire to achieve certain sales goals within a specific time frame. Incentives are also a function of the company's collaborators, such as distribution channels—many of which have gained considerable power and require significant concessions from manufacturers in the form of trade incentives. Competitors often influence incentives by making it necessary for companies to offer incentives to maintain competitive parity. The use of incentives is also a function of various context factors; for example, adverse economic conditions tend to lead to greater reliance on incentives to stimulate demand.

In addition to being influenced by the Five Cs, incentives also depend on the other marketing mix factors: product, service, brand, price, communication, and distribution. Thus, incentives are a function of the product and service aspect of the offering, whereby the increased commoditization leads to increased use of incentives. In the same vein, incentives are a function of the offering's brand, such that luxury brands are less likely to utilize monetary incentives. An offering's incentives are often set as part of its overall pricing strategy—for example, everyday low pricing involves limited use of incentives, whereas high-low pricing (see Chapter 10) relies heavily on incentives. An offering's incentives are a function of its communication, such that consumer-focused communications (pull strategy) are often complemented by consumer incentives, and retailer-focused communications (push strategy) are often complemented with trade incentives. Incentives are also a function of an offering's distribution, whereby consolidated, powerful channels typically require greater trade incentives.

Customer Incentives

Customer incentives can be offered by either the manufacturer (manufacturer incentives) or the channel member (retailer incentives). Manufacturer incentives can then be delivered either directly by the manufacturer or indirectly by the retailer (pass-through incentives). Based on the type of reward, customer incentives can be divided into two types: monetary and nonmonetary.

- **Monetary incentives** aim to reduce an offering's costs by providing customers with a monetary inducement to purchase the offering. Most common forms of monetary incentives include coupons, rebates, price reductions, and volume discounts.
  - *Coupons* entitle the buyer to receive a price reduction for a given product or service at the time of purchase.
  - *Rebates* involve cash refunds given to customers after they make a purchase.
  - *Price reductions* involve price discounts that do not require any action from customers.
  - *Volume discounts* involve price reduction offers conditional upon the purchase of multiple items.
- **Nonmonetary incentives** typically aim to enhance the value of the offering. The most common forms of nonmonetary incentives are premiums, prizes, contests, sweepstakes, games, and loyalty programs.
  - *Premiums* involve bonus products or services offered for free or at deeply discounted prices as an incentive for purchasing a particular offering. Premiums can be delivered instantly with the purchase (packaged with the product) or can require the customer to send in a proof of purchase to receive the premium.
  - *Prizes* offer customers the opportunity to win an award as an incentive for purchasing a particular offering. Unlike premiums, where the reward is given with every purchase, in the case of prizes the actual reward is given to a relatively small number of participants. Prizes can be both monetary and nonmonetary.
  - *Contests, sweepstakes, and games* involve prizes that typically require customers to submit some form of entry and are usually not contingent on customers purchasing the offering. Winners are selected by a panel of

judges (in the case of contests), by drawing (in the case of sweepstakes), or by an objective criterion, such as points collected (in the case of games).

- *Loyalty programs* involve rewards related to the frequency, volume, and type of products and services purchased. Loyalty programs can be both monetary (cash-back credit cards offering a reward based on purchase volume) and nonmonetary (frequent-flyer airline awards and frequent-stay hotel awards).

Companies typically use customer incentives to achieve three primary goals: to manage the timing of customers' purchases, to selectively reach specific segments, and to respond to competitive promotions.

- **Managing purchase timing**. Time-sensitive incentives can encourage customers to purchase a company's offering in a time frame consistent with the company's goals. Purchase timing is usually managed by offering widespread incentives, such as temporary price reductions, available to all target customers.

- **Optimizing the value of the offering to different segments**. A company might offer incentives to selectively enhance the value of an offering for particular customer segments. For example, a company might give discounts to economically disadvantaged customers, frequent buyers, and high-volume buyers.

- **Responding to a competitor's promotion**. Companies often attempt to lure customers by offering incentives, which, in turn, forces other companies serving these customers to respond by offering similar incentives.

Collaborator Incentives

Most collaborator incentives are offered to members of the distribution channel. These incentives, also referred to as trade incentives, can have multiple objectives, such as gaining distribution through a particular channel, encouraging channel members to stock the offering at certain inventory levels (to avoid stock-outs or to transfer the inventory from the manufacturer to retailers), and encouraging channel members to promote the company's offering. Similar to customer incentives, trade incentives can be either monetary or nonmonetary.

- **Monetary incentives** involve payments or price discounts given as encouragement to purchase the product or as an inducement to promote the product to customers. Typical monetary incentives include the following.
  - *Slotting allowance*: an incentive paid to a distributor to allocate shelf space for a new product.
  - *Stocking allowance*: an incentive paid to a distributor to carry extra inventory in anticipation of an increase in demand.
  - *Cooperative advertising allowance*: an incentive paid by the manufacturer to a distributor in return for featuring its offerings in a retailer's advertise-

ments. The magnitude of the allowance can be determined as a percentage of the distributor's advertising costs or as a fixed dollar amount per unit.

- *Market-development allowance*: an incentive for achieving a certain sales volume in a specific customer segment.
- *Display allowance*: an incentive paid by the manufacturer to a distributor in return for prominently displaying its products and/or services.
- *Spiffs*: incentives such as cash premiums, prizes, or additional commissions given directly to the salesperson (rather than the distributor) as a reward for selling a particular item. Because they encourage the retailer's sales personnel to "push" the product to customers, spiffs are often referred to as "push money."
- *Volume discount*: price reductions determined based on purchase volume.
- *Volume rebate* (also referred to as *volume bonus*): an incentive paid by the manufacturer to a distributor as a reward for achieving certain purchase-volume benchmarks (e.g., selling 1,000 units per quarter).
- *Off-invoice incentive*: any temporary price discounts offered by manufacturers to distributors.
- *Cash discount*: price reductions for payments made instantly or within a brief time frame.
- *Inventory financing* (also referred to as *floor planning*): loans provided to a distributor for acquiring manufacturers' goods.

- **Nonmonetary incentives** involve nonmonetary inducements designed to encourage channel support for a particular offering. Typical nonmonetary incentives include the following.
  - *Contests*: performance-based rewards (e.g., vacation trips, cars, and monetary compensation) given to the best achievers.
  - *Bonus merchandise*: free goods offered as a reward for purchasing a particular item.
  - *Buyback guarantees*: an agreement that the manufacturer will buy back from the distributor product quantities not sold within a certain time frame.
  - *Sales support and training*: various forms of aid offered to distributors that are designed to familiarize the distributor with the offering and facilitate sales.

Channel incentives can be used to achieve different goals: to acquire shelf space for new products (e.g., through slotting allowances), to encourage distributors to carry higher levels of inventory to avoid stock-outs (e.g., through stocking allowances, inventory financing, and volume discounts), to encourage distributors to promote new products (e.g., through advertising and display allowances), and to offset the impact of competitive promotions (e.g., through competitive price-matching incentives).

Company Incentives

In addition to incentives focused on target customers and collaborators, companies often offer incentives to motivate and reward their own personnel. Company incentives commonly involve rewards for employees who meet certain performance benchmarks. The importance of incentivizing employees is effectively captured in the words of the founder of The Virgin Group, Richard Branson: *If you take care of your employees, your employees will take care of your customers, and your customers will take care of your shareholders.*

Common company incentives include performance-based awards such as contests, monetary bonuses, employee recognition awards, free goods and services, vacation and travel incentives, prizes, sweepstakes, and games.

SUMMARY

Incentives offer solutions, typically short term, aimed at enhancing the value of the offering by providing additional benefits and reducing costs. Most incentives fall into one of three categories: incentives given to customers (coupons, loyalty programs, sweepstakes, contests, and premiums); incentives given to the company's collaborators, most often channel partners (price cuts, volume discounts, allowances, and co-op advertising); and incentives given to the company's employees (bonuses, rewards, and contests).

Managing incentives involves two types of decisions: *strategic* decisions—which are a function of the offering's target market defined by its customers, company, collaborators, competition, and context—and *tactical* decisions—which are a function of the other marketing mix variables: product, service, brand, price, communication, and distribution.

Most *customer incentives* serve one of two goals: temporarily increasing sales volume by giving target customers an additional reason to buy the offering, or serving as a segmentation tool by selectively enhancing the value of the company's offering for target customers. Customer incentives can be divided into two categories: monetary incentives that typically aim to reduce an offering's costs (coupons, rebates, price reductions, and volume discounts), and nonmonetary incentives, which often aim to enhance the offering's benefits (premiums, prizes, contests, and loyalty programs).

Most *collaborator incentives* are offered to members of the distribution channel and can have multiple objectives: (1) to gain distribution coverage, (2) to encourage channel members to stock the offering at certain inventory levels (to avoid stock-outs or to transfer the inventory from the manufacturer to distributors), and (3) to encourage channel members to promote the company's offering. Similar to customer incentives, trade incentives are either monetary (discounts and allowances) or nonmonetary (contests and bonus merchandise).

RELEVANT CONCEPTS

Freestanding Inserts (FSI): Leaflets or coupons inserted into newspapers.

Push and Pull Promotions: Based on the flow of promotions (i.e., incentives and communications) from the manufacturer to target customers, two core promotion strategies can be identified: push and pull (Figure 2). Push strategy refers to the practice of creating demand for a company's offering by incentivizing channel members, who in turn push the product downstream to end users. For example, the manufacturer can offer high margins on its products and services so that retailers have a vested interest in selling them. The manufacturer can also educate a retailer's sales force about the benefits of its offerings and provide the retailer with promotional materials, thus facilitating the sales process. In contrast, pull strategy refers to the practice of creating demand for a company's offering by promoting the offering directly to end users, who in turn demand the offering from intermediaries, and ultimately "pull" it through the channel. To illustrate, the manufacturer can extensively advertise its products and services to end users and promote its offerings using means such as direct mail, coupons, and contests.

Figure 2. Push and Pull Promotion Strategies

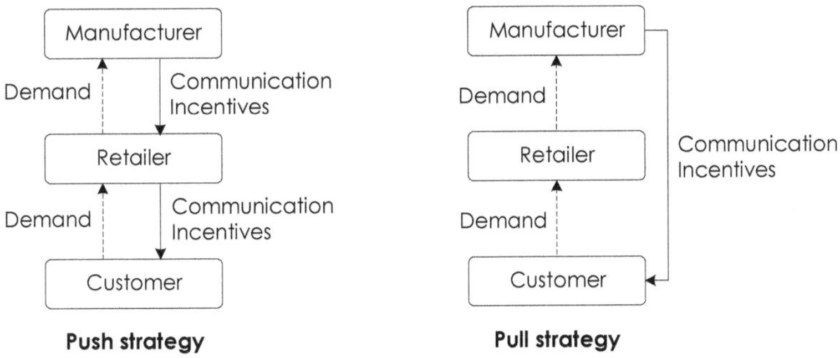

Run-of-Press Coupons: Coupons that appear in the actual pages of a newspaper (rather than being inserted as a separate page).

Slippage: The percentage of customers who fail to redeem a promotional offer made with the purchase.

Trade Allowance: A broad range of trade incentives, including slotting allowances, stocking allowances, and advertising allowances, offered as a reward for conducting promotional activities on behalf of the manufacturer. Trade allowances are typically implemented as a discount from the wholesale price rather than as a separate promotional payment. From an accounting standpoint, they are often considered as a discount to the channel rather than as a separate marketing expense.

ADDITIONAL READINGS

Blattberg, Robert C. and Scott A. Neslin (1990), *Sales Promotion: Concepts, Methods, and Strategies*. Englewood Cliffs, NJ: Prentice Hall.

Mullin, Roddy (2010), *Sales Promotions: How to Create, Implement, and Integrate Campaigns that Really Work* (5th ed.). Philadelphia, PA: Cogan-Page.

Neslin, Scott A. (2002), *Sales Promotion*. Cambridge, MA: Marketing Science Institute.

CHAPTER TWELVE

MANAGING COMMUNICATION

The single biggest problem in communication is the illusion that it has taken place.

—George Bernard Shaw, playwright
cofounder, London School of Economics

Communication aims to inform the market—customers, collaborators, company stakeholders, competitors, and society in general—about the specifics of a company's offering. The main aspects of developing and managing a communication campaign are the focus of this chapter.

Overview

Communication is the most visible component of an offering's marketing mix. Thousands of companies spend millions of dollars each year to advise buyers about the availability of their offerings, explain the benefits of these offerings, spread the word about price cuts, and promote product and corporate brands. In the words of Leo Burnett, the founder of Leo Burnett advertising agency, *Advertising says to people, "Here's what we've got. Here's what it will do for you. Here's how to get it."*

During the past decades there have been significant changes in the way companies design and manage communication. One of the most important changes is the evolution of the traditional forms of communication from mass media formats, including television and print, to one-on-one communication. Another important change involves the switch from company-driven communication to customer-driven social media interactions, whereby customers receive an increasing amount of information about the available offerings not from the companies but from other customers. These changes add an extra layer of complexity to the task of effectively managing communication, highlighting the importance of using a systematic approach to designing and implementing a communication campaign.

Communication as a Value-Creation Process

Communication informs target customers, collaborators, and/or the company employees and stakeholders about the benefits of the offering. The development of a communication strategy is influenced by five key factors—target customers, the company's goals and resources, its collaborators, competitors, and context. These Five Cs are the key decision factors that must be considered in order to design products and services that can create value for target customers, the company, and its collaborators (Figure 1).

Figure 1. Communication as a Value-Creation Process

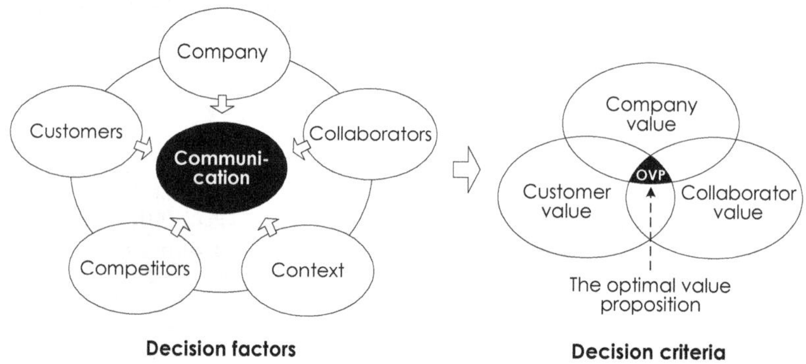

The Five Cs—customers, company, collaborators, competitors, and context—are the key decision factors that must be considered in designing an offering's communications. Thus, the choice of target customers plays an important role in managing communication: For customers unfamiliar with the offering, communication aims to create awareness of the offering, whereas for those already familiar with the offering, communication typically aims to strengthen their preferences and impel them to purchase the offering. Communication is also influenced by the company's goals and available resources, which determine the content (message), scale (budget), and the media selection (television, radio, print, or online). The communication campaign must be aligned with the company's collaborators, as in the case of co-developed and/or co-sponsored (co-op) advertising. Company communication is also often influenced by that of competitors, such that an increase in competitive spending frequently leads to a corresponding increase in the company's own communication budget. Communication is also a function of the context in which the company operates; it is influenced by technological advancements (e.g., the growth of online media), industry-specific regulations (e.g., tobacco, alcohol, and pharmaceuticals), and regulations concerning general advertising practices (e.g., claiming specific benefits and making product comparisons).

In addition to being driven by the Five Cs, communication is also influenced by the other marketing mix factors: product, service, brand, price, incentives, and distribution. Thus, communication reflects the balance of the product and service aspects of the offering: In the case of services that are mostly intangible, communication often aims to highlight their tangible aspects (e.g., by creating tangible symbols such as the Rock of Gibraltar for Prudential), whereas for tangible products, communication often highlights their intangible characteristics (e.g., warranty, reliability, and durability). Communication also is a function the offering's brand, such that the message, media, and creative aspects fit the identity and the meaning of the brand. Communication is also influenced by the offering's price and incentives, such that low-priced offerings featuring monetary incentives call for a different communication strategy compared to high-priced offerings featuring nonmonetary incentives. An offering's communication is also influenced by its distribution strategy: for example, online retailers offer multiple opportunities for point-of-purchase communication using a variety of media formats.

The Communication Process

Managing communication follows the G-STIC marketing framework, with the key difference that its focus is on the communication aspect of the company's marketing activities. In this context, managing communication involves seven key decisions: setting the communication goal, articulating the communication strategy, developing the message, selecting the media, developing the creative solution, implementing the communication campaign, and evaluating the campaign results (Figure 2).

Figure 2. Developing a Communication Plan

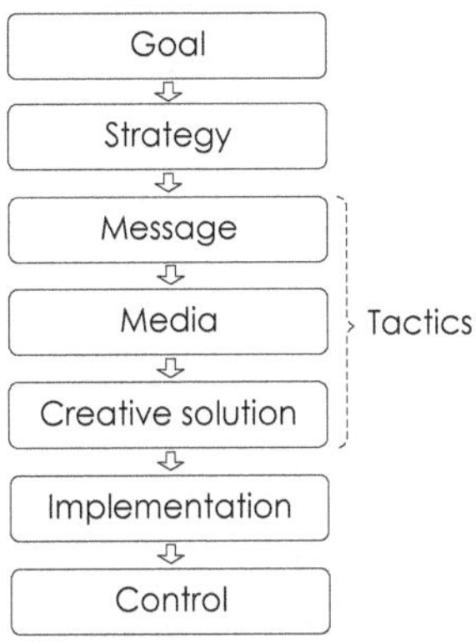

- The communication **goal** identifies the criteria to be achieved by the communication campaign within a given time frame.
- The communication **strategy** identifies the target audience and the value proposition to be communicated to this audience.
- The **message** articulates the information to be communicated to the target audience. The message can involve one or several of the other marketing mix variables: product, service, brand, price, incentives, and distribution. To illustrate, a company can choose to promote the benefits of its product and service, communicate the meaning of its brand, publicize its price, inform

customers about its current incentives, and inform customers about the offering's availability.

- The **media** are the means used by the company to communicate its message. The media decision involves three key aspects: budget, media type, and scheduling.
- The **creative solution** involves the execution of the company's message. Among the key aspects of the creative solution is the type of appeal used in the campaign (information, humor, or fear) and execution style (text, format, and layout).
- The **implementation** aspect of marketing communication identifies the logistics and the timeline for executing the message, media, and creative decisions.
- The **control** aspect of marketing communication involves evaluating the success of the communication campaign with respect to its goals.

The key aspects of developing a communication campaign are discussed in more detail in the following sections.

Setting Communication Goals

Setting a goal typically involves two decisions: identifying the *focus* of the communication campaign and identifying the specific *performance benchmarks* to be reached.

- Identifying the **focus** of the communication campaign involves setting the ultimate criterion for success. There are three core goals, any of which can be the focus of a given communication campaign:
  - Create and raise *awareness* of the company's offering.
  - Create and strengthen buyer *preferences* for the company's offering.
  - Incite an *action* such as purchasing the offering or contacting the company for information.

  These goals are interdependent, such that some can be viewed as prerequisites for others. Thus, enhancing an offering's attractiveness implies that target customers are aware of the offering's existence. Similarly, a call for action implies that customers are already aware of the offering and find it attractive.
- The **performance benchmarks** provide measurable *criteria* for success (e.g., creating awareness among 40% of a given market), as well as an identifiable *time frame* for achieving these criteria (e.g., two weeks prior to product launch).

Defining the Communication Strategy

Communication strategy follows directly from the offering's overall marketing strategy and comprises two key components: target audience and value proposition.

- **Target audience** defines the recipient of the communication campaign. An offering's target audience might not necessarily coincide with its target customers. In addition to aiming at the offering's target customers, the communication campaign might focus on entities influencing the decision process as well as those making the purchase, even when they are not the target customers. For example, in the case of gift buyers and parents buying food and clothing for their kids, the target audience (gift givers/parents) is different from target customers (gift recipients/kids).
- **Value proposition** defines the value that the communication campaign aims to convey to target customers. The value proposition conveyed in the communication campaign is typically related to the target audience, articulating the benefits of the offering to the recipients of the marketing communication.

The communication strategy articulates the target audience and the value proposition that guide the next steps in the development of the communication campaign: designing the communication tactics (message, media, and creative solution), developing an implementation plan, and measuring the success of the campaign.

Developing the Message

The message can involve one or more marketing mix variables: product, service, brand, price, incentives, and distribution. For each of these marketing mix factors, the message articulates the specifics of the company's offering as follows:

- **Product- and service-related messages** inform target customers of the characteristics of the company's products and services.
- **Brand-related messages** focus on the identity and the meaning of the company's or offering's brand.
- **Price-related messages** communicate the offering's price.
- **Incentives-related messages** communicate the incentives associated with the offering, such as temporary price reductions, volume discounts, rebates, coupons, and premiums.
- **Distribution-related messages** highlight the offering's availability in distribution channels.

The key principle when designing the message is that it should focus on the aspects of the offering that are likely to have the greatest impact. Thus, if customers are unaware of the benefits of the offering, the message should focus on its product and service aspects, whereas if customers are unaware of the offering's availability, the message should focus on distribution. A specific approach to identifying areas that can benefit from investing marketing resources, including communication, is outlined in Chapter 15.

Selecting the Media

The media decision involves deciding on the media budget, selecting the type of media used, and setting a media schedule. These three aspects are discussed in more detail in the following sections.

Media Budget

Deciding on the magnitude of communication expenditures is one of the key decisions in planning a promotional campaign, not only because it has a direct impact on the company's profitability but also because the overall budget often determines the type of media used. For example, mass-media television campaigns are predicated on the availability of substantial resources to secure this media. There are several approaches to determine the total communication budget:

- The **goal-driven** approach is based on an estimate of the resources required to achieve the company's strategic goal. This approach takes into account factors such as number of customers reached through a single exposure to the company's message per media dollar spent and the average number of exposures necessary to create awareness.
- The **percentage-of-sales** approach implies setting the budget as a percentage of the company's sales revenues.
- The **competitive-parity** approach implies setting the budget at par with that of a key competitor. The approach in which the budget is set proportionally to the desired share of total media expenditures in a given category is also referred to as share-of-voice budgeting.
- The **legacy** approach implies budgeting based on prior year expenditures.
- The **affordability** approach implies setting the budget based on resources available for promotional activities.

While all of the above budgeting strategies have merit (some more than others), the goal-driven approach dominates the others in its ability to estimate most effectively the resources required to achieve the company's communication goals. Competitive-parity and percentage-of-sales approaches can also provide useful inputs into the budgeting decision. Because they are detached from market realities, the legacy and affordability approaches are the least likely to provide an accurate budget estimate.

Media Type

Media type involves the means used by the company to convey its message. The most popular types of media include advertising, public relations and social media, direct marketing, personal selling, event sponsorship, product-based communications, and product samples. These media types are discussed in more detail below.

- **Advertising** involves nonpersonal marketing communications in which the company develops the message and absorbs most or all of the media (air time and print space) costs. The most popular forms of advertising involve audiovisual (television, video, and film), radio, print (promotional brochures, advertisements in newspapers and magazines, and newspaper and magazine inserts), online, mobile, outdoor (posters and billboards), and point of sale (front-of-the-store, end-of-aisle, and shelf-talkers—signs displayed in close proximity to the promoted item). In the United States, advertising is the most popular media type, with most of the advertising dollars spent on television commercials.
- **Public relations and social media** involve communications by third parties that are not directly controlled by the company. Unlike advertising, with public relations the company does not pay for the media and therefore cannot control the content of the message. Instead, it aims to encourage a third party (opinion leaders and press) to promote the offering. Because the message comes from a third party that typically has no vested interest in the company's offering, public relations communications are often viewed as more credible than communications directly sponsored by the company.
- **Direct marketing** involves individually targeted communications (catalogs, direct mail, telemarketing, and online advertising), typically designed to elicit a direct response.
- **Personal selling** involves direct, typically one-on-one, interaction with a company representative (a salesperson).
- **Event sponsorship** involves backing events and activities of interest to the offering's target customers. A form of event sponsorship is product placement, where the sponsor secures the rights to embed (place) its offering within a particular form of entertainment, such as a sports event, television show, or a movie.
- **Product-based communication** is embedded in the product itself, such as product labels, signs, and packaging.
- **Product samples** and **free trials** enable customers to experience product benefits directly. Samples and free trials are often used in new product introductions to encourage customers to try the offering. They are typically distributed via direct mail (in the case of consumer packaged goods); online (in the case of digital content products such as electronic newspapers, music samples, and movie trailers); or at the point of sale (in the case of items that can be readily consumed, such as food samples).

The allocation of resources across different media types is a function of the effectiveness and cost efficiency of each media format with respect to its ability to communicate the desired message. For certain types of products (gasoline, alcohol, and tobacco), the choice of advertising medium is also subject to stringent legal regulations.

In addition to deciding on the allocation of resources across different types of media, the media decision involves determining the specific media channels within each of the media types. For example, within the domain of television advertising, the media channel decision involves selecting particular shows and time slots in which the company's message will be best positioned to reach and influence its target customers. Thus, beer companies often choose to advertise during popular sport events with predominantly male audiences, whereas beauty products are typically advertised during shows with predominantly female audiences.

Media Scheduling

Deciding on media scheduling involves identifying the pattern of communication, its reach, and frequency.

- The **pattern** of communication can be continuous, concentrated, or intermittent. Continuous communication (also referred to as flighting) involves allocating exposures evenly throughout the individual periods within a given time frame. Concentrated communication involves allocating the majority of exposures in a single period (e.g., spending the entire advertising budget on a single Super Bowl commercial). Intermittent communication (also referred to as pulsing) involves alternating periods with high and low (or no) levels of advertising (e.g., advertising every other week). The decision to use a particular timing format is a function of the characteristics of the company's offering and the pattern of product adoption and/or usage by target customers.
- The **frequency** reflects the number of times target customers are exposed to a particular message over a given period. The number of exposures necessary for the company's message to register in a customer's mind is a function of factors such as communication goals, the novelty of the offering, the type of media (television, radio, print, mail, point of purchase, outdoor, or online), the creative solution used to generate awareness, and customers' level of involvement when viewing the advertisement. In some cases, a single exposure could be sufficient, although most often multiple exposures are required to achieve communication goals.
- The **reach** reflects the number of target customers who are exposed to a particular message at least once in a given period. The communication reach is typically a function of the size of the target market: the larger the market, the greater the potential reach.

Creative Solution

The creative solution involves translating the company's message into the language of the selected media format, such as television, print, radio, online, and point of purchase. Creative solutions vary on two main factors: their appeal and execution style.

- **Appeal** refers to the approach used to communicate the company's message. Most creative solutions involve at least one of two types of appeals: information-based and emotion-based. Information-based appeals typically rely on methods such as factual presentations (straightforward presentation of the relevant information), demonstrations (illustration of the offering's key benefits in a staged environment), slice-of-life stories (illustration of the offering's key benefits in everyday use), and testimonials (praise by an individual based on his or her experience with the offering and endorsements by ordinary users or celebrities). In contrast, emotion-based appeals typically play on emotions such as love, romance, humor, and fear. Some communication campaigns use a combination of the two approaches to achieve maximum impact.

- **Execution style** refers to the method used to convey a particular appeal using the language of the selected media format. Style decisions are media specific. Thus, print advertising involves decisions concerning the copy (wording of the headline and the body text), visual elements (pictures, photos, graphics, and logos), format (size and color scheme), and layout (the arrangement of different parts of the advertisement). Radio advertising involves decisions dealing with the text (wording of the dialogue and narration), audio (music, dialogue, and sound effects), and format (length). Television advertising involves decisions concerning the visual elements (imagery), text (wording of the dialogue, voice-over narration, and printed text), audio (music, dialogue, and sound effects), and format (length).

An important aspect of developing the communication campaign is keeping the balance between the marketing message and the entertainment component of the creative solution. Because of the ever-growing competition to capture buyers' attention, companies are often tempted to develop overly creative campaigns designed to break through the clutter of competitive messages. While creativity per se is a virtue, in business communication creativity should never be achieved at the expense of the marketing content. *I do not regard advertising as entertainment or an art form, but as a medium of information,* notes Ogilvy & Mather founder David Ogilvy. *A good advertisement is one which sells the product without drawing attention to itself.*

Implementing the Communication Campaign

The implementation of a communication campaign involves setting up the necessary infrastructure to execute the campaign; setting up the processes necessary to execute the message, media, and creative solutions; and outlining the implementation schedule.

- Setting up the organizational **infrastructure** of the communication campaign involves identifying the relevant collaborators (advertising, public relations, and social media agencies) and forming a team to manage the campaign.
- Setting up the **processes** involves identifying the specific actions to be taken during preproduction (identifying the technical aspects of the message, media, and creative solution), production (the actual filming, videotaping, recording, or printing of the advertisement), postproduction (editing, duplicating, ensuring legal compliance, and obtaining client approval), and distribution (airing, printing, and shipping).
- The **scheduling** aspect of implementation involves deciding on the timing and the optimal sequence in which individual tasks should be performed to ensure effective and cost-efficient execution of the communication campaign.

Evaluating Communication Effectiveness

I know that half of my advertising money is wasted. I just don't know which half. John Wanamaker's famous quote, uttered nearly a century ago, succinctly reflects the current state of evaluating communication effectiveness. There is little agreement on the part of marketers, advertising agencies, and research companies about the best way to measure advertising effectiveness. As a result, companies use diverse criteria to measure the effectiveness of an advertising campaign. The most commonly used criteria involve measuring six factors: exposure, comprehension, recall, persuasion, intent, and behavior.

- **Exposure** reflects the number of times a given advertisement has been seen by the target audience.
- **Comprehension** reflects the degree to which the target audience understands the message embedded in the advertisement.
- **Recall** reflects the degree to which the target audience remembers an advertisement. Recall can be either aided or unaided. In the case of *aided recall*, respondents are given a list of brand names following the presentation of a series of advertisements and are asked to recall whether they have seen any of these brands. In contrast, in the case of *unaided recall*, respondents are simply asked to recall all brands they have seen during the presentation.
- **Persuasion** reflects the degree to which the advertisement is able to strengthen or change preferences of the target audience. Because preferences for established brands (which often are among the largest advertisers) are difficult to change with a single advertisement, advertising agencies often measure the attitude toward the advertisement (rather than the attitude to-

ward the brand) on the premise that if the target audience likes the advertisement, then this attitude will translate into liking the brand.

- **Intent** reflects customers' mental disposition to act favorably toward the offering, such as buy the product, visit the store, or contact the company. Intent is typically measured by asking respondents to indicate the likelihood of purchasing the product within a given time frame.

- **Behavior** reflects the impact of an advertisement on respondents' actual behavior, such as purchasing the product, inquiring about product features, and researching the product on the Internet. Behavior is typically measured by the number of sales, sales inquiries, and website visits.

A great deal of disagreement exists about which of the above measures is the most reliable indicator of advertising effectiveness. Intuitively, it might seem that sales volume is the best measure of communication effectiveness. This, however, is not the case. The problem with relying on customers' behavior as a measure of effectiveness is that most often the impact of communication is not immediate (especially in cases of brand-building communication). As a result, the impact of communication is typically confounded with a variety of nonrelated factors, such as changes in price, incentives, competitive actions, and purchase cycle.

A more meaningful approach to measuring the effectiveness of a communication campaign should take into account three main factors: the goal of the campaign, the message being communicated, and the selected media format.

- **Communication goal**. Measuring the success of a communication campaign is a function of the nature of the communication goal. Thus, if the communication goal is to create awareness, then exposure, comprehension, and recall should be measured. If the communication goal is to strengthen preferences, then the persuasiveness of the advertisement should be measured. Finally, if the communication goal is to incite action, then behavior should be measured.

- **Communication message**. Evaluating the effectiveness of a communication campaign also depends on the type of message. Thus, communicating incentives tends to have an immediate impact on sales, whereas the impact of brand-building communication is delayed. As a result, using sales as a benchmark of effectiveness is likely to underestimate the impact of brand-building communication and overestimate the role of incentive-focused communication.

- **Media type**. Measuring the effectiveness of a communication campaign is also a function of the particular media type. Thus, in cases where the media are not directly linked to a particular performance measure, such as public relations and event sponsorship, performance tends to be gauged through indirect measures of awareness and preference. In contrast, in cases where the media are directly linked to performance measures (such as in direct marketing, personal selling, and click-through advertising), then actual behavior can be used to evaluate the effectiveness of the communication campaign.

SUMMARY

Managing communication involves *strategic* decisions—a function of the offering's target market defined by its customers, company, collaborators, competition, and context—and *tactical* decisions, which are a function of the other marketing mix variables: product, service, brand, price, incentives, and distribution.

Managing communication involves six key steps: setting the goal, developing the message, selecting the media, developing the creative solution, implementing the communication campaign, and evaluating the campaign results.

The *goal* identifies a set of criteria to be achieved by the communication campaign within a given time frame. The three most common communication goals are to create awareness, strengthen preferences, and incite action.

The *message* identifies the information communicated to target customers. The message can focus on one or several of the six value-design marketing mix variables: product, service, brand, price, incentives, and distribution.

The *media* are the means used by the company to convey its message. The media decision involves three aspects: setting the media budget, deciding on the media type (advertising, public relations and social media, personal selling, product samples, event sponsorship, and product placement), and outlining the media scheduling (pattern, reach, and frequency).

The *creative solution* involves the execution of the company's message in a given media. Among the key aspects of the creative solution are appeal type (information-based or emotion-based) and execution style (text, format, and layout).

The *implementation* aspect of marketing communication identifies the timeline and the logistics of executing the message, media, and creative decisions.

The *control* aspect of marketing communication involves evaluating the success of the communication campaign with respect to achieving its goals. The most commonly used criteria involve measuring the following six factors: exposure, comprehension, recall, persuasion, intent, and behavior. The decision about which metric to use is a function of three key considerations: the goal of the campaign, the message being communicated, and the selected media format.

RELEVANT CONCEPTS

Above-the-Line Communications: Company communications are often divided into two categories: Above-the-Line (ATL) communications, which encompass mass media advertising such as television commercials, radio, and print advertisements; and Below-the-Line (BTL) communications, which include public relations, event sponsorship, personal selling, and direct mail. Historically, the term ATL was used in reference to communications for which an advertising agency charged a commission to place in mass media, whereas the term BTL was used in reference to communications that involved a standard charge rather than a commission. Currently, the terms ATL and BTL are loosely used to indicate an emphasis on mass media (ATL) versus one-on-one communications (BTL). The current use of BTL often includes customer and trade incentives as well.

Advertising Allowance: A form of trade promotion in which retailers are given a discount in exchange for advertising manufacturers' products.

Advertising Awareness: The number of potential customers who are aware of the offering. Awareness is a function of the total volume of advertising delivered to the target audience and the number of exposures necessary to create awareness. In cases where a single exposure is sufficient to create awareness, the awareness level equals the advertising reach.

$$\text{Awareness} = \frac{\text{Advertising reach} \cdot \text{Frequency of exposure}}{\text{Number of exposures necessary to create awareness}}$$

Advertising Frequency: The number of times the target audience is exposed to an advertisement in a given period. Also used in reference to the number of times an advertisement is repeated through a specific medium during a specific period.

Advertising Reach: The size of the audience that has been exposed to a particular advertisement at least once in a given period (multiple viewings by the same audience do not increase reach). Reach can be stated either as an absolute number or as a fraction of a population. For example, if 40,000 of 100,000 different households are exposed to a given commercial at least once, the reach is 40%.

Affiliate Marketing: A communication strategy that involves revenue sharing between advertisers and online content providers. An affiliate is rewarded based on specific performance measures, such as sales, click-throughs, and online traffic.

Awareness Rate: The number of potential customers aware of the offering relative to the total number of potential customers. Depending on the manner in which it is measured, two types of awareness are commonly distinguished: aided awareness, in which respondents are provided with the name of the target offering (e.g., "Have you seen any advertisements for Coca-Cola in the past month?"), and unaided awareness, in which respondents are not provided with any offering-specific information (e.g., "Which soft drinks have you seen advertised during the past month?").

Below-the-Line (BTL) Communications: See *above-the-line communications.*

Carryover Effect in Advertising: Impact of an advertising campaign that extends beyond the time frame of the campaign. To illustrate, an advertising effort made in a given period might generate sales in subsequent periods.

Comparative Advertising: Advertising strategy whereby a given offering is directly compared with another offering.

Competitive Parity Budgeting: Budget allocation strategy based on (1) matching competitors' absolute level of spending or (2) the proportion per point of market share.

Cooperative Advertising: Advertising strategy in which a manufacturer and a retailer jointly advertise their offering to consumers. In this case, the manufacturer pays a portion of a retailer's advertising costs in return for featuring its products, services, and brands.

Cost Per Point (CPP): Measure used to represent the cost of a communication campaign. CPP is the media cost of reaching one percent (one rating point) of a particular demographic. See also *gross rating point.*

$$\text{CPP} = \frac{\text{Advertising cost}}{\text{GRP}}$$

Cost Per Thousand (CPM): Measure used to represent the cost of a communication campaign. CPM is the cost of reaching 1,000 individuals or households with an advertising message in a given medium (M is the Roman numeral for 1,000). For example, a television commercial that costs $200,000 to air and reaches 10M viewers has a CPM of $20. The popularity of CPM derives in part from its being a good comparative measure of advertising efficiency across different media (e.g., television, print, and Internet).

$$\text{CPM} = \frac{\text{Advertising cost}}{\text{Total impressions}} \cdot 1{,}000$$

Gross Rating Point (GRP): A measure of the total volume of advertising delivery to the target audience. It is equal to the percent of the population reached times the frequency of exposure. To illustrate, if a given advertisement reaches 60% of the households with an average frequency of three times, then the GRP of the media is equal to 180. GRP can also be calculated by dividing gross impressions by the size of the total audience. A single GRP represents 1% of the total audience in a given region.

$$\text{GRP} = \text{Reach} \cdot \text{Frequency}$$

Impression: A single exposure of an advertisement to one person.

Infomercial: A long-format television commercial, typically five minutes or longer.

Institutional Advertising: Advertising strategy designed to build goodwill or an image for an organization (rather than to promote specific offerings).

Integrated Marketing Communication (IMC): An approach to designing marketing communication programs that emphasizes the importance of consistency in all communication activities. In particular, this approach calls for consistency on at least three levels: strategic, tactical, and internal. *Strategic consistency* implies coordination among the different aspects of the communication campaign and the elements of the offering's overall marketing strategy. *Tactical consistency* implies coordination among communication and the other elements of the marketing mix to keep an offering's message consistent with the perceived product and service benefits, brand image, price, incentives, and distribution channel. *Internal consistency* implies that the message, media, creative solution, implementation, and control metrics evaluating the success of the campaign need to be consistent with the communication goal as well as in and of themselves. The concept of internal consistency can also be applied with respect to the different media types (e.g., advertising, public relations, and direct marketing) to ensure that they work in a coordinated fashion rather than independently of one another.

Net Promoter Score: A popular metric designed to measure customers' word of mouth about a company and/or its products.[1] The basic idea is fairly simple: A company's current and potential customers are asked to indicate the likelihood that they will recommend the company and/or its products to another person (e.g., "How likely is it that you would recommend this company to a friend or colleague?"). Responses are typically scored on a 0–10 scale, with 0 meaning extremely unlikely and 10 meaning extremely likely. Based on their responses, customers are divided into one of three categories: promoters (those with ratings of 9 or 10), passives (those with ratings of 7 or 8), and detractors (those with ratings of 6 or lower). The net promoter score is then calculated as the difference between the percentage of a company's promoters and detractors. For example, if 40% of a company's customers are classified as promoters and 25% are classified as detractors, the company's net promoter score is 15%.

Point-of-Purchase Advertising: Promotional materials displayed at the point of purchase (e.g., in a retail store).

Public Service Announcement (PSA): Nonprofit advertising that uses free space or time donated by the media.

Reminder Advertising: Advertising strategy designed to maintain awareness and stimulate repurchase of an already established offering.

Share of Voice: A company's communication expenditures relative to those of the entire product category.

$$\text{Share of voice} = \frac{\text{An offering's communication expenditures}}{\text{Product category's communication expenditures}}$$

Target Rating Point (TRP): A measure of the total volume of advertising delivery to the target audience. TRP is similar to GRP, but its calculation involves using only the target audience (rather than the total audience watching the program) as the base. Thus, a single TRP represents 1% of the targeted viewers in any particular region.

Teaser Advertising: Communication strategy designed to create interest in an offering while providing little or no information about it.

Top-of-Mind Awareness: The first brand identified by respondents when asked to list brands in a given product category.

Wearout: A decrease in the effectiveness of a communication campaign from decreased consumer interest in the message, often resulting from repetition.

ADDITIONAL READINGS

Belch, George E. and Michael A. Belch (2011), *Advertising and Promotion: An Integrated Marketing Communications Perspective* (9th ed.). Boston, MA: McGraw-Hill Irwin.

Ogilvy, David (1983), *Ogilvy on Advertising* (1st American ed.). New York, NY: Crown.

Sutherland, Max (2009), *Advertising and the Mind of the Consumer: What Works, What Doesn't, and Why* (3rd ed.). St. Leonards, NSW, Australia: Allen & Unwin.

NOTE

1 Reichheld, Fred (2003), "The One Number You Need to Grow," *Harvard Business Review*, (December), 1–11.

CHAPTER THIRTEEN

MANAGING DISTRIBUTION

If you make a product good enough, even though you live in the depths of the forest, the public will make a path to your door . . . But if you want the public in sufficient numbers, you better construct a highway.

—William Randolph Hearst, American newspaper publisher

Managing distribution involves designing and managing the process of delivering a company's offering to target customers. The key aspects of managing distribution channels are the focus of this chapter.

Overview

Distribution typically involves collaboration between a company and a set of distribution partners—retailers, wholesalers, and distributors—for the purpose of delivering a company's products to target customers. Retail distribution channels are represented by a variety of business models, such as traditional retailers (Target), franchises (McDonald's), personal selling (Amway), price clubs (Costco), and online retailers (Amazon.com).

One of the most important retail trends is the consolidation of fragmented retail outlets into powerful retail chains and superstores. In addition to creating large-scale mass merchandisers, such as Walmart, this consolidation has produced a number of specialized retailers concentrating on a single category such as home repairs (Home Depot), electronics (Best Buy), and books (Barnes & Noble). In addition, online retailing has gained ground on the traditional brick-and-mortar stores, with online shopping becoming the norm rather than the exception in many product categories. This consolidation and specialization of retailers, and the increasing importance of online retail formats call for the development of effective distribution strategies that accommodate the complex and dynamic nature of the retail environment.

Distribution as a Value-Creation Process

Distribution aims to deliver the offering to target customers in a way that creates value for the company and its collaborators. When designing a distribution strategy a manager must consider the Five Cs—customers, company, collaborators, competitors, and context—and design a distribution channel that optimizes the offering's value for the relevant market entities. The Five Cs are the key decision factors that must be considered in order to design products and services that can create value for target customers, the company, and its collaborators (Figure 1).

Figure 1. Distribution as a Value-Creation Process

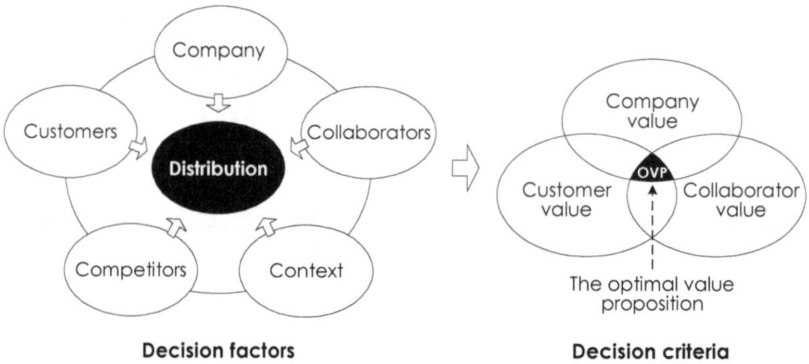

The Five Cs—customers, company, collaborators, competitors, and context—are the key decision factors that must be considered in designing the offering's distribution. Thus, the design of a distribution channel depends on the choice of target customers, such that offerings targeting mass markets are more likely to involve multiple distributors across different geographic markets, whereas niche offerings are likely to involve a more narrow distribution. The choice of a distribution channel is also a function of the company's goals and resources, such that a company seeking market dominance is likely to utilize diverse channels in order to achieve extensive coverage. An offering's distribution strategy also reflects the balance of power between the company and its collaborators, whereby a company might select multiple distributors or open its own retail stores in order to minimize the power of any particular channel. The choice of a distribution channel is also a function of competitors' offerings, such that companies seeking to avoid direct confrontation (e.g., to circumvent a price war) might seek alternative channels. Finally, distribution is a function of the economic, business, technological, sociocultural, regulatory, and physical context; for example, the preference for store size varies by culture and traditions, whereby customers in many countries favor smaller, individually operated retail outlets to consolidated superstore chains.

In addition to being influenced by the Five Cs, distribution also depends on the other marketing mix factors: product, service, brand, price incentives, and communication. Thus, an offering's distribution is a function of its product and service characteristics; for example, novel, complex, and/or undifferentiated products tend to benefit from channels offering higher levels of sales support. Distribution must also be aligned with the offering's brand, such that lifestyle brands (e.g., Ralph Lauren, Lacoste, and Cartier) benefit from using a direct distribution model that ensures a consistent brand image. Distribution is also a function of price, such that low-priced offerings are typically associated with channels offering lower levels of service, whereas high-price offerings typically involve higher levels of service. The choice of distribution channel is also a function of the offering's use of incentives: Incentive-rich offerings typically call for channels that offer frequent sales (e.g., department stores), whereas offerings that do not rely on incentives are a better fit with retailers using everyday low pricing (e.g., Walmart, Target, and Home Depot). The selection and design of a distribution channel are often a function of the channel's ability to effectively communicate the offering's benefits and "push" the offering to target customers.

Distribution Channel Design

The process of designing and managing distribution channels involves several key decisions: channel structure, channel coordination, channel type, channel coverage, and channel exclusivity. The main aspects of these decisions are outlined in the following sections.

Channel Structure

Channel structure defines the members of the distribution channel and the flow of goods and services from the manufacturer to customers. Based on their structure, channels can be direct, indirect, and hybrid (Figure 2).

Figure 2. Distribution Channel Structure

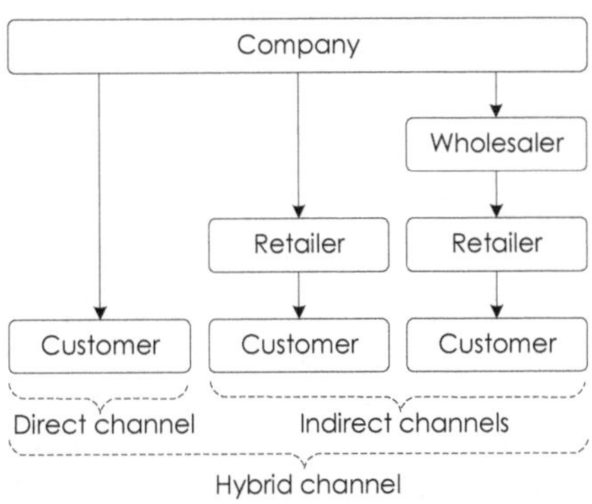

- **Direct channels** involve a distribution model in which the manufacturer and the end customer interact directly with each other without intermediaries. The direct distribution model affords multiple *advantages*: (1) a more effective distribution system resulting from better coordination of the different aspects of the value-delivery process; (2) greater cost efficiency resulting from eliminating intermediaries; (3) greater control over the environment in which the offering is delivered to customers (level of service, product display, and availability of complementary offerings); and (4) closer contact with end users, allowing the manufacturer to obtain firsthand information about their needs and their reactions to its offerings.

Despite its numerous advantages, the direct-distribution model also has a number of *disadvantages*: (1) establishing a direct-distribution channel, especially a brick-and-mortar one, takes time; (2) in most cases, it is difficult to achieve the same breadth of distribution outlets with direct distribution as with multiple intermediaries; (3) launching and managing a distribution channel requires different assets and competencies that many manufacturers do not have readily available; and (4) in most cases, direct-distribution channels require a large upfront fixed-cost investment.

- **Indirect channels** involve a distribution model in which the manufacturer and the end customer interact with each other through intermediaries, such as wholesalers and retailers. The indirect distribution model has a number of *advantages*: (1) rapid distribution that can be implemented instantly; (2) broad coverage that enables the company to reach all or the majority of its target customers; (3) greater effectiveness of the value-delivery process because manufacturers can benefit from the assets and core competencies of intermediaries; (4) potential economies of scale because intermediaries perform similar activities for a variety of manufacturers; and (5) no large upfront investment necessary because a manufacturer using intermediaries is "renting" shelf space for its products.

  Despite its advantages, the use of intermediaries in the indirect distribution model is associated with a number of *disadvantages*: (1) a more complex channel structure that could have a negative impact on the efficiency of the distribution system; (2) reliance on intermediaries could increase the overall distribution costs; (3) loss of control over the selling environment; (4) greatly diminished ability to communicate with and collect information directly from customers; and (5) potential for vertical channel conflicts resulting from different strategic goals and profit-optimization strategies for the manufacturer and its intermediaries.

- **Hybrid channels** involve a distribution model in which the manufacturer and the end customer interact with each other through multiple channels, both directly and through intermediaries. Hybrid channels have numerous *advantages* that stem from combining the benefits of direct and indirect distribution. At the same time, hybrid channels are also subject to many of the *disadvantages* of both direct and indirect channels. An additional problem with using hybrid channels is the potential for channel conflict in cases where both the company and its intermediaries target the same customers. Despite their disadvantages, hybrid channels are gaining popularity in categories where manufacturers can relatively easily establish direct online distribution.

Channel Coordination

Coordination benefits individual channel members by improving the effectiveness and cost efficiency of the channel as a whole. The conventional forms of coordination are: ownership-based, contractual, and implicit.

- **Common ownership** is a type of coordination in which different channel members are parts of the same company. Channel coordination based on common ownership of channel members offers numerous potential *advantages*: (1) better optimization of channel functions, resulting in greater effectiveness and cost efficiency (through joint profit optimization and system integration), (2) greater degree of information sharing, and (3) better control and performance monitoring.

  Despite its multiple advantages, single-ownership distribution channels have a number of potential *disadvantages*: (1) high initial investment; (2) potential internal inefficiencies because of lack of competition; (3) lower cost efficiency resulting from a smaller scale; and (4) the need to develop distribution channel expertise when moving from one business function to another (e.g., from manufacturing to distribution). In addition, in the case of hybrid distribution, in which some but not all channels are company owned, ownership often results in channel conflicts with independent distributors.

- **Contractual relationship** is a type of coordination that involves binding contractual agreements among channel members, including long-term contractual agreements, joint ventures, and franchise agreements. Channel coordination based on contractual relationships has several key *advantages*: (1) lower initial investment, (2) fast implementation, and (3) lower cost efficiency resulting from partners' scale and/or specialization.

  Despite its advantages, contractual channel coordination has a number of *disadvantages*: (1) potential inefficiencies stemming from less coordination, (2) strategic risk of creating a potential competitor (through forward or backward integration) by sharing know-how and strategic information (pricing policies, profit margins, and cost structure), and (3) decreased ability to monitor performance.

- **Implicit channel coordination** is achieved without explicit contractual agreements. Implicit coordination is similar to contractual coordination, with the advantage of being much more flexible. This flexibility, however, comes at the cost of the inability to predict the behavior of various channel members. Another shortcoming of implicit coordination is a lower level of commitment, resulting in an unwillingness to invest resources to customize the channel for a particular manufacturer. Implicit coordination is also likely to lead to lower cost efficiency resulting from a lower degree of channel coordination.

Channel Type

Channels vary in terms of the breadth and depth of their assortments. Based on the *breadth* of their assortments, channels can be classified into one of two types: specialized or broad. Specialized retailers, such as Foot Locker, Office Depot, CarMax, and Toys"R"Us, tend to carry a relatively narrow assortment focusing on relatively few product categories. In contrast, mass retailers, such as Walmart, Costco, and Carrefour, tend to carry much broader assortments.

Based on the *depth* of the assortment, channels can be classified into limited and extensive. Limited-assortment retailers, such as 7-Eleven and Circle K, carry a relatively small number of items within each category, whereas extensive-assortment retailers, such as Carrefour and Walmart, carry a fairly large number of items in each category. Specialized retailers carrying extensive assortments of items, such as Home Depot, Best Buy, Office Depot, and SportMart, are often referred to as category killers.

Channel Coverage

Channel strategies vary in their coverage as defined by the number of outlets at which offerings are made available to target customers. Extensive coverage implies that an offering is readily accessible to a fairly large proportion of customers in a given market; in contrast, limited coverage implies that the offering is likely to be available only in select markets and/or through specialized retailers. The downside of extensive coverage is that it typically comes at a high cost and often leads to channel conflicts. The downside of limited availability, on the other hand, is that it runs the risk of the offering being unavailable to some target customers.

Channel Exclusivity

Channel exclusivity refers to the degree to which an offering is made available through different distribution channels. Channel exclusivity is commonly used to reduce the potential for horizontal channel conflicts, which occur when distributors with different cost structures and profit margins sell identical offerings to the same customers. To mitigate the negative impact of a direct price comparison of the same offering across retailers, manufacturers often release channel-specific product variants that vary in functionality and, therefore, cannot be directly compared.

Value-Delivery Functions of Distribution Channels

The primary function of distribution channels is to deliver the company's offering to its target customers. This involves delivering different aspects of the offering: product, service, brand, price, and incentives.

- **Delivering products** involves transfer of the physical possession and ownership rights (title) of the product from the manufacturer to intermediaries (wholesales, distributors, and retailers) and, ultimately, to end users. It can involve value-added functions.

- **Delivering services** involves customer-focused activities such as customization, repair, technical assistance, and warranty support, as well as collaborator-focused activities, such as storage, inventory management, sorting, and repackaging.
- **Delivering brands** provides customers with an opportunity to experience the brand. Disney, Sony, and Harley-Davidson retail stores function as channels delivering these brands to their customers.
- **Delivering prices** involves collecting and processing payments from customers. Unlike other marketing mix variables where the flow of items is from the company to its customers, in the case of pricing the flow is reversed: Payments are collected from customers and delivered to the company.
- **Delivering incentives** involves distributing incentives such as coupons, rebates, and premiums to customers, as well as processing some of these incentives (e.g., redeeming coupons).

Note that in addition to delivering value, distribution channels often participate in designing and communicating the offerings they deliver. The value-design function of distribution channels can involve product assembly, financing and warranty services, enhancing the offering's brand, negotiating the sale price, and managing point-of-purchase incentives. In the same vein, the value-communication function of distribution channels can involve explaining product and service benefits of the offering, communicating the meaning of its brand, and informing customers about the offering's price and incentives. In addition to delivering the offering to target customers, the functions of distribution channels also involve managing reverse logistics, including processing returns and refunds. Channels also manage the reverse flow of information by soliciting and collecting customer feedback, suggestions, and complaints.

SUMMARY

Distribution decisions need to take into account two types of factors: strategic factors that involve customers, company, collaborators, competition, and context, and tactical factors that involve the other marketing mix variables: product, service, brand, price, incentives, and communication.

Designing and managing distribution channels involve several key decisions: channel structure (direct, indirect, and hybrid), channel coordination (ownership-based, contractual, and implicit), channel type (specialized vs. broad and limited vs. extensive), channel coverage (limited vs. extensive), and channel exclusivity.

Channels facilitate the value exchange between the company and its customers by delivering the different aspects of the company's offering to its target customers: they deliver the company's products and services, enhance the offering's brand, collect payments, and distribute and process incentives. Channels also facilitate reverse logistics by processing product returns and payment credits.

RELEVANT CONCEPTS

All-Commodity Volume (ACV): A measure of an offering's availability, typically calculated as the total annual volume of the company's offering in a given geographic area relative to the total sales volume of the retailers in that geographic area across all product categories (hence, the term "all-commodity volume"). Also refers to the gross sales in a specific geographic area (total sales of all stores).

$$ACV = \frac{\text{Total sales of stores carrying the company's offering}}{\text{Total sales of all stores}}$$

Category Killers: Specialty retailers that focus on one product category in which they offer a large assortment of options at competitive prices. Category killers include retailers such as Best Buy (electronics), Office Depot (office supplies), Home Depot (home improvement), and PetSmart (pet supplies).

Contractual Vertical Marketing System: Channel structure in which the relationships among channel members are set on a contractual basis (rather than common ownership).

Corporate Vertical Marketing System: Channel structure in which channel members have common ownership rather than a contractual relationship.

Detailers: Indirect sales force promoting pharmaceuticals to doctors and pharmacists so that they, in turn, recommend the brand to the consumer.

Direct Channel: Distribution strategy in which the manufacturer and the end customer interact directly with each other without intermediaries.

Forward Buying: Increasing the channel inventory, usually to take advantage of a manufacturer's promotion or in anticipation of price increases.

Gray Market: A market in which products are sold through unauthorized channels.

Horizontal Channel Conflict: Tension among entities in multiple distribution channels (e.g., a manufacturer and two retailers). See Chapter 7 for more details.

Hybrid Channel: Distribution strategy in which the manufacturer and the end customer interact with each other through multiple channels (directly and through intermediaries).

Indirect Channel: Distribution strategy in which the manufacturer and the end customer interact with each other through intermediaries.

Inventory Turnover: The number of times that inventory is replenished, typically calculated as the ratio of annual revenues generated by a given offering to average inventory.

Merchandisers: Indirect sales force that offers support to retailers for in-store activities, such as shelf location, pricing, and compliance with special programs.

Parallel Importing: The practice of importing products from a country in which the price is lower to a country in which the same product is priced higher. A hypothetical example of this practice is importing drugs from Canada to the United States. In most cases, parallel importing is illegal in the United States.

Reverse Logistics: The process of reclaiming recyclable and reusable materials and returns for repair, remanufacturing, or disposal.

Same-Store Sales: A metric used in the retail industry for measuring sales of stores that have been open for a year or more and have historical data by comparing the current year's sales to last year's sales. Same-store sales are a popular metric because it takes store closings and chain expansions out of the mix, indicating the portion of new sales that resulted from sales growth and the portion that resulted from the opening or closing of stores.

Share of Shelf Space: Shelf space allocated to a given offering relative to the total shelf space in a given geographic area.

Shrinkage: A term used by retailers to describe theft of goods by customers and employees.

Vertical Channel Conflict: Tension between entities in a single distribution channel (e.g., a manufacturer and a retailer). See Chapter 7 for more details.

Vertical Marketing Systems: Centrally coordinated distribution channel.

ADDITIONAL READINGS

Palmatier, Robert, Louis W. Stern, Adel I. El-Ansary, and Erin Anderson (2014), *Marketing Channel Strategy* (8th ed.). Upper Saddle River, NJ: Prentice Hall.

Ulin, Jeff (2009), *The Business of Media Distribution: Monetizing Film, TV and Video Content in an Online World.* New York, NY: Focal Press.

Zoltners, Andris A., Prabhakant Sinha, and Sally Lorimer (2004), *Sales Force Design for Strategic Advantage.* Basingstoke, NH: Palgrave Macmillan.

Part Four

Managing Growth

Introduction

You will either step forward into growth or you will step back into safety.

—Abraham Maslow, American psychologist

Managing growth is the most common route to profitability. Compared to cost-cutting—the alternative approach to profitability—ensuring top-line growth is the preferred long-term strategy by most organizations. In addition to enhancing profits, focusing on growth adds vitality to organizations by providing challenges and fostering creativity.

Four key issues in managing growth merit attention: gaining and defending market position, managing sales growth, developing new products, and managing product lines. These four issues are briefly outlined below and discussed in detail in the following chapters.

- **Gaining and defending market position** deals with issues concerning creating and sustaining growth in a competitive environment. The common strategies for managing market position are discussed in Chapter 14.
- **Managing sales growth** involves increasing sales volume and is typically achieved by acquiring new customers and selling more to existing customers. These two strategies for increasing sales volume—product adoptions by new customers and product usage by existing customers—are discussed in Chapter 15.
- **New product development** is essential to ensure sustainable growth. The key issues in developing new offerings—forecasting new product demand, understanding new product adoption, developing new products, and managing the product lifecycle—are the focus of Chapter 16.
- **Product-line management** aims to align the individual offerings in the company's product line. The key aspects of product line management—managing vertical and horizontal extensions, managing product-line cannibalization, and using product lines to gain and defend market position—are discussed in Chapter 17.

The selection of a growth strategy is ultimately determined by the company's goals, strategic resources, target customers, collaborators, competitors, and the overall market context. An integrative approach to analyzing these factors, such as the one described in the following chapters, is essential for the development of a successful growth strategy.

CHAPTER FOURTEEN

GAINING AND DEFENDING MARKET POSITION

In football, everything is complicated by the presence of the other team.

—Jean-Paul Sartre, French philosopher

The constantly evolving nature of the competitive landscape calls for developing dynamic strategies to manage a company's market position. Managing market position presents companies with two perennial questions: how to gain market position and how to defend their current market position. These two questions and strategies to address them are the focus of this chapter.

Gaining Market Position

From a competitive standpoint, a company can gain share by using three core strategies: (1) stealing share from competitors already serving this market, (2) growing the market by attracting new customers to the category, and (3) creating new markets.

Steal-Share Strategy

The steal-share strategy refers to a company's activities aimed at attracting customers from its competitors rather than trying to attract customers who are new to the product category. Apple targeting Windows users (rather than aiming at customers who have never had a computer) is an example of a steal-share strategy. A company's steal-share strategy can vary in breadth: It can narrowly target customers of a specific competitor (e.g., Pepsi targeting Coke customers), or it can broadly focus on the competitor's market as a whole (e.g., RC Cola trying to steal share from all competitors, including Coke and Pepsi). The steal-share strategy is illustrated in Figure 1 where the dark-shaded segment represents the company's current market share and the light-shaded segment represents the share it aims to gain from the competition. Because of its focus on attracting only competitors' customers, the steal-share focus is also referred to as *selective demand* strategy.

Figure 1. Steal-Share Strategy

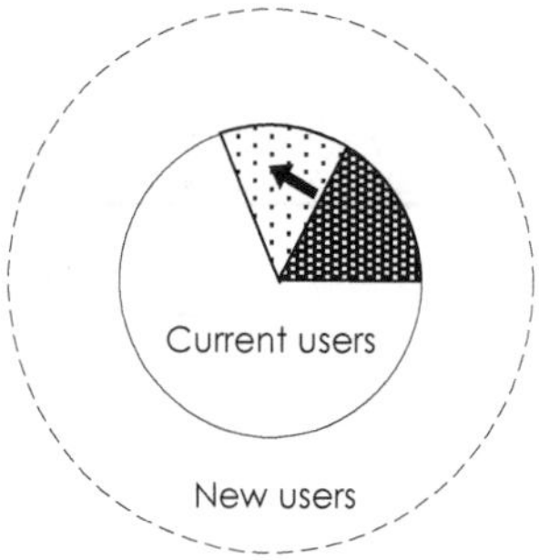

To succeed in attracting competitors' customers, a company needs to present these customers with a compelling value proposition. In this context, there are two basic steal-share strategies: a differentiation strategy and a similarity strategy.

- **Differentiation strategy** aims to steal share from the competition by demonstrating the superiority of the company's offering. The differentiation might involve superior benefits, such as better performance and/or lower costs.
- **Similarity strategy**, also referred to as a "me-too" strategy, aims to establish multiple points of parity and steal share from a competitor, typically the market leader, by showing that a company's and a competitor's offerings are, in fact, identical. One particular form of the "me-too" strategy is cloning, which involves emulating the incumbent's offering, usually with slight variations to avoid patent and trademark infringement liability.

Market-Growth Strategy

Unlike the steal-share strategy, which targets customers who are using competitors' offerings, the market-growth strategy aims to attract customers who are new to the category (Figure 2). For example, an advertising campaign promoting the consumption of milk (the *Got Milk?* campaign) builds the entire category, whereby switching occurs between substitute products (milk vs. non-milk) rather than among different milk producers. Because of its focus on increasing the overall category demand, the market-growth strategy is sometimes referred to as *primary demand* stimulation.

Figure 2. Market-Growth Strategy

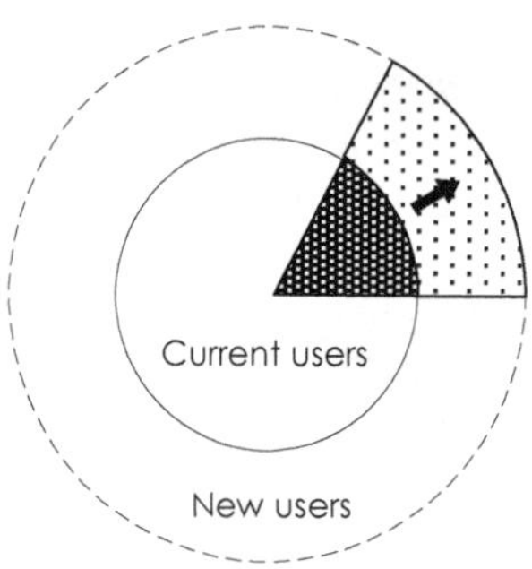

Because the market-growth strategy is aimed at growing the entire category, it typically benefits all companies competing in that category. Therefore, this strategy is usually adopted in the early stages of an offering's life cycle when the overall market growth is high and competition is not yet a primary issue. Moreover, because offerings tend to gain share proportionately to their current market position, in the case of relatively mature products the market-growth strategy is likely to benefit the market leader.

A notable exception to the scenario illustrated in Figure 2 involves a case in which a company's offering has a superior value proposition relative to the competition (because of a technological breakthrough, the addition of unique product benefits, or a price advantage), making it likely to gain a disproportionately large share (relatively to its current share) of new customers. In this case, a small-share offering can be more successful in growing the market than the leader (Figure 3).

Figure 3. Market-Growth Strategy for an Offering with a Superior Value Proposition

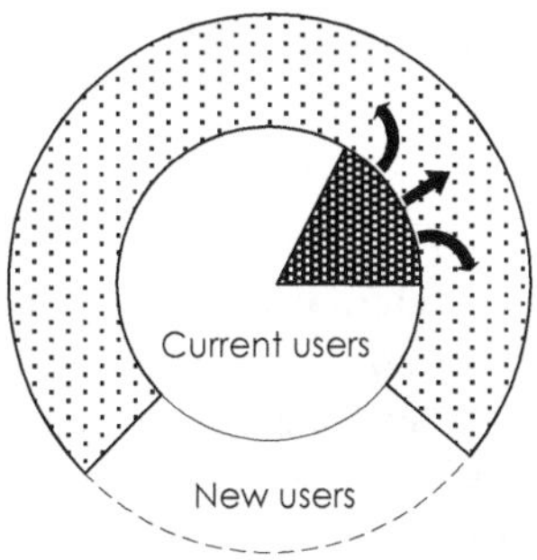

Market-Innovation Strategy

The market-innovation strategy is similar to the market-growth strategy in that a company gains market position by attracting customers who are not using any products and services in a given category (Figure 4). The key difference is that instead of converting new customers to the existing category in which the company faces its current rivals, it defines an entirely new category in which direct competitors are absent. Because of its focus on uncontested markets, the market-innovation strategy, also referred to as the Blue Ocean Strategy, often leads to high profit margins and rapid growth—a scenario that almost inevitably attracts new market entrants.

Figure 4. Market-Innovation Strategy

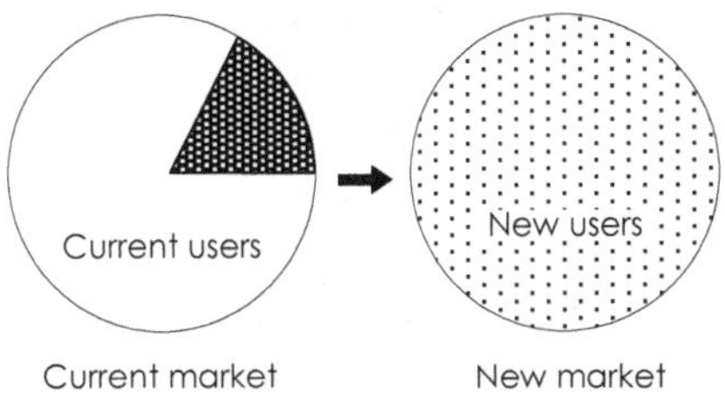

Because it targets customers who are new to the particular product category, the market-innovation strategy typically involves pioneering new markets. The key aspects of creating new markets are discussed in the following sections.

Pioneering New Markets

The term *pioneer* or *first mover* refers to the first company to establish its presence in a particular domain. Based on the domain in which the company is the first mover, there are four common types of pioneers.

- **Technology pioneer:** the company that first introduces a new technology to a category
- **Product pioneer:** the company that is first to commercially introduce an entirely new ("new-to-the-world") product
- **Business model pioneer**: the company that is first to introduce a new business model
- **Market pioneer:** the company that first introduces a given offering to a particular target market

For the purposes of marketing analysis, the term *pioneer* is used in reference to the first company to introduce its offering to a given market defined by a particular customer need. Thus, a pioneer in a market is the company that first reached a given customer segment with its offering. Even though, from a chronological standpoint, another company might have pioneered a product by introducing it to a different customer segment, the company that first introduced it to target customers is considered the pioneer for these customers. For example, Apple's iPod, which was introduced in the United States in 2001, is typically thought of as the pioneer of portable hard drive MP3 players, even though MPMan, which used similar technology, was introduced in Asia in 1998 by the Korean company Saehan.

The Benefits of Pioneering

Pioneering a market offers the incumbent a number of advantages that are not available to later entrants. These advantages include shaping consumer preferences, creating switching costs, gaining access to scarce resources, creating barriers to competitive entry, and taking advantage of the learning curve.

- **Preference formation**. A pioneering company has the unique opportunity to shape customer preferences, creating a close association between its brand and the underlying customer need. For example, Jeep, Google, Amazon.com, eBay, Twitter, and Xerox not only helped shape customer preferences but also became synonymous with the entire category.
- **Switching costs**. As a pioneer, a company has the opportunity to build loyalty by creating switching costs for its customers. These switching costs could be functional (loss of the unique features of the pioneer's offering), monetary (the cost of replacing proprietary equipment or a penalty for

breaking a contract), or psychological (the cost of learning the functionality of a competitor's offering).

- **Resource advantage**. The pioneer can benefit from preempting scarce resources such as raw materials, human resources, geographical locations, and collaborator networks. For example, the pioneer might be able to lock out the competition by securing exclusive access to strategically important mineral resources. Similarly, the pioneer might preempt competitors' access to a particular human resource in short supply, such as engineers, designers, and managers. The pioneer may also preempt strategically important geographic locations in both real space (Starbucks, McDonald's, and Walmart) and cyberspace (flowers.com, drugstore.com, and cars.com). The pioneer can also preempt the competition by forging collaborator alliances with strategically important partners such as distributors or advertisers. For example, sporting goods manufacturers offer exclusive long-term contracts to promising athletes early in their careers, thus precluding competitors from collaborating with these athletes when their careers take off.
- **Barriers to entry**. The pioneer can create technological barriers to prevent competitors from entering the market. For example, the pioneer might secure the exclusive rights to use a particular invention or design that is essential for developing offerings that will successfully address a specific customer need. Being the pioneer also enables a company to establish a proprietary technological standard (e.g., operating system, communication protocol, and video compression) that ensures the sustainability of its technological advantage in the marketplace.
- **Learning curve**. The pioneer often benefits from learning curve advantages, allowing it to heighten production effectiveness and efficiency as its cumulative output increases over time. Simply put, being in business longer than its competitors often gives the pioneer a competitive edge in technological know-how, level of workforce experience, and productivity.

The Drawbacks of Being a Pioneer

Being a pioneer does not always benefit the company. Pioneers face a distinct set of disadvantages that might impede rather than facilitate their market success. The three most common disadvantages include free riding, incumbent inertia, and market uncertainty.

- **Free riding**. A later entrant might be able to free ride on the pioneer's resources, including its investments in technology, product design, customer education, regulatory approval, infrastructure development, and human resource development. To illustrate, after spending millions of dollars to develop the technology and educate the American audience about the advantages of a personal digital recorder, the pioneer TiVo found itself in competition with cable and satellite operators selling similar services to its already educated target customers. Alternatively, a follower could reverse-engineer the pioneer's product and improve on it, while investing only a fraction of the resources required to develop the original product. Federal Express built on DHL's idea to start overnight deliveries in the United States. IBM launched its personal computer by building on the earlier product introductions from Apple and Atari. Best Buy launched a rapid expansion of superstores based on the success of the business model introduced by Circuit City.

- **Incumbent inertia**. Being a market leader often leads to complacency, thus leaving technological and market opportunities open to competitors. To illustrate, IBM's reliance on mainframes, even when mainframes were being replaced by networked computers, enabled competitors such as Dell and Hewlett-Packard to gain a foothold in IBM's markets and steal some of its most valuable clients. Incumbent inertia might also be driven by a reluctance to cannibalize existing product lines by adopting a new technology or a new business model. For example, brick-and-mortar booksellers such as Barnes & Noble and Borders failed to recognize the importance of e-commerce, allowing Amazon.com to establish a dominant presence in online book retailing. Incumbent inertia might also result from a "sunk-cost mentality," whereby managers feel compelled to utilize their large investments in extant technology or markets even when technological advancements and market forces make these investments unfeasible. For example, one of the reasons Ford lost its leading market position to General Motors in the 1930s was its reluctance to make the necessary investments to modify existing manufacturing facilities to diversify its product line.
- **Market uncertainty**. Another potential disadvantage in being a pioneer is the uncertainty associated with the offering. Indeed, whereas the pioneer has to deal with the uncertainty surrounding the technology and market demand, a follower can learn from the pioneer's successes and failures and design a superior offering. Because of the uncertainty associated with the introduction of a new offering, companies with strong brands and distribution capabilities often choose to be late-market entrants, which enables them to learn from the pioneer's experience and develop an effective and cost-efficient market-entry strategy. These companies use their brand and channel power to manage the risk associated with new product development and new market entry, allowing them to be successful late entrants into a given market. To illustrate, the first sugar-free soft drink was introduced in the United States by Cott in 1947, and the first sugar-free cola was introduced by Royal Crown in 1962, only to be overtaken by Coca-Cola and PepsiCo, which used their branding and distribution power to dominate the consumer soft drink market.

The numerous drawbacks of being a market pioneer suggest that when entering new markets, a company should strive not only to gain share but also to create a business model that cannot be easily copied by its current and future competitors. Because market success inevitably attracts competition, creating a sustainable competitive advantage is the key to a successful pioneering strategy.

Defending Market Position

Because business success inevitably attracts competition, in addition to strategizing how to expand its offerings, a company needs to develop strategies to defend its market position. In this context, there are three basic ways in which a company can react to a competitor's activities: not taking action, repositioning the existing offerings (reducing costs, moving downscale, increasing benefits, moving upscale by launching new, more exclusive offerings), and adding new (premium or economy) offerings. These strategies are illustrated in Figure 5 and discussed in more detail below.

Figure 5. Defensive Market Strategies[1]

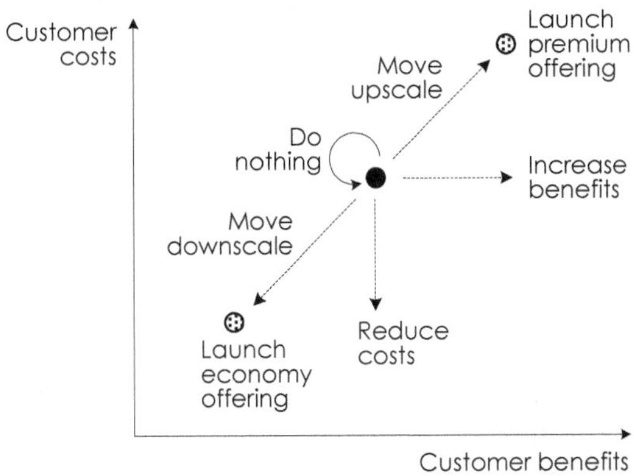

Not Taking Action

The decision to ignore a competitor's action(s) reflects a company's belief that these actions either will have no material impact on the company's market position or that the competitive threat is not sustainable and will dissipate by itself. For example, a company might decide that its upscale offering will not be affected by the entry of a low-price, low-quality competitor and, therefore, not consider this action a direct threat. In the same vein, a company might not react to a competitor's price reduction if it believes that this low-priced position is not sustainable in the longer term.

Repositioning the Existing Offering

A company might choose to reposition its offering in one of two ways: It might change the offering's value proposition to increase its appeal to current customers or, alternatively, it might reposition the offering to appeal to a different customer segment.

- **Repositioning to increase the offering's value for current customers**. Because value is a function of benefits and costs, enhancing the value of an offering might be achieved in two ways: by increasing benefits and by decreasing costs.

- *Increasing an offering's benefits.* To increase the attractiveness of its offering, a company might choose to (1) enhance the functional benefits of the offering (by improving the offering's performance), (2) increase the monetary benefits (by adding monetary rewards), and (3) increase the psychological benefits (by enhancing the offering's image). For each of these strategies to succeed, the increase in benefits must actually be perceived as such by customers; improving the offering's performance on attributes that are unobservable by customers is not likely to enhance its customer value.
- *Decreasing an offering's costs.* As in the case of increasing benefits, decreasing an offering's costs can be achieved by decreasing its functional, monetary, and psychological costs. Because the price of an offering is typically the most important component of customers' costs, price reduction and adding monetary incentives are the most common forms of cost decreases.

- **Repositioning to attract new customers**. In addition to increasing an offering's value for existing customers, a company might decide to reposition its offering to better address the needs of different target customers. Repositioning implies a change in the value proposition of a given offering in one of two ways: vertical or horizontal.
  - *Vertical repositioning* refers to a scenario in which a company modifies the value proposition of an offering by moving it into a different price tier, either upscale or downscale. In the case of upscale repositioning, the company increases the price of an offering while augmenting its benefits. In contrast, downscale repositioning involves a decrease in an offering's price and a corresponding decrease in benefits.
  - *Horizontal repositioning* refers to a scenario in which a company modifies the value proposition of an offering by altering its benefits without necessarily moving it to a different price tier. To illustrate, in an attempt to break away from the traditional association of prunes as a means to regularity for the elderly and make them appealing to younger customers, California prune manufacturers began marketing prunes as "dried plums," highlighting their high level of antioxidants.

Extending the Product Line

In addition to repositioning its existing offerings, a company can respond to competitive actions by adding new offerings to its product line. Product-line extension is similar to repositioning, with the key distinction that instead of modifying the value proposition of an existing offering, the company launches a new offering with a different value proposition. There are two common product-line extension strategies: vertical and horizontal.

- **Vertical extensions** are new offerings differentiated by both benefits and price (e.g., an economy car vs. a luxury car). A company can use both upscale and downscale extensions to defend its market position. One popular strategy to fight low-priced rivals involves launching a *fighting brand*—a downscale offering introduced to shield the core offering from low-priced competitors. A slightly more complex approach to dealing with low-priced competitors is the *sandwich strategy*, which involves both the introduction of a downscale offering and upscale repositioning of the core brand. A third commonly used approach to deal with low-priced rivals is the *good-better-best strategy*, which involves introducing both an upscale and a downscale offering, resulting in a three-tier product line.

- **Horizontal extensions** are new offerings that are differentiated primarily by functionality and not necessarily by price (e.g., a sedan vs. a minivan). As product categories mature, their user base becomes more diverse, calling for specialized offerings customized to the needs of different customer segments. Consequently, the pioneer might preempt the competition by extending its product line with offerings tailored to each strategically important customer segment.

A more detailed discussion on managing product lines is offered in Chapter 17.

Core Competencies as a Source of Competitive Advantage

To gain and defend market position, a firm needs to develop core competencies that will give it a competitive advantage. Core competencies involve expertise in an area essential to the company's business model, allowing the company to create market value. From a marketing standpoint, there are six key areas in which a company can develop a core competency: business innovation, operations management, technology development, product development, service management, and brand building.

- **Business innovation**. Competency in business management refers to proficiency in managing business processes, such as identifying business goals, designing strategies and tactics to achieve these goals, and implementing a company's business plan. Business innovation competency also involves the company's ability to build the collaborator network required for efficient functioning of the business. This competency typically leads to strategic benefits such as *business model leadership*. Examples of companies with demonstrated competency in business innovation include McDonald's, Amazon.com, IKEA, PayPal, Netflix, and Starbucks.

- **Operations management**. Competency in operations management refers to expertise in manufacturing and supply-chain management. Companies with this competency are proficient at optimizing the effectiveness and cost efficiency of their business processes. This can lead to two strategic benefits: *logistics leadership* and *cost leadership*. Logistics leadership involves proficiency in supply-chain management that enables a company to provide unsurpassed levels of integration and effectiveness in manufacturing and/or distribution. For example, Foxconn—arguably the world's largest electronics contract manufacturer and the supplier of BlackBerry, iPad, iPhone, iPod, Kindle, Xbox, PlayStation, and Wii—stands out for its dynamic, high-volume production of complex electronics products. Other examples of companies with demonstrated competency in logistics include UPS, FedEx, and Amazon.com. Cost leadership reflects the company's position as the lowest cost (although not necessarily the lowest price) producer in the market. For example, Walmart's competency in operations management is reflected in its dominant position as the low-cost player in the market. Other examples of companies with demonstrated cost leadership include Costco, Carrefour, H&M, and Zara.

- **Technology development**. Competency in technology development refers to a company's ability to devise new technological solutions. This competency typically leads to the strategic benefit of *technological leadership*. Examples of companies that have demonstrated this competency include Motorola, BASF, Google, and Intel. Competency in developing new technologies does not necessarily imply competency in developing commercially successful products. To illustrate, Xerox and its Palo Alto Research Center (PARC) have invented numerous new technologies including photocopying, laser printing, graphical user interface, client/server architecture, and the Ethernet but have been slow in converting these technologies into commercial products.

- **Product development**. Competency in product development describes a company's ability to develop products that deliver superior customer value. This competency typically leads to the strategic benefit of *product leadership*. Examples of companies with demonstrated competency in this area include Apple, Microsoft, and Merck. Note that the competency in product management is not contingent on the company's competency in technology management; technologically inferior products delivering need-based functionality are often more successful than technologically superior products that fail to meet customer needs.

- **Service management**. Competency in service management reflects a company's ability to develop services that deliver superior customer value in the context of a service encounter. This competency typically leads to the strategic benefit of *service leadership*. Examples of companies with demonstrated competency in this area include Ritz-Carlton, American Express, Amazon.com, Zappos.com, and Nordstrom. The competency in service management does not necessarily stem from a competency in product development. Indeed, unlike products that can be physically separated from the manufacturer and inventoried, services are delivered and consumed at the same time, and hence require a different set of skills and resources.

- **Brand building**. Competency in brand building describes a company's ability to build strong brands that deliver superior customer value. This competency typically leads to the strategic benefit of *brand leadership,* which reflects a company's ability to build and sustain strong brands. Examples of companies with demonstrated competency in this area include Harley-Davidson, Nike, Nestlé, and Unilever.

Note that the above core competencies are not mutually exclusive; achieving excellence in one area does not prevent the company from excelling in another. To stay competitive, a company must develop competencies in multiple areas. For example, the success of Amazon.com stems from building core competencies in all of the above domains—from business model development to brand building.

The concept of core competencies is related to that of strategic assets (discussed in more detail in Chapter 4). Thus, while core competencies reflect the company's expertise in specific functional areas and result from a focused utilization of strategic assets, a company's assets often stem from its competencies. For example, competency in database software development is likely to enhance competency-specific assets such as business infrastructure, collaborator network, human capital, and intellectual property.

SUMMARY

The constantly evolving nature of the competitive landscape calls for developing dynamic strategies to manage a company's market position. There are three basic strategies to gain market position: stealing share from competitors serving this market (steal-share strategy), growing the market by attracting new customers to the category (market-growth strategy), and creating new markets (market-innovation strategy).

Gaining market position often involves pioneering new markets. The key benefits of market pioneering include the opportunity to shape customer preferences, create switching costs, preempt scarce resources, create technological barriers to entry, and reap learning curve benefits. The key drawbacks of being a pioneer include free riding by competitors, incumbent inertia, and uncertainty associated with the offering's technology and with customer demand.

Because business success inevitably attracts competition, a company needs to develop strategies to defend its market position. There are three basic ways in which a company can react to a competitor's actions: by not taking an action, by repositioning its existing offerings (increasing benefits, decreasing costs, and moving upscale or downscale), and by adding a new offering to its product line.

To gain and defend market position, a firm needs to develop core competencies that will give it a competitive advantage over the competition. Core competencies involve expertise in one or more of six key areas essential to the company's business model: business innovation, operations management, technology development, product development, service management, and brand building.

RELEVANT CONCEPTS

Blue Ocean Strategy: Term coined by Chan Kim and Renée Mauborgne suggesting that instead of competing in overcrowded existing markets (red oceans), a company should focus its efforts on uncovering new, uncontested markets (blue oceans). Consistent with the concept of product life cycle, the Blue Ocean Strategy argues that mature markets are red oceans that should be avoided and priority given to the search for the blue oceans—new markets that a company can shape and in which it can be the dominant player. According to this strategy, technological innovation is most often not the key driver in discovering uncontested markets; instead, it is the company's ability to find an innovative way of creating value for target customers that determines its success in discovering blue oceans.

Strategic Group: Competitors that target the same customers and follow similar strategies to serve the needs of these customers. Competitors in the same strategic group often have similar products and services, similar branding strategies, similar pricing and incentive strategies, similar communication campaigns, and similar distribution channels. As a result, competition among companies within the same strategic group tends to be more intense than competition among companies from different strategic groups.

RELEVANT FRAMEWORKS: PRODUCT–MARKET GROWTH FRAMEWORK

The product-market growth framework (also referred to as the Ansoff matrix) offers a practical approach to evaluating market opportunities by linking customer segments to product development opportunities.[2] This framework is often presented as a 2×2 matrix in which one of the factors is the type of offering (current vs. new) and the other factor is the type of customers (current vs. new). The resulting four product–market strategies are commonly referred to as market penetration, market development, product development, and diversification (Figure 6).

Figure 6. Product–Market Growth Matrix

	Current customers	New customers
Current products	Market penetration	Market development
New products	Product development	Diversification

- *Market-penetration* strategies aim to increase sales of an existing offering to a company's current customers. A common market-penetration strategy involves increasing usage rate. To illustrate, airlines stimulate demand from current customers by adopting frequent-flyer programs, cereal manufacturers enclose repurchase coupons in their offerings, and orange-juice producers promote drinking orange juice throughout the day rather than only for breakfast.
- *Market-development* strategies aim to grow sales by promoting an existing offering to new customers. Popular market-development strategies include price promotions (e.g., price reductions, coupons, and rebates), new distribution channels, and communication strategies focused on new customer segment(s).

- *Product-development* strategies endeavor to grow sales by developing new (to the company) offerings for existing customers. The two most common product-development strategies include developing entirely new offerings or extending the current product line by modifying existing offerings.
- *Diversification strategies* aim to grow sales by introducing new offerings to new customers. Because both the offering and the customers are new to the company, this strategy tends to be riskier than the other product-market strategies. The primary rationale for diversification is to take advantage of growth opportunities in areas in which the company has no presence.

The four strategies identified above are not mutually exclusive: A company can pursue multiple sales-growth strategies. However, the company needs to prioritize these strategies and focus on those that will enable it to achieve its strategic goals.

RELEVANT FRAMEWORKS: SWOT

The SWOT framework is a relatively simple, extremely flexible, and intuitive approach for evaluating a company's overall business condition. As implied by its name, the SWOT framework entails analyzing four key factors: the company's *strengths* and *weaknesses*, and the *opportunities* and *threats* presented to the company by the environment in which it operates. These four factors are typically organized in a 2 × 2 matrix based on whether they are internal or external to the company, and whether they are favorable or unfavorable from the company's standpoint. Analysis of the internal factors (strengths and weaknesses) focuses on the company, whereas analysis of the external factors (opportunities and threats) focuses on the market in which the company operates (Figure 7).

Figure 7. The SWOT Framework

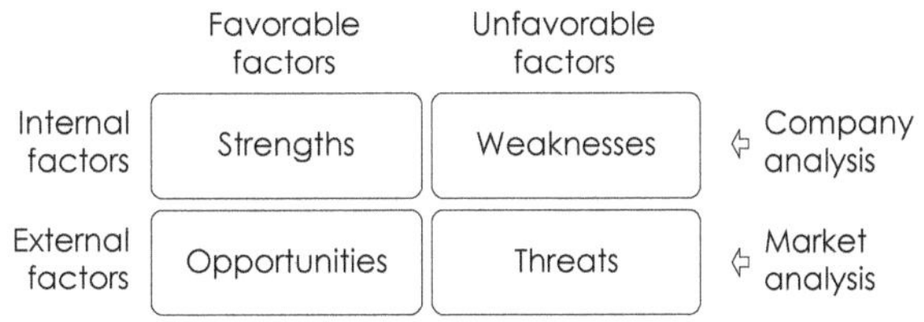

To illustrate, factors such as loyal customers, strong brand name(s), strategically important patents and trademarks, know-how, experienced personnel, and access to scarce resources are typically classified as strengths, whereas factors such as disloyal customers, diluted brand name(s), and lack of technological expertise are classified as weaknesses. Similarly, factors such as emergence of a new, underserved customer segment and a favorable economic environment are typically classified as opportunities, whereas a new competitive entry into the category, increased product commoditization, and increased buyer and supplier power are classified as threats.

ADDITIONAL READINGS

Day, George S., David J. Reibstein, and Robert E. Gunther (2004), *Wharton on Dynamic Competitive Strategy*. New York, NY: John Wiley & Sons.

Kim, W. Chan and Renée Mauborgne (2005), *Blue Ocean Strategy: How to Create Uncontested Market Space and Make the Competition Irrelevant*. Boston, MA: Harvard Business School Press.

Prahalad, C. K. and Gary Hamel (1990), "The Core Competence of the Corporation," *Harvard Business Review*, (May-June), 79-91.

NOTES

[1] Adapted from Hoch, Stephen J. (1996), "How Should National Brands Think about Private Labels?" *Sloan Management Review*, 37 (2), 89-102.

[2] Ansoff, H. Igor (1979), *Strategic Management*. New York, NY: John Wiley & Sons.

CHAPTER FIFTEEN

MANAGING SALES GROWTH

He who moves not forward, goes backward.
—Johann Wolfgang von Goethe
German writer and philosopher

Sales growth is a key aspect of a company's efforts to achieve sustainable profitability. Understanding the main factors influencing sales volume and identifying strategies for effectively managing sales growth are the focus of this chapter.

Overview

There are two basic strategies for increasing sales: increasing the rate of adoption of a company's offering by new customers and increasing the offering's sales to existing customers (Figure 1). Balancing a company's resources across these two strategies is essential for a company's ability to gain and defend its market position and ensure long-term profitability.

Figure 1. Managing Sales Growth

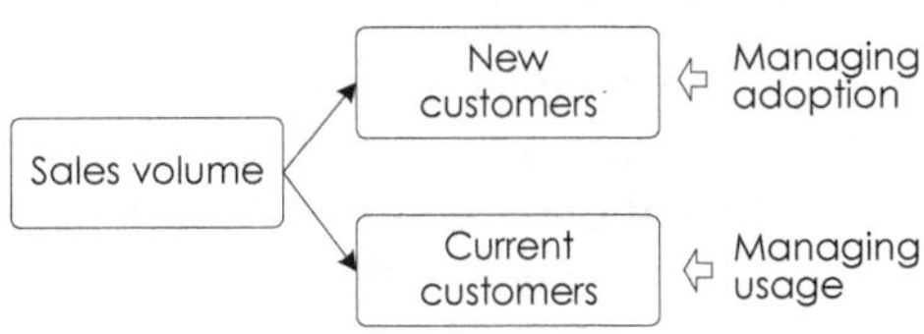

The two strategies for increasing the sales volume of a company's offerings—managing product adoption by new customers and managing product usage by current customers—are discussed in more detail in the following sections.

Managing Product Adoption

To identify the optimal strategy for increasing sales volume, a company first needs to understand the process by which its target customers adopt new products, then identify the impediments to new product adoption in different stages of the process, and, finally, develop an action plan to remove these impediments. These aspects of managing product adoption are discussed in more detail below.

Understanding the Adoption Process

From a customer's perspective, product adoption can be viewed as a multistage process comprising four key steps: awareness, attractiveness, affordability, and availability. Thus, for customers to adopt an offering, they must (1) be aware of its availability, (2) find its benefits attractive, (3) perceive the offering to be affordable, and (4) have access to purchase the offering. Because the number of potential customers who ultimately purchase the offering tends to decrease with each step, the adoption process is also referred to as an *adoption funnel* (Figure 2).

Figure 2: The Adoption Funnel

The adoption funnel illustrates how users progress through the experience of purchasing a new offering. The key steps of the adoption funnel are as follows:

- **Awareness** reflects customers' knowledge of the offering. Awareness can be generated by the company's direct communications to its target customers, by communications initiated by its collaborators (distribution partners, supplier partners, codevelopers, and copromoters), as well as by third-party communications, such as social media and press coverage.

- **Attractiveness** reflects the benefits that buyers expect to receive from the offering. An offering's attractiveness reflects its ability to satisfy a particular customer need better than the competition. Attractiveness implies that buyers are not only aware of the offering but also understand and value its benefits.

- **Affordability** reflects customers' perceptions of the costs associated with the offering and their ability to cover these costs. Considered together, affordability (costs) and attractiveness (benefits) determine the overall value (utility) of the offering to target customers. Affordability can involve monetary as well as nonmonetary costs (e.g., time and effort involved in acquiring and using the offering). Affordability related to monetary costs is often the key impediment to adoption of an offering in developing countries and in financially strained demographic areas.

- **Availability** reflects the degree to which customers have access to the offering. An offering's availability is a function of the density of the distribution channels catering to a given customer segment and the in-stock availability of the offering in these channels on a day-to-day basis.

Identifying and Closing Adoption Gaps

Managing product adoption calls for identifying and eliminating impediments at different stages of the adoption process. These impediments, often referred to as *adoption gaps*, can be illustrated by mapping the dispersion of customers across different stages of the adoption process. The goal of this analysis is to provide a better understanding of the dynamics of the adoption process and identify problematic areas that require specific actions.

To visualize the potential hurdles in the adoption process, the dispersion of customers across different stages of the adoption process can be represented by a series of bars, as shown in Figure 3. Here, the blank part of each bar corresponds to the share of potential customers who have not transitioned to the next stage of the adoption process. The ratio of the blank part to the shaded part reflects the effectiveness of the company's actions at each step in acquiring new customers.

Figure 3: Identifying Adoption Gaps

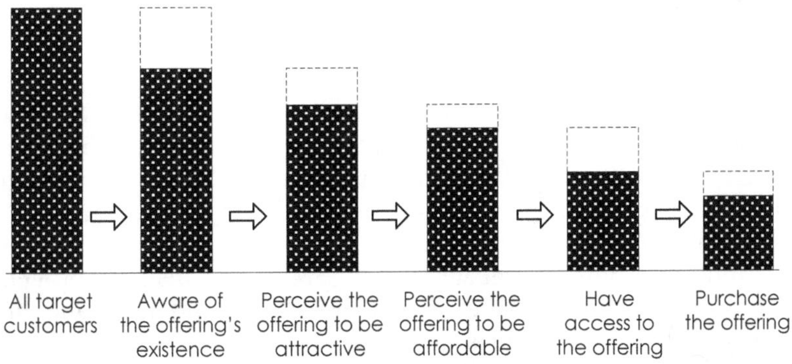

Evaluating the loss of potential customers at each step of the process offers a simple way to identify adoption gaps, which describe steps with a disproportionate drop in product adoption. The gap analysis can be used both to pinpoint the problem spots in product adoption and identify specific solutions to close adoption gaps. Some of the common solutions for closing these performance gaps at the different stages of the adoption process are outlined below.

- **Awareness gaps** call for increasing awareness of the offering among target customers. This type of gap calls for improving company communications (by increasing overall communication spending, streamlining the message, developing a better creative solution, and using more effective media in a more cost-efficient manner). In addition to directly communicating the availability of the offering to target customers, the company can also involve its collaborators in creating awareness of the offering among target customers (e.g., by joint advertising), as well as foster third-party communications that promote the offering (e.g., by encouraging product adoption by opinion leaders and facilitating publicity about the offering).

- **Attractiveness gaps** call for improving the benefits of the offering. This typically is achieved by reformulating/redesigning the offering, which can involve permanent changes in the product, service, branding, and pricing aspects of the offering as well as by temporarily enhancing the value of the offering through incentives. Note that attractiveness gaps do not always imply that the offering lacks the benefits desired by target customers; they can also stem from the fact that buyers do not understand the offering's benefits. Such gaps in customers' understanding of the offering's benefits can be closed by improving communication and providing target customers with an option to experience the offering via product samples and demonstrations.
- **Affordability gaps** call for lowering the costs of the offering. Lowering monetary costs might involve lowering the offering's price, adding monetary incentives, as well as redesigning the offering to improve its affordability. Lowering nonmonetary costs might involve decreasing the amount of time and effort involved in acquiring and using the offering. Note that affordability gaps do not always imply that the actual costs of the offering are high; they might also result from customers' perception of the offering's actual costs. Such gaps in customers' understanding of the offering's costs can be closed by correcting price misperceptions.
- **Availability gaps** indicate that target customers do not have access to the offering. For example, an offering might be in short supply because a company underestimated its appeal to target customers or because of inadequate distribution coverage. Depending on the cause of the availability gap, improving an offering's availability can involve ramping up production to meet demand, improving the geographical coverage of distribution channels to give target customers better accessibility to the offering, and improving channel operations to reduce stock-outs.
- **Purchase gaps** indicate that even though customers might find the company's offering attractive, affordable, and accessible, they have not purchased the offering within the time frame defined by the company's goals. This can result from the fact that customers have not formed an intent to purchase the offering in the near future or that they have formed such an intent but have fail to act on it—for example, because of time or budgetary constraints. Closing purchase intent gaps typically involves introducing time-sensitive incentives, such as short-lived price discounts, coupons, and financing options.

Managing Usage

The discussion so far has focused on growing sales volume by increasing product adoption by new customers. An alternative approach to growing an offering's sales volume involves increasing its consumption by current customers.

Understanding Consumption

Most purchases are recurring in nature, be it products for daily usage such as food, apparel, and cosmetics, or durable goods such as cars, household appliances, and electronics. Therefore, managing recurring consumption can have a significant impact on sales volume.

The total quantity of offerings purchased over time by individual customers depends on several key factors, including the overall satisfaction with the offering, the frequency with which consumers use the offering, the quantity used on each usage occasion, the frequency of replacement, and the availability of the offering (Figure 4). These five factors are summarized in more detail below.

Figure 4: Key Factors Influencing Consumption Quantity

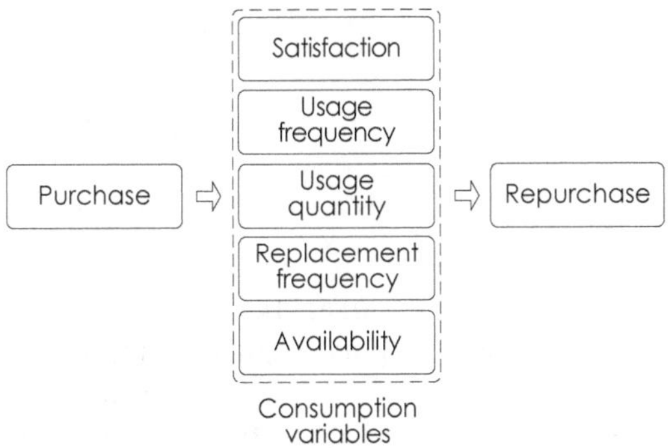

- **Satisfaction** reflects customers' experience with the offering. Unlike the attractiveness stage in product adoption, which is based on expectations of an offering's value, satisfaction reflects the postconsumption evaluation that takes into account customers' actual use of the offering.
- **Usage frequency** reflects the number of occasions on which the offering is used. For example, for cars, usage frequency refers to how often customers drive; for toothpaste, it refers to the number of times people brush their teeth.
- **Usage quantity** is particularly relevant when customers determine the quantity consumed on each occasion. For example, usage quantity for toothpaste depends on the amount of toothpaste people use to brush their teeth.
- **Replacement frequency** is particularly relevant in cases of unit-based products such as cars, printer cartridges, water filters, and razor blades, where customers determine when to replace the item.
- **Availability** indicates whether customers have a replacement available or can conveniently repurchase it.

Identifying and Closing Consumption Gaps

A practical approach to managing usage calls for identifying and eliminating impediments at the different stages of product usage. The potential impediments in product usage can be visualized by a series of bars, as shown in Figure 5. Here, the blank part of each bar corresponds to the share of customers whose consumption behavior is suboptimal, and the ratio of the blank part to the shaded part reflects the effectiveness of the company's actions at each step in managing consumption.

Figure 5: Identifying Consumption Gaps

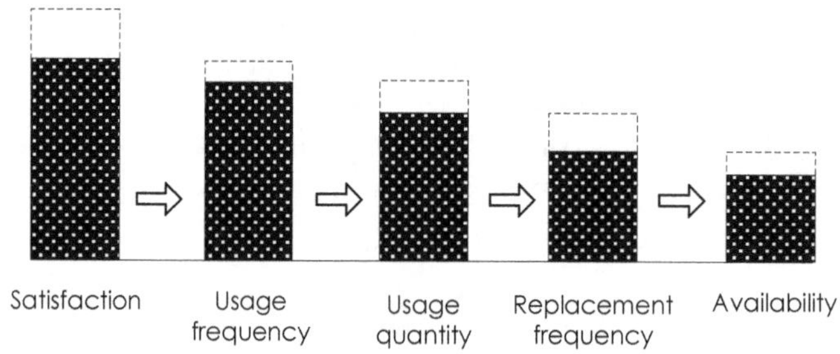

Evaluating the effectiveness of each stage of the repurchase process offers a simple way to identify disproportionate drops in product usage. Common solutions for closing such consumption gaps are outlined below.

- **Satisfaction gaps** call for improving customers' experience with the offering. Depending on the cause of the satisfaction gap, this might involve enhancing the benefits and reducing the costs of the offering to make it more competitive, better aligning the offering's value proposition with changes in customer preferences, and adding variants to the offering's product line to reduce boredom and address variety seeking.

- **Usage-frequency gaps** call for increasing the frequency with which customers use the offering. For example, sales of a laundry detergent can be increased if customers wash their clothes more often; sales of toothpaste can be increased if customers brush their teeth more frequently; and sales of razors can be increased if customers shave more frequently. Sales volume can also be increased by identifying new ways to use the offering. To illustrate, Campbell Soup Company promotes the use of its soup (usually consumed in winter time) during summer and Arm & Hammer promotes baking soda not only for baking but also as a household cleaner and deodorizer.

- **Usage-quantity gaps** call for increasing the amount of product used on each occasion. Thus, usage quantity can be increased by educating customers about the optimal usage quantity. A classic example of this approach is the "rinse and repeat" shampoo instruction. Another approach involves increasing the size of the packaging in categories where bigger package size typically leads to using a larger quantity. For example, Pepsi's introduction of the two-liter bottle in 1970 resulted in increased consumption of its products. Usage volume also can be increased by designing the product in a way that ensures dispensing the optimal quantity per usage occasion. For example, Heinz introduced a plastic squeeze bottle, increased the size of the opening in the bottle neck, and designed the "upside-down bottle" so ketchup can be poured without having to wait for the contents to slide down to the opening of the bottle. Similarly, laundry detergents often include measuring cups to determine the optimal usage quantity.

- **Replacement-frequency gaps** call for increasing the frequency with which customers replace the product. This type of gap is particularly relevant when consumption volume is defined by the number of times an item is used before being replaced, as in the case of printer cartridges, razor blades, and water filters. In this case, replacement frequency can be managed by informing customers about the optimal usage duration and replacement frequency. For example, to encourage customers to replace their toothbrush, Gillette added blue bristles on its Oral-B Indicator toothbrush, which fade to alert users that they need to replace their brush.
- **Availability gaps** call for ensuring continuous consumption without disruptions caused by buyers running out of the product. For example, printer manufacturers include toner-level indicators to alert users that the cartridge will soon need replacement. Repurchase can also be facilitated by incentives that encourage customers to buy the offering in advance of the need to replace it so that they never run out. A side benefit of advance purchasing and stockpiling is that it can promote consumption in categories where usage is "elastic" with respect to the quantity available. For example, the consumption of food and beverages is often influenced by the quantity at hand, such that greater quantity leads to greater consumption (referred to as the "pantry effect").

Because they deal with recurring purchases, consumption gaps often hold greater potential to increase sales volume than acquisition gaps. This is especially true for companies with a dominant position in the market because of the relatively large installed base of users. Optimizing the consumption experience in this case can have a significant impact on the company's ability to grow sales volume.

SUMMARY

Sales growth is a key factor for achieving sustainable profitability. The two core strategies for increasing the sales volume of a company's offerings are (1) increasing product adoptions by new customers and (2) increasing product usage by current customers.

Product adoption can be viewed as a multistage process comprising four key factors: awareness (knowledge of the existence of the offering), attractiveness (perceived benefits that customers expect to receive from the offering), affordability (perceived costs associated with the offering), and availability (degree to which the offering is accessible by target customers). A useful approach to managing product adoption involves identifying and eliminating impediments (adoption gaps) at the different stages of the adoption process.

In addition to increasing adoption by new customers, in many cases an offering's sales volume can also be increased by influencing its usage (and, hence, repurchase frequency) by current customers. Product repurchase is a function of the following five factors: satisfaction (the degree to which customers find the offering attractive after having experienced it), usage frequency (rate at which customers use the offering), usage quantity (amount of the offering that customers consume on each usage occasion), replacement frequency (the rate at which consumers replace the offering), and availability (the extent to which the offering is readily available for repurchase and use). A practical approach to managing product usage involves identifying and eliminating impediments (usage gaps) at the different stages of the repurchase process.

RELEVANT CONCEPTS

Conversion Rate: The number of potential customers who have tried the product/service relative to the total number of customers aware of the product/service.

$$\text{Conversion rate} = \frac{\text{Current and former customers}}{\text{Potential customers aware of the offering}}$$

Customer Attrition Rate (Churn Rate): The number of customers who discontinue using a company's product or service during a specified period relative to the average total number of customers during that same period.

$$\text{Customer attrition rate} = \frac{\text{Number of customers who disadopt an offering during a specific period}}{\text{Total number of customers during that period}}$$

Pareto Principle: The 80/20 relationship discovered in the late 1800s by the economist Vilfredo Pareto. Pareto established that 80% of the land in Italy was owned by 20% of the population. He later observed that 20% of the peapods in his garden yielded 80% of the peas that were harvested. The Pareto Principle, or the 80/20 Rule, has proven its validity in a number of other areas. In marketing, the most common illustration of the 80/20 rule is that 80% of revenues (or profits) are often generated by 20% of customers (or products).

Penetration Rate: The number of customers who have tried the offering at least once relative to the total number of potential customers.

$$\text{Penetration rate} = \frac{\text{Current and former customers}}{\text{Potential customers}}$$

Retention Rate: The number of customers who have repurchased the offering during the current buying cycle (month, quarter, or year) relative to the number of customers who purchased the offering during the last cycle. Also used in reference to the number of customers who have repurchased the offering relative to the total number of customers who have tried the product at least once.

$$\text{Retention rate} = \frac{\text{Active customers during the current period}}{\text{Active customers during the last period}}$$

ADDITIONAL READINGS

Aaker, David A. (2009), *Strategic Market Management* (9th ed.). New York, NY: John Wiley & Sons.

Best, Roger J. (2012), *Market-Based Management: Strategies for Growing Customer Value and Profitability* (6th ed.). Upper Saddle River, NJ: Prentice Hall.

Kumar, Nirmalya (2004), *Marketing as Strategy: Understanding the CEO's Agenda for Driving Growth and Innovation.* Boston, MA: Harvard Business School Press.

CHAPTER SIXTEEN

MANAGING NEW PRODUCTS

I don't design clothes. I design dreams.

—Ralph Lauren, fashion designer and entrepreneur

New products and services are the key to sustainable growth; they enable companies to gain and sustain their market position by taking advantage of the changes in the market to create superior customer value. The main aspects of designing and managing new product offerings are the focus of this chapter.

Forecasting New Product Demand

The decision to launch a new offering stems from a company's belief that there is market demand for the benefits provided by this offering. To define the strategy and design tactics involved in the development of the new offering, the company needs to know the specifics of the target market and, in particular, the size of the market for its offering. This process of estimating the size of the potential market is referred to as demand forecasting.

There are two common types of demand forecasts: market forecasts and sales forecasts. *Market forecasts* estimate the total sales volume that ultimately can be achieved by all companies in a given market. Forecasts of market potential are typically used to make market entry and exit decisions, resource allocation decisions, and to set goals and evaluate performance. Unlike market forecasts, which indicate the sales volume that potentially can be achieved in a particular market, *sales forecasts* impose a specific time frame for achieving the sales volume. Thus, sales forecasts are an estimate of the total sales volume attainable within a given time frame. Similar to estimates of market potential, sales forecasts typically are used to make entry and exit decisions, allocate resources, plan production capacity, and evaluate the impact of various marketing mix variables on sales.

Based on the type of data they utilize, there are two types of demand-forecasting methods: collecting and analyzing primary data (data collected especially for the purpose of demand forecasting) and analyzing secondary data (existing data). These two types of methods are discussed in more detail in the following sections.

Forecasting Demand Using Primary Data

Primary-data forecasting involves collecting and analyzing new data to gain insight into the adoption process and estimate the offering's potential market size and speed of adoption. There are two types of primary-data demand forecasts: expert-judgment forecasts and customer-research forecasts.

- **Expert-judgment forecasts** rely on experts' opinions to estimate market demand. Depending on the nature of the expert's background, there are three main categories of forecasts: the executive forecast, sales force forecast, and industry forecast.
  - *Executive forecast* is a top-down approach in which the forecast is based on the aggregated opinion of a company's top executives and senior managers.
  - *Sales force forecast* is a bottom-up approach in which the forecast is based on the aggregated opinion of a company's sales force and sales managers.
  - *Industry forecast* is based on the aggregated opinion of industry experts, such as industry analysts, executives, managers, and sales forces from competitive companies.

  Because most expert-judgment forecasts are based on aggregating the opinions of multiple experts, an important issue concerns the process of aggregating individual judgments to arrive at the final estimate. A popular method for eliciting expert judgments is the Delphi method, described in more detail at the end of this chapter.

- **Customer-research forecasting** examines customers' reaction to the offering at different stages of the product development process. The two most popular methods of customer-based forecasting are concept testing and market testing.
  - *Concept testing* is the process of evaluating consumer response to a particular offering prior to its introduction to the market. Concept testing can be based on a description of the offering or, alternatively, can involve a fully functional prototype. One approach to concept testing involves using a representative sample of the target segment (a focus group) for the purpose of gleaning insights, ideas, and observations related to the key aspects of the offering. Another methodology involves estimating the probability of the offering's purchase by target customers based on a description of its main benefits and costs. Because it is based on customers' estimates of their future behavior, concept testing provides only rough estimates of sales volume.
  - *Market testing* relies on test markets to estimate market potential and future sales volume. It is often used as the litmus test for a go or no-go decision to launch a new product, as well as for testing specific aspects of the offering's marketing mix. Test markets aim to replicate all relevant aspects of the environment in which the company's offering will be launched (offering-related advertising and incentives, competitive offerings, and point-of-purchase environment) so that the test market outcome can be extrapolated to more general (national) sales forecasts. To

ensure greater validity of the results, multiple test markets, typically located in different geographic areas, are used. Because of its relatively high costs, market testing is normally used only for products that successfully pass the concept testing stage.

Forecasting Demand Using Secondary Data

Secondary-data forecasting relies on already existing data. Based on the type of data included, three different secondary-data forecasting methods can be used:

- **Offering-specific forecasting** is based on past data from the sales of the same offering for which the demand is being forecast. A popular approach relies on past sales data to identify trends, then extrapolates these trends to a sales forecast. A variety of time-series statistical approaches might be employed for this type of analysis, such as linear trend analysis, moving-average analysis, and exponential smoothing. Another popular approach involves identifying the relationships between the offering's sales and a variety of internal (the offering's price, incentives, and communication) and external factors (competitors' price, incentives, and communication) to predict the likely sales volume.
- **Forecasting by analogy** involves forecasting an offering's performance by comparing its adoption cycle to a functionally similar product for which sales data are available. This approach is especially useful for new products for which adoption data are not available, or for nontraditional marketing activities involving existing products (drastic price change, novel incentives, nontraditional communication campaign) for which market reaction is unknown. For example, one could forecast the adoption of 3-D TVs by comparing it to the adoption of analogous products, such as color, flat-screen, and high-definition TVs. The key assumption of analogy-based forecasts is that the pattern of adoption of the new product (speed and depth of market penetration) will follow a similar pattern to that of the analogous product.
- **Category-based forecasting** involves utilizing available product-category data to estimate a particular product's performance. One category-based forecasting approach to quantifying sales potential involves estimating the degree to which sales in a given category have captured the total market potential in a particular geographical area based on the population of that area and average consumption per user nationally (also referred to as the Category Development Index, or CDI). An alternative approach to category-based demand forecasting involves estimating the degree to which sales of a specific offering (rather than the entire category) have captured the total market potential in a particular market (also referred to as the Brand Development Index, or BDI). Comparing these two indexes reveals an offering's performance relative to the category (discussed in more detail at the end of this chapter). Thus, a combination of high BDI and low CDI indicates that the brand is doing better than competitive offerings, whereas a combination of low BDI and high CDI indicates that the brand is doing worse than competitive offerings.

Understanding New Product Adoption

Managing new products calls for understanding how customers adopt these products—a process often referred to as diffusion of innovations. The diffusion of new products is often represented by an S-shaped curve, which depicts the total number of adoptions at any given point in time (Figure 1A). The pattern of the diffusion process can be defined by two factors: (1) *market potential*, indicating the total number of users that will ultimately adopt the innovation, and (2) the *speed of diffusion*, which can be defined by the time frame for reaching the inflection point—the point at which the rate of growth slows down and starts declining (and where the shape of the diffusion curve turns from convex to concave).

Figure 1. New Product Adoption

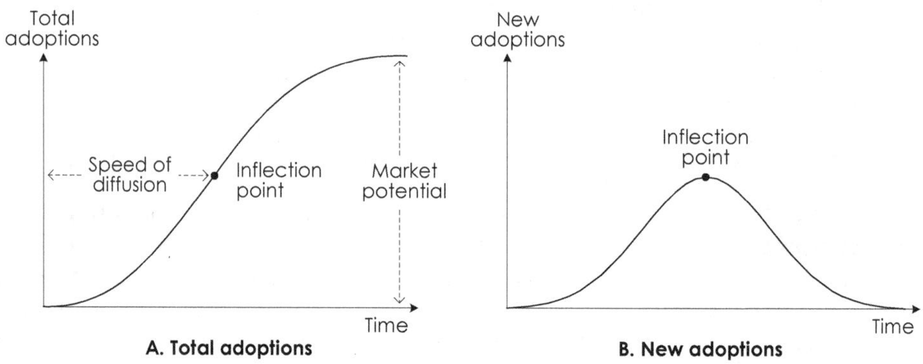

The diffusion process can also be represented by the number of new (rather than total) adoptions at any given point in time. In this context, new product adoption can be represented by a bell-shaped curve, whereby, after a relatively slow start, an increasing number of people adopt the innovation until it reaches a peak, then starts declining as the number of potential adopters decreases. The pattern of new adoptions directly corresponds to that of total adoptions, with the key difference that it represents the dispersion of new adoptions over time instead of the total number of adoptions (Figure 1B). A popular interpretation of the bell-shaped curve of new adoptions involves classifying customers into distinct categories based on their adoption pattern. The two most influential frameworks offering such classifications—Rogers' model and Moore's model—are discussed at the end of this chapter.

The adoption of an innovation does not always follow a normal distribution represented by the bell-shaped curve: Some innovations are adopted very rapidly, whereas others take a substantial amount of time to achieve their peak adoption period. A new offering might be adopted almost instantly by a large segment of the population, then it might be diffused at a much slower rate until it is adopted by all target customers; alternatively, adoption might start at a much slower rate and reach the point at which the majority of target customers have adopted it relatively late in the adoption process. The speed with which customers adopt a new offering is a function of the value provided by the offering. Specifically, several factors can influence the diffusion of new offerings:

- **Inherent value of the offering**. The greater the inherent value of the new offering, the more likely it is to be adopted.
- **Relative advantage**. The greater the relative advantage of an offering over the product it replaces, the more likely it is to be adopted.
- **Transparency**. An offering is more likely to be adopted when its relative benefits are readily observable and can be experienced by customers.
- **Compatibility**. An offering compatible with customers' existing systems and processes is more likely to be adopted than an incompatible one.
- **Perceived risk**. An offering is more likely to be adopted when the perceived risk associated with the new product is low. This might involve customers' uncertainty about their own preferences, about the product's performance, and about the magnitude of the risks associated with the new product.

In addition to being a function of the offering's inherent benefits, the likelihood that customers will adopt a new offering is a function of a company's promotional and distribution activities. Thus, the greater the promotional activity (advertising, public relations, monetary and nonmonetary incentives) associated with a new offering and the greater the availability of the offering across distribution channels, the more likely it is to be adopted by customers.

Managing New Product Development

New product development involves converting ideas into successful market offerings. One of the main challenges with developing new products is streamlining the innovation process in a way that facilitates market success. The key aspects of the new product development process are discussed in the following sections.

Understanding the New Product Development Process

New product development can be viewed as a stepwise process comprising the following six stages:

- **Idea generation** involves generating ideas that can become the basis for new products. Ideas can come from different sources: They can stem from the company (e.g., by virtue of marketing research and/or employee suggestions), from customers (e.g., via crowdsourcing), and from collaborators (e.g., dealers, retailers, and wholesalers). Idea generation is typically complemented by idea screening, which involves evaluating the idea from the viewpoint of its technological and market feasibility.
- **Concept development** involves creating a detailed sketch of the initial idea by delineating the key technological and market aspects of the proposed offering. At this stage, the goal is to define the key product attributes, the underlying technology processes, and the offering's tactics (product, service, brand, price, incentives, communication, and distribution). The process of

concept development is typically complemented with concept testing, which aims to examine whether the new product is technologically feasible and whether it is likely to be accepted by target customers.

- **Business analysis** involves evaluating the viability of the offering's business model. This stage examines the offering's concept that was defined in the previous stage with respect to its ability to create an optimal value proposition for target customers, the company, and collaborators. An important aspect of business analysis involves forecasting market demand (discussed in more detail later in this chapter).
- **Product development** involves designing and manufacturing the offering. Typically, product development is initially implemented on a smaller scale to allow for testing of its technological and business viability. In cases when manufacturing the actual product is complex and/or costly, the company might consider developing a physical prototype or a mock-up before producing a limited quantity of the product for a test market.
- **Market testing** involves assessing the viability of the new product or prototype, typically on a small scale (in a simulated usage environment and/or in a test market area). Market testing enables the company to more realistically assess the likelihood of success of a given offering. In addition to assessing customers' response to the offering, market testing (also referred to as beta testing) is also conducted to improve the design and functionality of the product before commercializing it.
- **Business deployment** involves deploying the new product on a large scale, including full-scale manufacturing, promotion, and distribution.

Note that although the above six stages are presented as a stepwise process, this particular sequence—although the most common one—is not fixed, allowing a certain level of flexibility. Thus, when product development requires substantial resources, prototype-based market testing can precede the development of the actual product. On the other hand, when commercial deployment does not require substantial resources, the new product development process can skip the market-testing stage and use full-scale product deployment as a de facto market test.

Managing Risk in New Product Development

One of the key challenges in new product development is managing the uncertainty of success associated with launching new offerings. Because uncertainty increases the risk of failure, minimizing risk is one of the key aspects of new product development. Managing risk involves minimizing the chance that the new offering will fail (e.g., during unfavorable market conditions), thus wasting the resources expended on its development. The risk involved in new product development can be classified into one of two categories: market risk and technology risk.

- **Market risk** reflects the uncertainty associated with the factors (the Five Cs) defining the market. Thus, the customer need that the new product aims to fulfill might be transient or might exist only for a *customer* segment that is not large enough to justify the development, production, promotion, and distribution costs. The company's *collaborators* (suppliers, distributors, codevelopers) might not allocate the necessary support to ensure the success of the offering. The *company* might end up without sufficient resources to develop and launch the offering due to factors such as cost overruns, inadequate manufacturing infrastructure, and the loss of key personnel. *Competitors* might gain pioneering advantage by being first to market, or they might gain second-mover advantage by emulating the company's technology to design a cheaper product or by building on the company's technology to develop a functionally superior offering. Finally, the success of a new offering can be influenced by changes in the market *context,* such as the development of superior technologies, fluctuating sociocultural trends, new regulatory restrictions on product specifications and the product development process, as well as new import/export tariffs, taxes, and fees.

- **Technological risk** reflects the uncertainty associated with the technological viability of the new offering. For example, the desired product features might not be achievable with currently available technologies, product design might not be compatible with the functional requirements, and product reliability might be compromised by the use of new, unproven technologies. Technological risk might also extend the timeframe for developing the new offering, which in turn can increase the market risk associated with changes in the market environment during a longer period of time.

A common approach to managing risk involves evaluating the outcomes of each of the six stages discussed in the previous section, and before proceeding to the next stage screening out the ideas, concepts, and products that are unlikely to succeed. Thus, the process of new product development can be thought of as a funnel, with numerous new product ideas entering the process and only a few ending up being commercialized. A popular strategy for managing risk in new product development is the *stage-gate approach,* which involves introducing benchmarks (gates) that must be met in order for an idea, concept, or product to proceed to the next stage of development. The stage-gate approach to product development is illustrated in Figure 2.

Figure 2: The Stage-Gate Approach for Minimizing Risk in New Product Development

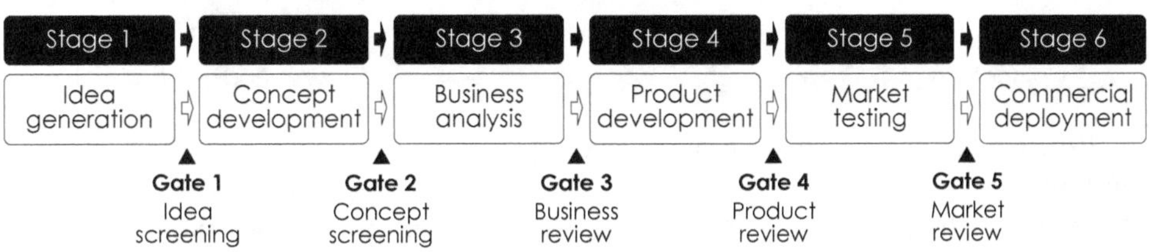

To manage the risk associated with a new product launch, a manager must define the hurdle set by each of the five gates—idea screening, concept screening, business review, product review, and market review—depicted in Figure 2. The more stringent the hurdle, the greater the likelihood that the offering will succeed. At the same time, setting overly stringent hurdles (gates) can make the company overlook a potentially viable new product, thus giving the competition the opportunity to gain pioneering advantage by being the first to bring the product to market. Therefore, setting the "right" hurdles at each stage of product development is essential for growing the company's new product pipeline while minimizing the risk of new product failure.

Managing the Product Life Cycle

The concept of a product life cycle is based on the idea that products have a limited life in which they pass through distinct stages. Typically, four key product life cycle stages are identified: introduction, growth, maturity, and decline. During the *introduction* stage, product awareness is low and there are few competitors. As the product takes off during the *growth* stage, the number of competitors entering the market increases. At *maturity*, the number of competitors tends to peak, the market becomes saturated, and industry profitability starts to decline because of intensifying competition. Finally, the *decline* stage is characterized by falling demand for the product, relatively low profitability, and a decreasing number of competitors stemming from consolidation and exit from the market. The four stages of the product life cycle and the corresponding market conditions at each stage are illustrated in Figure 3.

Figure 3. Managing the Product Life Cycle[1]

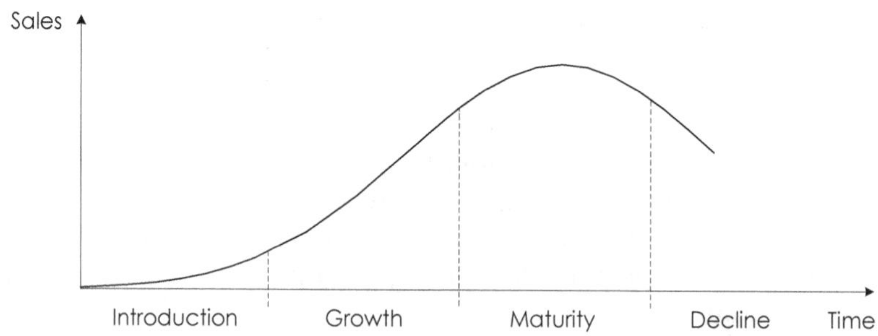

	Introduction	Growth	Maturity	Decline
Market size	Small	Moderate	Large	Moderate/Small
Market growth	Low	High	Low	Negative
Competition	Low	Moderate	High	Moderate/Low

Product strategies vary across an offering's life cycle. At the introduction stage, companies typically offer a single product variant targeted to the most likely adopters. As the product enters the growth stage, the number of customers adopting the product increases, and so does the heterogeneity of these customers. To address the diverse needs of current and potential customers, companies add product extensions designed to better meet the needs of various customer subsegments. The number of product variants typically peaks at maturity and starts decreasing as the product enters its decline stage; profit margins shrink, and companies focus on best-selling products, phasing out products with insufficient volume to meet their profitability benchmarks.

In the same vein, the stage of an offering's life cycle can influence its communication. Thus, in the early stages of product introduction, the communication campaign aims primarily at creating awareness among early adopters, as well as among channel partners. As the product enters the growth stage, a company's communication goals shift to creating awareness of the product within the mass market while at the same time differentiating its offerings from those of competitors. As the product enters its maturity stage and the majority of customers are aware of the category benefits, the communication focus shifts from creating awareness of the category benefits to differentiating the company's offering by highlighting its benefits vis-à-vis the competition. This emphasis on product differentiation continues as the product enters its decline stage; however, at this point overall communication expenditures tend to decline.

An important aspect of new product decisions involves managing the evolution of the company's products over time. As products become obsolete, they are often replaced by a new generation of products that take advantage of changes in target markets, such as changes in customer preferences, alterations in the competitive landscape, advances in technology, and changes in the regulatory environment. Innovation enables companies to extend the life cycle of their individual products (Figure 4). To illustrate, consider Gillette's product development strategy leading to the introduction of Fusion, its eighth-generation wet-shaving razor. Gillette's original razor, introduced in 1903 was replaced by the second-generation razor Trac II (1971), followed by Sensor (1990), Sensor Excel (1995), Mach3 (1998), Mach3 Turbo (2002), M3Power (2004), Fusion (2006), Fusion ProGlide (2010), and Fusion FlexBall (2014).

Figure 4. Extending Product Life Cycle through Innovation[2]

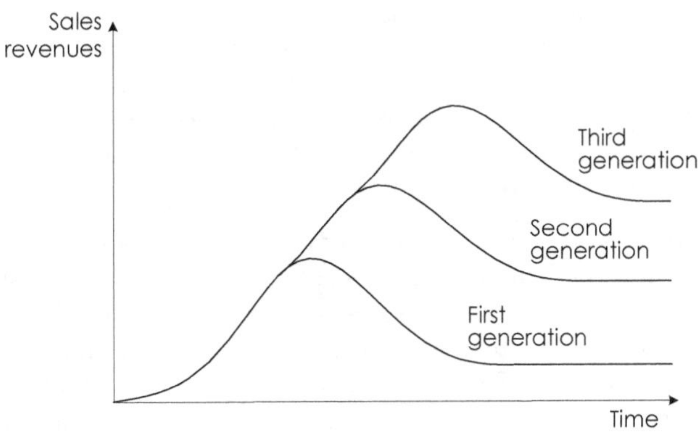

When developing a new generation of products, companies often develop strategies to make the earlier generation obsolete, a process often referred to as planned obsolescence. Planned obsolescence involves designing new products in a way that makes prior generations inferior (and, therefore, obsolete) on key dimensions such as functionality, compatibility, and style. To illustrate, to facilitate user migration to later versions of their software, companies systematically terminate support (e.g., software upgrades) for earlier versions. In addition, the added functionality of the new generation of software often limits its backward compatibility; as a result, once the new software has been adopted by a critical mass of users, the earlier versions become obsolete because of their incompatibility. Another important implication of planned obsolescence for new product design involves managing a new product's costs by optimizing its performance during its expected lifetime, a process often referred to as value engineering. For example, a company expecting its product to be obsolete within a given time frame might optimize costs by designing the durability of a product's components according to the expected product lifetime.

SUMMARY

The decision to launch a new offering stems from a company's belief that there is market demand for the benefits provided by this offering. To define the strategy and design tactics involved in the development of the new offering, the company needs to know the specifics of the target market and, in particular, the size of the market for its offering.

Understanding market demand is essential for managing new products. There are two basic types of demand forecasting methods: methods that involve collecting primary data (data collected especially for the purposes of demand forecasting) and methods that involve analyzing secondary data (existing data). Primary-data forecasting comprises two types of methods: expert-judgment forecasts and customer-research forecasts. Forecast methods involving already existing (secondary) data include offering-specific forecasting, forecasting by analogy, and category-based forecasting. Because most forecasting methods are based on a variety of assumptions, a more accurate forecast can be achieved by using multiple methods.

The process of new product adoption can be represented by an S-shaped curve that depicts the total number of adoptions at any given point in time, as well as by a bell-shaped curve depicting the number of new (rather than total) adoptions of the innovation at any given point in time. New product adoption is influenced by several factors: the inherent value of the product, its relative advantage over similar offerings, the transparency of product benefits, its compatibility with related products, and the perceived risk that consumers associate with product adoption.

The process of converting ideas to market offerings can be viewed as a process comprising the following six stages: idea generation, concept development, business analysis, product development, market testing, and business deployment. To minimize the market and technical risk associated with the offering, the stage-gate approach to new product development calls for introducing benchmarks (gates) that must be met in order for an idea, concept, or product to proceed to the next stage of development.

Managing product life cycle involves optimizing the market value of products and services as they progress through different stages in the marketplace: introduction, growth, maturity, and decline. At introduction, product awareness is low and there are few competitors. As the product gains traction with customers, the number of competitors entering the market increases. At maturity, the number of competitors tends to peak, the market becomes saturated, and industry profitability starts to decline because of intensifying competition. Finally, the decline stage is associated with falling demand for the product, relatively low profitability, and a decreasing number of competitors stemming from consolidation and exit from the market. Because the stages in the product life cycle are characterized by different market conditions, different stages require different marketing strategies.

RELEVANT CONCEPTS

Brand Development Index (BDI): A measure of the degree to which sales of a given offering (or a product line associated with a particular brand) have captured the total market potential in a particular geographical area. BDI quantifies the sales potential of a given brand in a particular market.

$$\text{BDI} = \frac{\text{Percent of an offering's total US sales in market X}}{\text{Percent of the total US population in market X}}$$

Category Development Index (CDI): A measure of the degree to which sales in a given category have captured the total market potential in a particular geographical area. CDI quantifies the sales potential of a given category in a particular market.

$$\text{CDI} = \frac{\text{Percent of a category's total US sales in market X}}{\text{Percent of the total US population in market X}}$$

Delphi Method: A popular method for eliciting group expert judgments, named after the site of the most revered oracle in ancient Greece, the Temple of Apollo at Delphi. The Delphi method involves multiple rounds of collecting anonymous expert opinions. The primary goal of the Delphi method is to ensure an accurate forecast from a group of experts by controlling for many of the potential decision biases, such as social conformity (agreeing with the majority), status (seniority within the organization), confirmation bias (ignoring new information that is inconsistent with the original forecast), and other related effects (experts' ability to eloquently articulate their forecast). To achieve this degree of control, individual forecasts are collected by a moderator who ensures anonymity of the experts' opinions. Each forecast typically consists of two parts: the forecast and its rationale. In the Delphi method, after each round of forecast elicitation, the moderator provides the experts with the anonymous forecasts and their rationale, and gives them the option to revise their opinion. This process is repeated until a consensus is reached. In cases where consensus is unlikely after several rounds, the individual forecasts are typically aggregated into an overall estimate (e.g., by averaging the individual numeric forecasts).

RELEVANT FRAMEWORKS: ROGERS' MODEL OF ADOPTION OF INNOVATIONS

The key premise underlying the Rogers model is that some consumers are inevitably more open to innovations than others.[3] Based on the relative time of adoption of innovations, the Rogers model distinguishes five categories of customers (Figure 5): innovators (the first 2.5% of the adopters), early adopters (the 13.5% of the adopters following the innovators), early majority (the next 34% of adopters), late majority (the next 34%), and laggards (the remaining 16%).

Figure 5. Rogers' Categorization of Customers Based on the Time of Adoption of Innovation

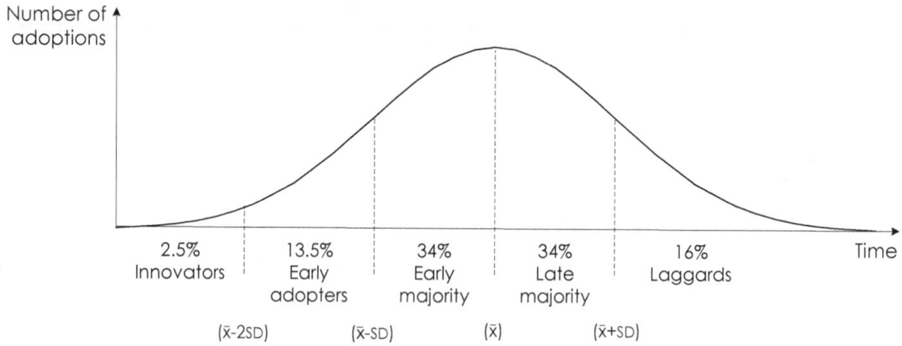

The respective percentage values associated with each category are based on the assumption that the process of adoption of innovations can be represented by a normal distribution, which is defined by two key parameters: its mean ($\overline{x}$) and its standard deviation (SD), a measure of the variation from the mean. In this context, the early and late majorities are defined as being one standard deviation from the mean (34%), whereas early adopters are defined as being two standard deviations from the mean. This classification is not symmetric: There are three categories on the left of the mean and only two on the right. The reason is that the segment on the far left end is further divided into two categories: innovators and early adopters, which cumulatively add up to the size of the laggards segment on the right. The rationale for this division is that these two categories display distinct patterns of adoption behavior and, therefore, from a theoretical standpoint, need to be considered separately.

Despite its popularity, the Rogers model has a number of limitations. One of its key limitations is that it is essentially a classification model; although it identifies the five different categories of adopters of innovation, it does not explain the factors that determine this classification. For example, this model does not offer a decision rule to help determine whether a particular individual will become an early adopter or a laggard. Another limitation is that classification into one of the five categories is linked to relatively stable personality traits, even though in reality individuals who are innovators in one domain often might be laggards in another. Additional limitations can be traced back to some of its assumptions, such as the normally shaped distribution of adoption of innovation across the population and the preset percentage allocation of individuals into each of the five categories. As a result, the application of the Rogers model is limited to a general description of the adoption of innovations process and to classifying adopters into one of the five categories for descriptive purposes.

RELEVANT FRAMEWORKS: MOORE'S MODEL OF ADOPTION OF NEW TECHNOLOGIES

A popular application of Rogers' diffusion theory to technology products is Moore's "chasm" model.[4] Moore argued that the adoption of technology-based innovations is discontinuous because different groups of adopters have different adoption patterns and, therefore, require different marketing strategies. Moore's model identifies five distinct categories of customers based on their attitudes toward technology, which correspond to Rogers' five categories: technology enthusiasts (innovators), visionaries (early adopters), pragmatists (early majority), conservatives (late majority), and skeptics (laggards). These five categories of adopters can be described as follows:

- **Technology enthusiasts** (innovators) are fundamentally committed to new technology and derive utility from being the first to experience new technologies.
- **Visionaries** (early adopters) are among the first to apply new technologies to solve problems and exploit opportunities in the marketplace.
- **Pragmatists** (early majority) view technology innovation as a productivity tool. Unlike enthusiasts, they do not appreciate technology for its own sake. Unlike visionaries, they do not use technology innovations to change existing business models but rather to optimize the efficiency and effectiveness of existing business models.
- **Conservatives** (late majority) are generally pessimistic about their ability to significantly benefit from new technological innovations and are reluctant to adopt them.
- **Skeptics** (laggards) are critics of any innovative technology and are not likely to adopt such technologies even when they offer distinct benefits.

Unlike Rogers' model, which implies smooth and continuous progression across segments during the life of an offering, Moore's model assumes that the adoption of technology-based innovations follows a discontinuous pattern. This discontinuity in the adoption process is attributed to the fact that different groups of adopters have different adoption patterns and, therefore, require different marketing strategies. Thus, once a technology has reached its market potential within a given segment, it might not naturally roll over to the next segment.

To illustrate, even though an innovation has been adopted by technology enthusiasts, it might never be widely accepted by the visionaries. In this context, a company's biggest hurdle in promoting technology innovations is to bridge the gaps among different segments. According to Moore, the key gap among segments—referred to as a "chasm"—is the one between the early market (enthusiasts and visionaries) and the mainstream market (pragmatists, conservatives, and skeptics). In this context, the chasm describes the impediments to mainstream commercialization of technology innovations that prevent pioneers from gaining mainstream acceptance of their offerings (Figure 6). Thus, to be successful, an offering needs to "cross the chasm" between the early and the mainstream market.

Figure 6. Moore's Application of Rogers' Model to Technology Markets

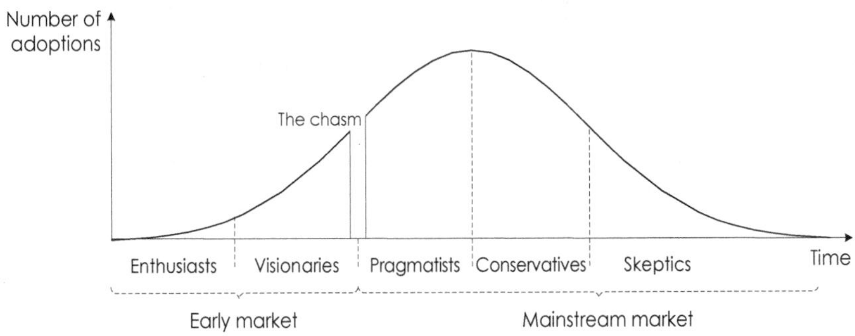

To avoid the perils of discontinuity of adoption of innovations, Moore's model suggests promoting innovations first to technology enthusiasts so that they help educate visionaries. Visionaries, in turn, are likely to serve as a reference for pragmatists, one of the two largest market segments. Leveraging its success with pragmatists, the company should be able to gain the know-how and achieve the economies of scale necessary to make the product reliable and inexpensive, allowing it to meet the needs of conservatives. With respect to skeptics, referred to as the "gadflies of high tech," the prescription is to let them be and not promote the innovation to them.

Despite the intuitive appeal of the idea that customers vary in terms of the speed and likelihood of adopting new technologies, Moore's model of technology adoption is subject to several important assumptions that limit the validity of its predictions. Dividing adopters into five distinct categories, as well as predefining the size of each category (e.g., enthusiasts/innovators are the first 2.5% of adopters), often involves an unrealistic assumption that does not apply to all high-tech innovations. This assumption is not an issue for Rogers' model, which assumes continuous adoption across different segments. In contrast, because the presence of gaps among segments is the cornerstone assumption of Moore's model, the identification and size of each segment are crucial. To illustrate, the assumption that a pronounced discontinuity (chasm) in the adoption process is likely to occur after 16% of customers (the "early market") have adopted the product is not likely to hold universally across different innovation types and industries. In the same vein, relative segment sizes are likely to be a function of the degree to which the technology appeals to the broader market. Indeed, certain types of innovations are likely to have much broader appeal than others and, as a result, the dynamics of their adoption patterns are likely to vary.

ADDITIONAL READINGS

Christensen, Clayton (1997), *The Innovator's Dilemma: When New Technologies Cause Great Firms to Fail.* Boston, MA: Harvard Business School Press.

Grieves, Michael (2006), *Product Lifecycle Management: Driving the Next Generation of Lean Thinking.* New York, NY: McGraw-Hill.

Rogers, Everett M. (2003), *Diffusion of Innovations* (5th ed.). New York, NY: Free Press.

NOTES

[1] Adapted from Levitt, Theodore (1965), "Exploit the Product Life Cycle," *Harvard Business Review*, 43, (November–December), 81–94.

[2] Adapted from Christensen, Clayton (1997), *The Innovator's Dilemma: When New Technologies Cause Great Firms to Fail.* Boston, MA: Harvard Business School Press.

[3] Rogers, Everett M. (1962), *Diffusion of Innovations.* New York, NY: Free Press.

[4] Moore, Geoffrey A. (1991), *Crossing the Chasm: Marketing and Selling High-Tech Products to Mainstream Customers.* New York, NY: HarperBusiness.

CHAPTER SEVENTEEN

MANAGING PRODUCT LINES

The essence of the beautiful is unity in variety.

—William Somerset Maugham, British novelist

Product line refers to a set of related offerings that function in a similar manner, are sold to the same target customers, and/or are distributed through the same channels. Product-line management aims to optimize the value delivered by the individual offerings that are contained in a company's product line. The key aspects of managing a company's product line—managing vertical and horizontal extensions, managing product-line cannibalization, and using product lines to gain and defend market position—are the focus of this chapter.

Product Lines as a Means for Creating Value

The increased fragmentation of many markets calls for developing customized offerings that create value for each individual segment. The times when a company can easily fulfill the needs of all its customers are long gone. To successfully compete in today's environment, a company must develop and manage a portfolio of offerings that targets the "long tail" of the market. Even companies that once were able to cover the market with a single product now find it imperative to extend and constantly reinvent their product lines to address the needs of different customer segments.

Product-line management calls for the company to shift its focus from optimizing the value it derives from a single offering to the bigger picture of optimizing the value it derives from the entire product line. Accordingly, an offering that is part of a product line might not create superior value for the company when considered by itself but instead might create value indirectly by complementing other offerings in the company's product line. In this context, product-line management involves more than optimizing the value it creates and receives from each individual offering; rather, it should optimize the value of the entire product line. Accordingly, the key principle in creating and managing product lines is that the offerings—considered individually and as a whole—should be optimally positioned to create superior value for each of the relevant market participants: the company, its target customers, and its collaborators.

Product lines can create value for each of the market entities in the value exchange: target customers, the company, and its collaborators. The means by which product lines create market value are outlined in more detail below.

Product lines can benefit the *company* by creating additional sources of revenue and profits as well as by supporting other profitable and/or strategically important offerings. Product lines can also increase the adoption of individual offerings by distribution channels that seek a single supplier to provide the entire range of products sought by its customers. Product lines can also create value for the company by helping it deal with the competition. Thus, product lines can help a company deter market entry by new competitors, which are less likely to target customers whose needs are already fulfilled by an existing offering. In addition, product lines can "crowd out" existing competitors by taking up premiere shelf space in distribution channels featuring the company's entire product line.

Product lines also benefit *customers* by offering a better match between a customer's preferences and the benefits provided by the company's offerings: The more extensive a company's product line, the greater the chance that each individual customer will find the "ideal" option. Product lines also benefit customers who seek to explore new options and who might otherwise choose a competitor's offering because they feel that their choice is constrained by a limited roster of options.

Product lines can also benefit *collaborators* by enabling the company to customize its offering for the specific needs of different collaborators. For example, product lines can help channel partners—manufacturers and distributors—manage their relationships. Specifically, product lines can help minimize conflicts that are likely to occur among distribution channels (e.g., mass-market retailers and specialty stores) that offer the same product at different price points to the same customers. Manufacturers can address such conflicts (also referred to as horizontal channel conflicts) by developing product lines comprising different versions of the same product that vary on minor attributes (color, packaging, and optional features), which makes their offerings in different distribution channels difficult to compare.

Despite its multiple benefits, product lines have several important drawbacks. From a company's perspective, product lines lead to an increase in product development, production, distribution, and management costs. There is also the potential danger that instead of stimulating new customer demand, the new offerings will ultimately cannibalize sales of the company's existing offerings. Increasing the number of available options can also lead to customer confusion stemming from the inability to choose among the options. Indeed, although the premise for offering a greater variety of options is that it allows consumers to identify the "ideal" option, in cases when consumers do not have well-defined preferences, offering more choice can backfire, leading to greater confusion. As a result, buyers might defer their choice or choose a competitor's offering that provides greater simplicity of choice. Finally, product-line proliferation might face resistance from channel partners' profit-optimization strategy to carry only the most profitable offerings from competing manufacturers rather than the company's entire product line (also referred to as vertical channel conflict; see Chapter 7 for more details).

A key principle of managing product lines is that each individual offering should be optimized with respect to a particular target segment, such that each offering has its own unique value proposition that fits the needs of a particular customer segment. When offerings are too similar to one another, they are likely to end up targeting the same needs of the same customers, which, in turn, inevitably leads to cannibalization (discussed in more detail later in this chapter). Thus, the primary rationale for extending a company's product line is the presence of customers for whom the company can create value with its new offering.

The logic of a company's product line can be illustrated using a typical positioning map (see Chapter 4 for more details), which represents customers' beliefs about the relative performance of the offerings in the company's product line (rather than that of competitive offerings) on the two most important attributes. Such a product-line positioning map is illustrated in Figure 1, which shows the perceived benefits provided by each offering in the company's product line (the black dot) as well as the offering's target customers (the circle around the dot). Here larger circles represent the size of each customer segment, whereby larger segments typically display greater heterogeneity due to the mere fact that they comprise a greater number of customers.

Figure 1. Product-Line Positioning Map

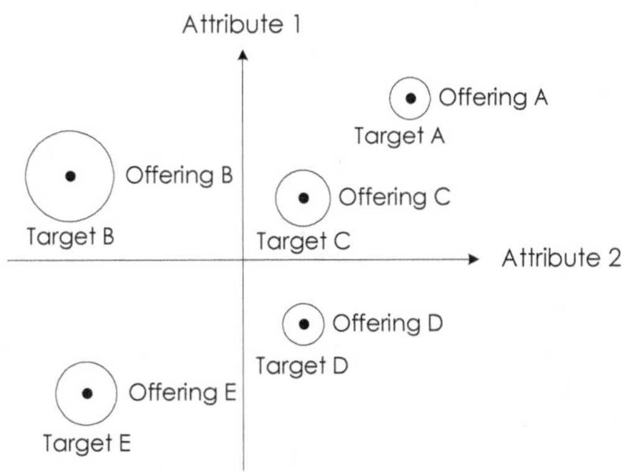

The product-line positioning map is complemented by an attribute value map, which goes beyond the two-attribute representation of the positioning map to provide a multi-attribute scenario illustrating the performance of the individual offerings on *all* relevant attributes (Figure 2). Such a representation allows a more accurate picture of the similarities and differences across the product-line offerings on all relevant attributes. To succeed in creating value for customers, the company, and its collaborators, the attribute-value profile of each offering should match the needs of the targeted customer segment.

Figure 2. Product-Line Attribute Value Map

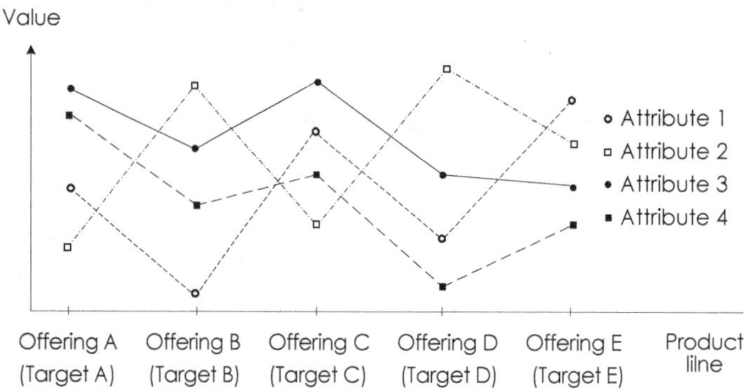

To ensure that the company's offerings are not only optimally positioned in the context of the company's product line but are also superior to the competition, product-line positioning and attribute value maps can include competitive offerings. In fact, competitive positioning and value maps can be viewed as a more general case of product-line maps because product-line offerings "compete" with one another for a share of a customer's wallet. Accordingly, product-line differentiation is as important as competitive differentiation.

Note that while in the majority of cases each offering must be designed to address a unique customer need, in some cases the offerings in a company's product line can deliberately target the same need of the same customer in order to satisfy the customer's desire for variety. Thus, in addition to being uniquely appealing to different customer segments, offerings that are differentiated on relatively minor attributes (e.g., flavor, scent, and/or color) are often designed to target the same customer in order to fulfill this customer's variety-seeking behavior.

Product lines can create value not only for target customers but also for the company collaborators. Consider an offering that is sold through multiple channels with different levels of service and cost structures. Because retailers vary in their profit-maximization strategies, those following a high-volume/low-margin strategy end up pricing the product lower than those following a low-volume/high-margin strategy. This differential pricing is likely to lead to a conflict (referred to as a horizontal channel conflict), whereby shoppers at the high-end channel are likely to be displeased by the fact that they could have purchased the same item at a lower price elsewhere. One strategy for addressing this problem involves extending a company's product line to include higher end versions of its offering to be sold exclusively at high-end retailers and lower end versions to be sold at low-end retailers. Thus, by developing a collaborator-focused product line, the company can use product lines to optimize the market value of its offerings.

A common approach to building product lines involves starting with a single offering and then adding other offerings, commonly referred to as product-line extensions. Depending on the relationship between the incumbent offering and the added offering, product-line extensions can be divided into two types: vertical and horizontal. These two types of extensions are discussed in more detail in the following sections.

Managing Vertical Product-Line Extensions

Vertical product-line extensions involve adding new offerings in different price tiers, such that some of the newly added offerings deliver a higher level of benefits at a higher price (in the case of upscale vertical extensions) whereas others deliver a lower level of benefits at a lower price (in the case of downscale vertical extensions). The two types of vertical extensions—upscale and downscale—are illustrated in Figure 3 and discussed in more detail below.

Figure 3. Vertical Product-Line Extensions

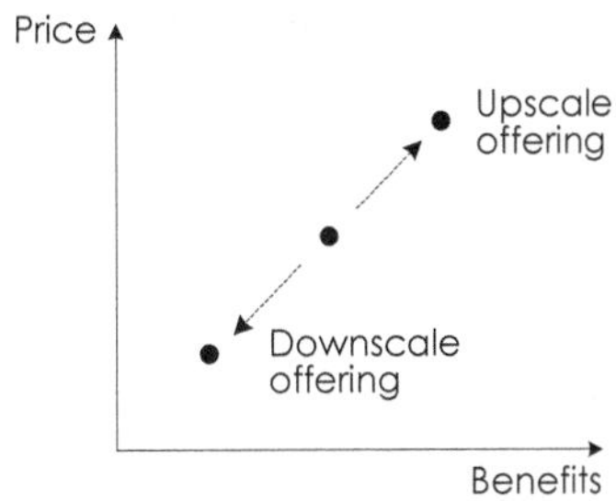

Upscale Product-Line Extensions

Upscale extensions involve extending the company's product line by adding an offering that delivers a higher level of benefits at a higher price. One of the main reasons for introducing an upscale extension is that it enables a company to capture a more lucrative, higher margin market. For example, to gain a foothold in the growing market for professional tools, leading home improvement company Black & Decker introduced DeWalt—a line of professional, high-end power tools. Upscale extensions are often used to follow customers through different stages of their life cycle by creating offerings that fit their evolving needs and changing buying power. For example, building on the success of its low-priced cars, Volkswagen introduced the more upscale Jetta, Passat, and Phaeton, aimed at customers who seek larger, better performing vehicles.

In addition to providing access to higher end markets, upscale extensions can provide synergies with existing offerings. For example, adding an upscale offering can lift the image of the lower end offerings in the company's product line. Thus, by introducing a line of premium, award-winning Gallo-branded wines, E. & J. Gallo Winery helped strengthen the image of its lower end offerings. Companies also introduce upscale extensions to gain a competitive advantage in developing advanced technologies. For example, car manufacturers often develop high-performance versions of their vehicles to strengthen their core competencies and further the advancement of technologies that can be used in their mass-produced lower end models.

Despite their multiple advantages, upscale extensions present numerous challenges. Developing upscale offerings usually requires specific resources that a company specialized in lower tier offerings might not readily possess. The lack of such resources might prevent a company from developing an offering that can successfully compete in the upscale market. For example, launching an upscale apparel brand requires a variety of specific resources, such as knowledge of fashion trends, product development know-how, high-end manufacturing capabilities, a reputable brand, and access to specialized suppliers and upscale distribution channels that a lower end manufacturer might not have.

Because most companies do not readily have the resources necessary to introduce higher quality offerings, "organic" upscale extensions (internally developed by the company) usually take time to implement and are not very common. Instead, companies often gain access to upscale markets by acquiring existing high-end offerings. This acquisition strategy is illustrated by Fiat's entry into the racing car market with the acquisition of Ferrari, Gap's purchase of Banana Republic, and Marriott's acquisition of Ritz-Carlton.

Downscale Product-Line Extensions

Downscale extensions involve extending the company's product line by adding an offering that delivers a lower level of benefits at a lower price. Downscale extensions are driven by a company's desire to increase its customer base by attracting less affluent customers who are currently not served by its offerings. Examples of downscale extensions include Armani's launch of Armani Exchange, Mercedes' introduction of the A-class, and Gap's introduction of Old Navy stores.

The main appeal of downscale extensions is the high volume of sales resulting from serving customers in lower socioeconomic tiers. Downscale extensions also enable companies to gain access to customers early in their life cycle by providing a lower entry point for a company's offerings. For example, Audi and BMW's "1" series cars provide access to younger customers, who despite current constrained resources are likely to evolve into a lucrative customer segment in the future.

Downscale extensions are especially beneficial to companies operating in industries requiring high fixed-cost investments—such as the airline, hotel, and automotive industries—in which economies of scale might be achieved. For example, many upscale car manufacturers—including Mercedes, BMW, and Porsche—have opted to use their design and manufacturing resources to develop downscale product offerings. Downscale extensions are quite popular among managers seeking to achieve quick results because they build on the company's existing resources and are often easier to implement than upscale extensions.

Despite their numerous advantages, downscale extensions have a number of significant drawbacks. A key concern is the threat of cannibalization of higher end offerings by the downscale extension (discussed in more detail later in this chapter). In cases when the extension carries the same brand as the upscale offering, the downscale offering can also weaken the brand by creating undesirable associations with a low-quality/low-priced offering. Another area of concern is that downscale extensions yield lower margins compared to higher end offerings and, as a result, they need to generate substantial sales volume to be profitable. Furthermore, serving price-conscious customers can be challenging because these customers tend to be less loyal than performance-focused customers.

Managing Horizontal Product-Line Extensions

Offerings in a horizontally differentiated product line typically belong to the same price tier and differ primarily in the type of benefits they offer (Figure 4). Unlike vertical extensions, in which the different levels of offering benefits can be clearly ordered in terms of their attractiveness (e.g., Ritz-Carlton is likely to be regarded as more attractive than Marriott), horizontal extensions do not imply such universal preference ordering. Instead, horizontal extensions are differentiated on benefits that are idiosyncratic and are likely to vary in their attractiveness across customers. For example, different designs, styles, colors, and flavors are likely to appeal to different tastes without necessarily implying differential pricing. Thus, even though prices might vary across horizontally differentiated offerings, they are not the key differentiating factor.

Figure 4. Horizontal Product-Line Extensions

Horizontal extensions create value by providing customers with offerings that better match their preferences. Unlike vertical extensions, which provide a better preference match at different price–quality tiers, horizontal extensions aim to accommodate customers' tastes within a given price–quality tier. By providing an assortment of diverse options, horizontal extensions help companies fulfill the needs of customers with different tastes while at the same time satisfying the variety-seeking behavior of these customers. For example, Colgate-Palmolive, Procter & Gamble, and Unilever have introduced more than 100 varieties of toothpaste to appeal to consumers' diverse tastes while providing individual customers with a greater variety of options to choose from.

Because they draw on a company's existing resources, horizontal extensions are often easier to implement than vertical extensions. Moreover, because they are sold at similar price points and have a similar cost structure, horizontal extensions have profit margins comparable to those of the existing offerings, thus eliminating any cannibalization concerns—a key advantage over downscale extensions.

Despite their multiple advantages, horizontal extensions have several important drawbacks. A key concern is the cost efficiency of offering horizontal extensions. Indeed, because it is difficult to identify customers who share a particular taste, companies need to make their entire product line available to consumers so that they can self-select the options that fit their taste. The problem with this approach is that making the entire product line available to all customers can be resource intensive and ultimately cost inefficient. In addition to increasing the company's costs, extensive assortments of similar options can lead to customer confusion and choice deferral, especially in cases when customers are unable to readily ascertain which of the available options best matches their preferences.

Managing Product-Line Cannibalization

When extending its product line, a company expects that the new offerings will generate additional sales by stealing share from the competition or bringing new users into the category. Ideally, all the sales generated by the new offering will come from competitors' offerings or from growing the overall category (Figure 5B). In reality, however, this is rarely the case. A common side effect of launching a new offering is that in addition to stealing share from competitors it takes away share from a company's current offerings, a process commonly referred to as cannibalization (Figure 5C).

Figure 5: Product-Line Cannibalization

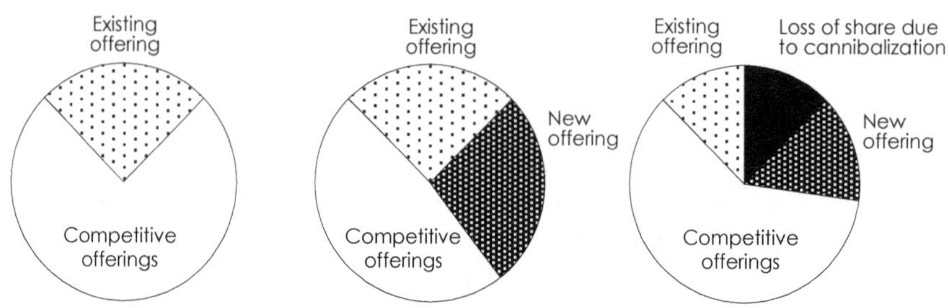

A. Single-offering scenario B. Dual-offering scenario without cannibalization C. Dual-offering scenario with cannibalization

Cannibalization describes a scenario in which the sales of one of the company's offerings come at the expense of the sales of another offering. The presence of cannibalization is not always indicative of a problem in the company's strategy and, accordingly, is not always a cause for concern. In fact, on certain occasions a company might actively seek to cannibalize the sales of some of its offerings. For example, a market leader launching a "new and improved" version of its flagship product has no choice but to cannibalize its current flagship offering. Such was the case with the introduction of the five-bladed Gillette Fusion, which inevitably cannibalized the sales of the three-bladed Gillette Mach3.

Cannibalization is a primary concern in the case of downscale product-line extensions because they typically have lower profit margins than the offerings they are likely to cannibalize. To minimize the possibility of cannibalization, a company needs to ensure that its downscale extension is substantially differentiated from the existing offerings. This means that differentiation on price must also involve differentiation on benefits, such that lower price is associated with a lower level of benefits. When the new offering provides the same benefits as the incumbent offering but at a lower price, customers have no reason to prefer the higher priced offering and will ultimately gravitate toward the lower priced extension. Meaningful differentiation is key to sidestepping cannibalization.

The importance of differentiation in vertical product-line extensions can be illustrated by examining the dispersion of the price-benefit tradeoffs across the different offerings in a company's product line (Figure 6). Here, the value-equivalence line represents offerings for which the ratio of perceived benefits and perceived price is the same: higher benefit, higher priced offerings are toward the upper right; lower benefit, lower priced offerings are toward the lower left. Ideally, all offerings should lie on the value-equivalence line (e.g., offerings A, B, and C). In reality, however, offerings might vary in the value they deliver to customers; some offerings (e.g., offerings E and F) deliver superior value (higher benefits at a lower price), whereas others (e.g., offering D) deliver inferior value (lower benefits at a higher price). These value discrepancies are likely to influence the market shares of the offerings, such that value-advantaged options are likely to gain share, whereas value-disadvantaged options are likely to be share losers. This implies that, over time, the sales of offerings A, B, and D are likely to be cannibalized by the sales of offerings E, F, and C, respectively (provided that customers seek a certain level of benefits and then search for the lowest price for these benefits).

Figure 6: Product-Line Cannibalization and the Price-Benefit Tradeoff

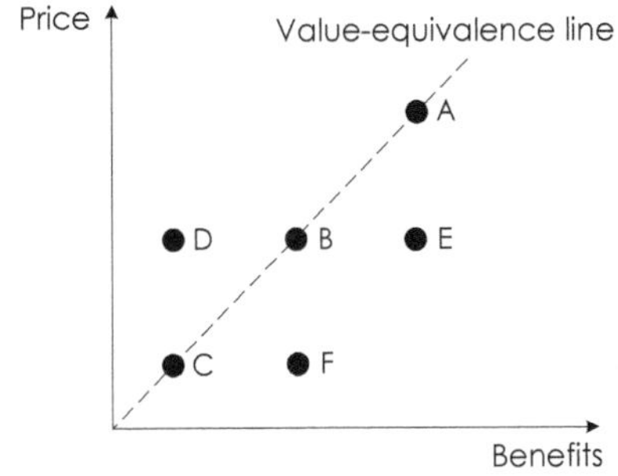

When differentiating its downscale extension, a company walks a fine line between curbing potential cannibalization by ensuring that the downscale extension is not more attractive than the incumbent offering and building the market for the downscale extension by bolstering its appeal, sometimes to the detriment of the incumbent offering. In its desire to minimize cannibalization, a company can stretch its downscale extension so far that it becomes inferior to those of its direct competitors. For example, in an effort to avoid cannibalization, Intel overstretched its downscale extension, Celeron, making it inferior to its low-priced competitors AMD and Cyrix. Over-differentiation can also result from overpricing the lower end offering. For example, Gap Warehouse, the forerunner of Old Navy, failed because in an effort to avoid cannibalizing sales in Gap's core stores it set relatively high prices, which put it at a disadvantage relative to its direct competitors.

In general, cannibalization is of primary concern when the margins of the new offering are lower than those of the offering being cannibalized, whereby every time a customer buys the new, lower margin offering instead of the higher margin one, the company generates lower profits. A key question, therefore, is how much cannibalization a company can afford before the new offering produces a net loss. The maximum amount of cannibalization of an existing offering by a new one is given by a metric commonly referred to as the break-even rate of cannibalization. Specifically, the break-even rate of cannibalization indicates the maximum proportion of the new offering's sales volume that could come from the existing offering(s) without the company incurring a loss. Calculating break-even cannibalization rates is discussed in more detail at the end of this chapter.

Cannibalization by lower margin offerings (as in the case of poorly differentiated vertical extensions) is not the only way that profitability can be eroded through cannibalization; poorly differentiated horizontal extensions can result in cannibalization as well. Even when offerings in horizontal product-line extensions are priced at parity and have similar margins, in cases when increasing the number of offerings does not lead to a corresponding increase in sales volume, the overall profitability of the product line is likely to decrease because a larger number of company offerings is chasing the same number of customers. Thus, when the newly added offerings in a company's product line address the same need of the same target customer as the existing offerings, extending product lines ultimately leads to substitution rather stimulating new demand.

Managing Product Lines to Gain and Defend Market Position

In addition to creating value for target customers, product-line extensions can help companies gain and sustain market position. Three of the most popular competitive product-line strategies—the fighting-brand strategy, the sandwich strategy, and the good-better-best strategy—are outlined in more detail below.

The Fighting-Brand Strategy

A popular strategy to compete with low-priced rivals involves launching a fighting brand – an offering that matches or undercuts the competitor's price (Figure 7). For example, to compete with low-price rivals while preserving the market position of its flagship Marlboro brand, Philip Morris aggressively priced its Basic cigarette label, effectively making it a fighting brand. Similarly, Procter & Gamble launched Oxydol laundry detergent as a low-price alternative to its flagship brand Tide.

Figure 7. The Fighting-Brand Strategy

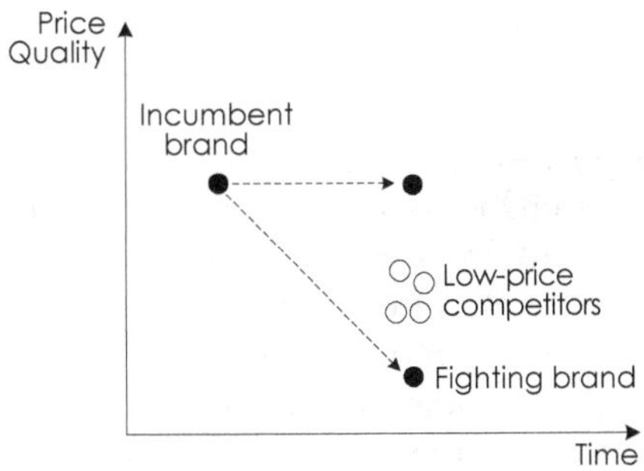

The fighting-brand strategy assumes a two-tiered market in which some buyers are quality focused and others are willing to sacrifice quality for price. In this context, the fighting-brand strategy involves introducing a lower priced, lower quality offering to address the needs of the price-conscious buyers while leaving intact the value proposition of the original offering. By recognizing the diversity (heterogeneity) of the underlying market, the fighting-brand strategy develops a new offering aimed at the price-sensitive customer segment.

The Sandwich Strategy

The sandwich strategy involves introducing a two-tier product line comprising a high-quality offering and a low-priced offering, effectively sandwiching low-priced competitors. This strategy is typically achieved by launching a downscale extension while simultaneously moving the existing offering upscale (Figure 8). For example, in anticipation of an inflow of cut-price competitors following the patent expiration of its blockbuster prescription drug Prilosec, AstraZeneca introduced a low-priced, over-the-counter version (Prilosec OTC) and at the same time replaced Prilosec with Nexium – a premium-priced and slightly more effective version of the drug.

Figure 8. The Sandwich Strategy

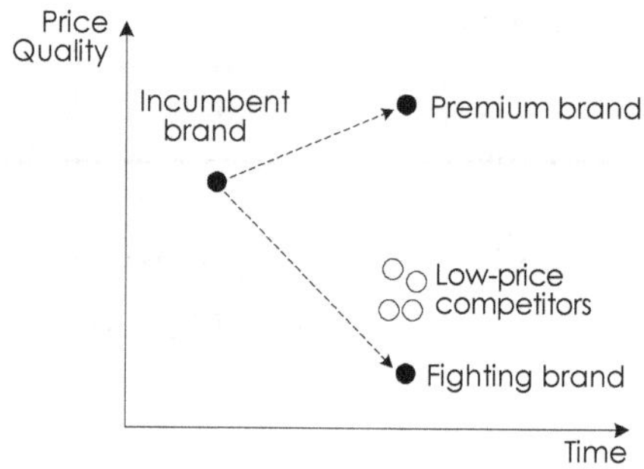

The sandwich strategy resembles the fighting-brand strategy because in both cases the incumbent brand introduces a low-priced offering. Despite their similarities, the sandwich strategy differs from the fighting-brand strategy in that in addition to introducing a downscale offering it also repositions the core offering by moving it upscale. The upscale repositioning of the incumbent offering in the sandwich strategy reflects the change in the target market following the introduction of low-price offerings by competitors. After the incumbent brand loses some of its price-sensitive customers to low-price rivals, the remaining customers are, on average, less price sensitive and more quality oriented. As a result, the incumbent brand is no longer optimally positioned to meet the needs of its target customers and can benefit from moving upscale.

The Good-Better-Best Strategy

The good-better-best strategy involves introducing a downscale offering (fighting brand) as well as an upscale offering (premium brand) while preserving the core brand. Thus, the good-better-best strategy is similar to the sandwich strategy in that it involves the introduction of a low-priced offering. However, instead of a two-tier product line that involves an upscale repositioning of the core brand, the good-better-best strategy calls for launching a new premium offering that yields a three-tier product line (Figure 9).

Figure 9. The Good-Better-Best Strategy

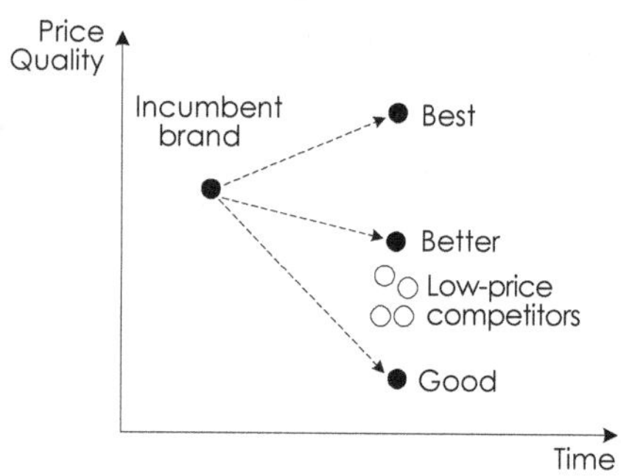

The good-better-best strategy can be illustrated with Apple's response to low-priced competitors of its iPod music player. Instead of directly competing with lower priced offerings, Apple extended its product line downscale by first introducing the iPod Nano and then the iPod Shuffle. iPod's good-better-best product line reflects Apple's view of the market as comprising three key segments: a segment seeking a fully functional player (iPod), a segment seeking basic functionality (iPod Nano), and a segment seeking a low-priced offering with limited functionality (iPod Shuffle). The good-better-best strategy also has been successfully employed by a number of other companies such as Microsoft (Works, Office Home Edition, and Office Professional), and Gap (Old Navy, Gap, and Banana Republic).

The good-better-best strategy works well in tiered markets comprising three key segments: a quality-focused segment, a price-focused segment, and a segment seeking a compromise between high quality and low price. In such three-tiered markets, the two-pronged sandwich strategy would not work because moving the core offering upscale without having a mid-tier option leaves the company vulnerable to competitive offerings of mid-point quality and price.

In addition to being an effective tool to fence off cut-price competitors in three-tiered markets, the good-better-best strategy can be used in markets in which buyers have uncertain preferences. In such markets, buyers tend to prefer options that offer a compromise among the extreme alternatives. To illustrate, when choosing from a set composed of a high-priced/high-quality brand, a low-priced/low-quality brand, and an average-priced/average-quality brand, buyers often select the middle option because it allows them to avoid trading off price and quality. Buyers' tendency to choose the middle option in the absence of articulated preferences has important implications for choosing a strategy to compete with low-priced rivals. In this case, trying to "sandwich" the low-priced brand by simply launching a fighting brand and moving the core brand upscale without offering a mid-priced/mid-quality option might backfire because the "sandwiched" competitor might benefit from becoming the compromise option.

SUMMARY

Product-line management aims to optimize the value delivered by the individual offerings in a company's product line. The development of offerings that are part of a company's product line is similar to the development of freestanding offerings, with the main difference being that in addition to developing a strategy to manage each individual offering, the company needs to develop a product-line strategy that delineates the relationships among the individual offerings in the company's product line.

A key principle of managing product lines is that each individual offering should be optimized with respect to a particular target segment, such that each offering has its own unique value proposition that fits the needs of a particular customer segment. In addition to creating value for target customers, offerings contained in a company's product line should create value for the other two entities participating in the market exchange: the company and its collaborators.

Depending on the relationships among the individual offerings in a company's product line, there are two types of extensions: vertical and horizontal. Vertical extensions involve adding new offerings that are in different price tiers. Because higher price is typically associated with better performance, vertically differentiated offerings differ in benefits such that more attractive offerings come at a higher price. Depending on the price tier of the newly added offering, there are two basic types of vertical extensions: upscale extensions in which the newly added offering is in a higher price tier and downscale extensions in which the new offering is in a lower price tier.

Horizontally differentiated offerings typically belong to the same price tier and differ primarily in the type of benefits they offer. Horizontal extensions create value by providing customers with offerings that better match their preferences. Unlike vertical extensions, which provide a better preference match at different price–quality tiers, horizontal extensions aim to accommodate customers' tastes within a given price–quality tier.

Cannibalization is a primary concern in the case of downscale extensions. The maximum amount of cannibalization of an existing offering by a new one is given by a metric commonly referred to as the break-even rate of cannibalization, which indicates the maximum proportion of the new offering's sales volume that could come from the existing offering(s) without the company incurring a loss.

In addition to creating value for target customers, product-line extensions can help companies gain and sustain market position. Three of the most popular competitive product-line strategies are the fighting-brand strategy, the sandwich strategy, and the good-better-best strategy.

Relevant Concepts: Break-Even Analysis of Cannibalization

The break-even rate of cannibalization indicates the maximum proportion of the sales volume of the new offering that could come from the company's existing offering(s) without incurring a loss. The break-even rate of cannibalization is calculated as the ratio of the cannibalized sales volume of the existing offering to the sales volume generated by the new offering at which a company neither makes a profit nor incurs a loss.[1]

$$BER_C = \frac{Margin_{NewOffering}}{Margin_{OldOffering}}$$

For example, consider a company launching a new product priced at \$70 with variable costs of \$60, which might cannibalize the sales of an existing product priced at \$100 that also has variable costs of \$60. In this case, $Margin_{NewOffering}$ = \$70 – \$60 = \$10 and $Margin_{OldOffering}$ = \$100 – \$60 = \$40. Therefore, the break-even rate of cannibalization can be calculated as follows:

$$BER_C = \frac{Margin_{NewOffering}}{Margin_{OldOffering}} = \frac{\$10}{\$40} = 0.25$$

The break-even rate of cannibalization in this case is 0.25 or 25%, which means that to be profitable to the company, no more than 25% of the sales volume of the new offering should come from the current offering, which in turn implies that at least 75% of the sales volume should come from competitors' offerings and/or from increasing the overall size of the market.

RELEVANT CONCEPTS: BEHAVIORAL ECONOMICS OF PRODUCT-LINE EXTENSIONS

Attraction Effect: People's tendency to evaluate options based on their relative advantage (rather than on their inherent values), whereby adding an option that is inferior relative to one of the options in the set tends to increase the choice share of the (relatively) superior option. Consider the case of Williams-Sonoma, which used to offer one home bread maker priced at $275. Later, it extended its product line by adding a second home bread maker that had similar features, was slightly larger size, and was priced more than 50% higher than the original bread maker. The company did not sell many of the new (relatively overpriced) bread makers, but the sales of the less expensive bread maker nearly doubled.[2]

Compromise Effect: People's tendency to avoid options with extreme values in favor of the option with moderate values on all attributes.[3]

Attribute-Balance Effect: People's tendency to evaluate options with equal values on key attributes as being less extreme (more "balanced") and, consequently, to choose these options when seeking a compromise. For example, consider three snacks; one has 6g fat and 6g sugar, the second one has 5g fat and 7g sugar, and the third one has 4g fat and 8g sugar. The first snack is typically viewed as the compromise option that offers the optimal balance of fat and sugar among the three options even though in reality it is an extreme option that has the highest amount of fat and the lowest amount of sugar (the "real" compromise option is the second snack).[4]

Diversification Effect: People's tendency to overestimate their future variety-seeking behavior. To illustrate, people tend to buy a greater variety of yogurt for future consumption than they do if they buy it on a day-to-day basis, when they tend to display much less variety seeking.[5]

ADDITIONAL READINGS

Jain, Dipak C. (2010), "The Sandwich Strategy: Managing New Products and Services for Value Creation and Value Capture," in *Kellogg on Marketing* (2nd ed.), Alice Tybout and Bobby Calder, Eds. New York, NY: John Wiley & Sons.

Kotler, Philip and Kevin Lane Keller (2011), *Marketing Management* (14th ed.). Upper Saddle River, NJ: Prentice Hall.

Lehmann, Donald R. and Russell S. Winer (2006), *Product Management* (4th ed.). Boston, MA: McGraw-Hill/Irwin.

NOTES

[1] The break-even rate of cannibalization can be derived as follows: To avoid loss of profit across all offerings, profit from the new product must be equal to or greater than the lost profits from cannibalization.

$$Profit_{NewOffering} \geq LostProfit_{OldOffering}$$

Because profit is a function of unit volume and unit margin, the above equation can be modified as follows:

$$Volume_{NewOffering} \cdot Margin_{NewOffering} \geq LostVolume_{OldOffering} \cdot Margin_{OldOffering}$$

The above equation can be restructured as follows:

$$\frac{LostVolume_{OldOffering}}{Volume_{NewOffering}} = \frac{Margin_{NewOffering}}{Margin_{OldOffering}}$$

The left part of the equation is the ratio of sales volume of the old offering that was lost because of cannibalization by the new offering, which is the definition of the break-even rate of cannibalization (BER_C). Hence:

$$BER_C = \frac{Margin_{NewOffering}}{Margin_{OldOffering}}$$

Note that the above equation assumes that the launch of the new offering is not associated with an increase in the fixed costs or that such costs—if they do exist—are included in the margins of the old and the new offering.

2 Simonson, Itamar (1999), "The Effect of Product Assortment on Buyer Preferences," *Journal of Retailing*, 75 (Autumn), 347-370.

3 Simonson, Itamar (1989), "Choice Based on Reasons: The Case of Attraction and Compromise Effects," *Journal of Consumer Research*, 16 (September), 158-174.

4 Chernev, Alexander (2004), "Extremeness Aversion and Attribute-Balance Effects in Choice," *Journal of Consumer Research*, 31 (September), 249-263.

5 Simonson, Itamar (1990), "The Effect of Purchase Quantity and Timing on Variety-Seeking Behavior," *Journal of Marketing Research*, 27 (May), 150-162.

Part Five

Strategic Marketing Workbooks

INTRODUCTION

There is nothing so useless as doing efficiently something that should not be done at all.

—Peter Drucker, founder of modern management theory

The first four parts of this book presented the key aspects of the theory of marketing and outlined a framework for applying this theory to marketing management. The application of this conceptual knowledge is facilitated by a set of tools that help managers accomplish commonly encountered business tasks, such as identifying target customers, designing a business model, and writing positioning statements. These three activities are briefly outlined below and discussed in more detail in the following chapters.

- **Identifying target customers** involves deciding which customers the company should tailor its offering to and which customers it should ignore. An algorithm for identifying target customers, which builds on the theory presented in Chapter 4, is outlined in Chapter 18.
- **Generating a business model** involves developing the key aspects of an offering's strategy and tactics. An algorithm for generating a business model, which builds on the theory presented in Chapter 2, is outlined in Chapter 19.
- **Writing a positioning statement** involves crafting a succinct outline of an offering's targeting and positioning strategy to inform all relevant entities about the essence of the company's value-creation model. The key aspects of developing a positioning statement, which build on the theory presented in Chapter 5, are the focus of Chapter 20.

A key aspect of the theory presented in this book—in addition to its streamlined, logical, and value-focused approach—is that it can be readily applied to help managers solve practical problems in a way that enables them to achieve their strategic goals. In this context, the three topics discussed in Part Five help bridge the marketing theory outlined earlier in this book with managerial practice.

CHAPTER EIGHTEEN

SEGMENTATION AND TARGETING WORKBOOK

Where your talents and the needs of the world cross, lies your calling.
—Aristotle, Greek philosopher

The process of segmentation and targeting can be formalized in an algorithm that outlines a sequence of steps a company should undertake in order to identify its "ideal" target customers. The algorithm outlining these steps is presented in this chapter.

Overview

Deciding which customers to serve is a defining aspect of a company's marketing strategy. It influences all other aspects of the target market—competitors, collaborators, the company's resources necessary to serve these customers, and the relevant economic, political, regulatory, sociocultural, and physical context in which the company operates. This interdependency of market factors involved in identifying target customers further complicates the targeting decision and highlights the importance of a systematic approach to targeting.

The process of identifying target customers can be described in terms of four key analyses: segmentation analysis, strategic targeting analysis, tactical targeting analysis, and customer strategy formulation. Each of these analyses comprises multiple factors that must be considered when choosing target customers. These factors, in turn, can be represented as a sequence of specific decisions delineating the process of identifying target customers. These specific decisions are summarized in Figure 1 and discussed in more detail in the following sections.

Figure 1. Identifying Target Customers: Key Steps

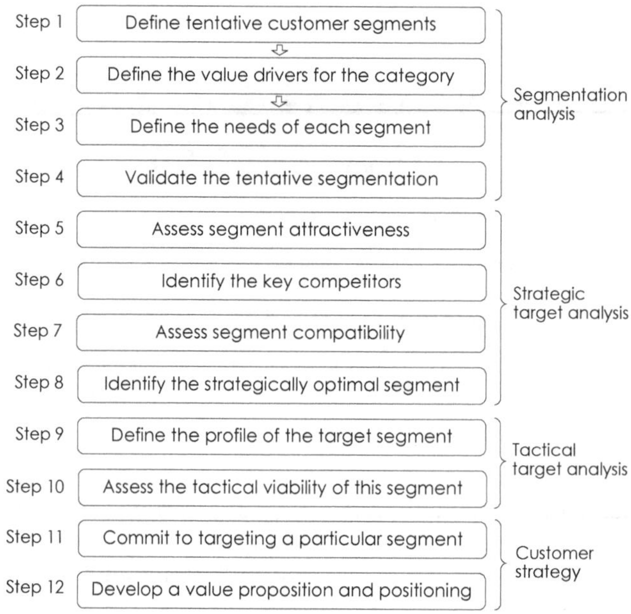

The process of identifying target customers is discussed in the context of a company-specific example, which illustrates the decisions involved at each step of the targeting analysis. The particular example (set in the early 1990s) involves Black & Decker, a large US manufacturer of power tools and accessories. Specifically, the discussion focuses on Black & Decker's analysis of its current customer base, the identification of the key customer segments, and the decision to single out one customer segment as having the greatest market potential.[1]

Segmentation Analysis

Segmentation analysis aims to group individual customers into segments in a way that facilitates targeting. Because the aim of targeting is to identify customers for whom the company can create superior value relative to the competition, value analysis is central to segmentation and targeting. The key steps involved in segmentation analysis are outlined in steps 1–4 below.

Step 1: Define Tentative Customer Segments

A common approach to segmentation is to start by identifying tentative customer segments based on the value they are likely to seek from a given product category. A good starting point is to ask the following value-related questions: *What are the reasons that motivate customers' purchases? On what occasions do customers purchase from this product category? What needs are customers trying to fulfill?* The goal of these questions is to identify tentative market segments—that is, groups of customers who are very similar in their buying behavior within each segment and at the same time are very different across segments.

Defining tentative segments is often a trial-and-error process that stems from a manager's intuition about the different types of buyers in a given market. Accordingly, the goal of the ensuing analysis (Steps 2–4) is to validate this intuitive segmentation by developing a deeper understanding of the needs of each of the identified segments to ensure that they indeed represent different groups of customers.

EXAMPLE: In Black & Decker's case, a manager might ask why and on which occasions buyers need power tools. The answer to this question might yield two groups of customers: *consumers*—buyers who use power tools around the house, and *commercial*—buyers who purchase power tools for business use. These two segments represent Black & Decker's tentative market segmentation, which will be enriched (in terms of content) and validated (in terms of its ability to facilitate targeting) in Steps 2–4.

Step 2: Define the Value Drivers for the Category

The next step involves identifying the value drivers—the relevant attributes that buyers consider when making a choice. When identifying the value drivers, it is important to ensure that they are indeed *relevant*, meaning that buyers definitely consider them when making a choice, and *comprehensive*, meaning that all relevant attributes are identified and included in the analysis. Furthermore, the attributes must be *specific* rather than a broad combination of multiple attributes. For example, "reliability" is a specific attribute, whereas "quality" is not because it typically refers to the combination of all nonprice attributes. Finally, attributes must be *uncorrelated* (independent) to avoid double-counting the effects of individual attributes. For example, "precision" and "accuracy" are likely to overlap in meaning and hence produce similar evaluations.

EXAMPLE: In Black & Decker's case, analysis reveals five key attributes—power, reliability, service, brand image, and price—that define the key factors typically considered by buyers when making a choice. These are the attributes on which Black & Decker will have to create superior value (relative to the other power tool manufacturers) for its target customers.

Step 3: Define the Needs of Each Segment

Following the identification of the relevant value drivers (attributes) is the identification of their relative importance for each of the tentative customer segments. The analysis performed at this step provides deeper insights into the value sought by each segment.

A practical approach to defining the value sought by each segment involves rating the importance of each attribute for all of the tentatively identified segments.

For example, one might use a three-point rating scale with levels "high," "moderate," and "low," where "high" indicates that a particular attribute is very important to a given segment and "low' indicates that it is relatively unimportant. Note that the three-point scale described here is for illustration purposes only; any scale that rank orders the importance of different attributes can work. In general, the more nuanced the scale, the greater its ability to detect relatively minor differences among segments.

Note also that not all of the identified value drivers might differentiate the segments: some attributes might be equally important to all segments. For example, durability might be considered an important factor by all segments, whereas color might be viewed as relatively unimportant by all. This is not problematic; it merely indicates that these attributes are non-diagnostic with respect to the ability to differentiate among the tentatively identified segments.

EXAMPLE: In Black & Decker's case, power and reliability are very important for commercial buyers but are of much lower importance to consumers who care most about price and are moderately concerned with the brand of the power tools they buy (Table 1). The importance of service, brand, and price for commercial users, however, is much more difficult to pinpoint. Thus, there are valid reasons to argue that these three attributes are relatively unimportant to these buyers and there are valid reasons to argue that they are extremely important. (This variance is addressed in the next step of analysis.)

Table 1. Customer Value Analysis Matrix (Black & Decker)

Attributes	Customer segments	
	Consumer	Commercial
Power	Low	High
Reliability	Low	High
Service	Low	Medium - High
Brand image	Medium	Low - High
Price	High	Low - Medium

Step 4: Validate the Tentative Segmentation

The next step is to ensure that the tentatively identified segments can indeed serve as the basis for identifying target customers. Specifically, this involves validating that market segments are *homogeneous* (meaning that customers in that segment have similar needs and preferences), *mutually exclusive* (meaning that customers with similar needs and preferences are assigned to a single segment), and *collectively exhaustive* (meaning that segments are comprehensive, such that each customer is assigned to a segment and there are no "unassigned" customers).

Given that the starting point of analysis (Step 1) was an intuitively derived segmentation, it is quite possible that the first attempt at identifying viable market segments does not conform to these criteria. In such cases, one must go back to the "drawing board" (Step 1) and revise the initial segmentation in a way that meets the above criteria. The number of iterations to achieve a valid segmentation depends largely on a manager's experience and knowledge of the particular market. Some managers might derive the "right" segmentation from the beginning, whereas others less experienced and less familiar with the market might go through several iterations to arrive at a valid customer segmentation.

EXAMPLE: In Black & Decker's case, the consumer/commercial segmentation does not meet the validity criteria because the commercial segment exhibits significant variation in the importance that customers in this segment assign to service, brand image, and price (shown in Figure 2). This means that this segment is not homogeneous and needs to be segmented further to produce homogeneous segments that have minimal within-segment variance in customer needs. The subsequent analysis reveals that the commercial segment comprises two subsegments: *tradesmen*—small businesses and independent contractors, such as carpenters, plumbers, and electricians working in residential construction—using power tools on the job; and *industrial buyers,* such as companies that purchase power tools for employee use. The resulting segments are fairly homogeneous with respect to customer preferences within each segment and yet reflect significant differences across customers in these segments (Table 2).

Table 2. Customer Value Analysis Matrix (Black & Decker: Revised)

Attributes	Customer segments		
	Consumer	Tradesman	Industrial
Power	Low	High	High
Reliability	Low	High	High
Service	Low	High	Medium
Brand	Medium	High	Low
Price	High	Low	Medium

The customer value analysis summarized in Table 2 shows that whereas customers in the two commercial segments—tradesmen and industrial buyers—share the belief that power and reliability are paramount, tradesmen place much greater importance on brand image and service. Thus, having fast diagnostic and repair service provided by the manufacturer is more important for tradesman than for industrial buyers, many of whom have internal service support. Furthermore, having tools that carry a professional brand not readily promoted to consumers can help enhance the professional image of tradesmen and is more important to them than to the industrial buyer, who is purchasing the power tools for use by employees on commercial projects. Finally, the larger volume purchased by industrial buyers is likely to make them more price sensitive than the tradesman, who is often buying a single tool.

Strategic Targeting Analysis

Once the key target segments have been identified, the next step is to assess the strategic viability of the individual segments. This involves evaluating the attractiveness and compatibility of each segment in terms of the company's ability to create superior value for this segment as well as capture value in a way that enables the company to reach its strategic goals.

Step 5: Assess Segment Attractiveness

Segment attractiveness reflects a segment's ability to create value for the company. Evaluating segment attractiveness aims to answer the question of whether a particular segment has the resources to create value for the company and whether it can create greater value than the non-chosen segments. Segment attractiveness is company specific: a segment considered appealing by some companies can be viewed as unappealing by others.

The evaluation of segment attractiveness is based on the assessment of two types of value: monetary value, which reflects a segment's ability to generate profits for the company, and strategic value, which reflects a segment's ability to create nonmonetary benefits that are of strategic importance for the company. Because monetary and strategic value is often expressed in terms of different metrics, converting all types of value into the same metric (e.g., monetizing nonmonetary benefits and costs) can facilitate the evaluation of the viability of the different segments.

A practical approach to assessing segment attractiveness involves evaluating each segment with respect to its ability to create monetary and strategic value for the company. For example, one might use a three-point rating scale with levels "high," "moderate," and "low," where "high" indicates that a particular segment is extremely attractive and "low" indicates that it is relatively unattractive. Note that the three-point scale described here is for illustration purposes only; a more nuanced scale is more likely to detect relatively minor differences in segment attractiveness.

EXAMPLE: In the Black & Decker case, the analysis reveals that all three segments—consumer, tradesmen, and industrial—are attractive with respect to their ability to create value for the company. At the same time, even though the tradesmen segment is the fastest growing of the three segments, Black & Decker's share of that segment is significantly lower compared to that of the other two segments. Accordingly, the tradesmen segment is viewed as presenting the greatest market opportunity and is rated as a priority for Black & Decker.

Step 6: Identify the Key Competitors

Following the analysis of segment attractiveness is evaluating segment compatibility—that is, the degree to which the company can create superior value for this segment. In order to provide this assessment, however, one needs to know the competitive context in which customers will evaluate the company's offering.

Therefore, the first step in evaluating segment compatibility involves identifying the competitors for each of the identified customer segments.

Because customer segments were chosen based on their needs, each segment has a different set of competitors aiming to fulfill its specific needs. Accordingly, competitive analysis is focused on the segment that has been prioritized by the company as being the most attractive. (Similar analysis needs to be conducted for all segments that are evaluated as potential targets.)

EXAMPLE: Black & Decker's top competitors for the tradesman segment include Makita (the market leader with nearly a 50% share), Milwaukee Tools, and Ryobi.

Step 7: Assess Segment Compatibility

Once relevant competitors have been identified, the next step is to evaluate the company's ability to fulfill the needs of each target segment better than the competition. In cases when the company already has an existing market offering, segment compatibility can be assessed by evaluating this offering relative to the competition on each of the relevant attributes (identified in Step 2). For example, one might use a three-point rating scale with levels "high," "moderate," and "low," where "high" indicates that a particular offering performs very well on a given attribute and "low" indicates that it performs rather poorly (although a more nuanced scale can offer greater accuracy). In cases when the company does not have an existing market offering and/or when its offering fails to create superior value for target customers, the company needs to assess whether its resources enable it to create superior value for target customers relative to the competition. Specifically, common resources include business infrastructure and collaborator networks, human capital, intellectual property, strong brands, established customer base, synergistic offerings, access to scarce resources, and access to capital.

In cases when the company has the resources necessary to create superior value for a given segment, this segment is deemed compatible, whereas in cases when the company is lacking resources to create value for this segment, it is incompatible and should not be targeted by the company. In the same vein, if the company's existing market offering fails to create superior value for its target customers but the company has the resources to improve its offering in a way that will appeal to its target market, this segment is deemed compatible. In contrast, when the company lacks resources to improve its current offering to create superior customer value, this segment is incompatible and should not be targeted by the company.

EXAMPLE: In Black & Decker's case, analysis of the compatibility of the tradesman segment involves evaluating the performance of Black & Decker's offerings vis-à-vis its key competitors—Makita, Milwaukee Tools, and Ryobi—on each of the attributes identified in Step 2. The resulting attribute performance matrix is given in Table 3. The customer analysis ratings depicted in Table 3 reflect the importance of each attribute to the particular customer segment (tradesman), and competitive analysis ratings reflect the performance of each competitor on these attributes.

Table 3. Segment Compatibility Analysis (Black & Decker)

Attributes	Customer analysis	Competitive analysis			
	Tradesman	B&D	Makita	Milwaukee	Ryobi
Power	High	Medium	High	High	Medium
Reliability	High	High	High	High	High
Service	High	Medium	Medium	Medium	Low
Brand	High	Low	High	High	Low
Price	Low	Medium	High	High	Medium

The analysis depicted in Table 3 shows that Black & Decker is at parity with its key competitors in terms of reliability and service, and is lagging Makita and Milwaukee Tools in terms of power and brand image. With respect to price—an attribute that is of relatively low importance to tradesmen—Black & Decker is superior to Makita and Milwaukee Tools and on a par with Ryobi. This analysis suggests that to be at parity with the competition in the tradesman segment, Black & Decker must increase the power of its offerings and dramatically improve its brand image. Furthermore, Black & Decker could create a competitive advantage in terms of service, which would put it ahead of the competition. Finally, given the relatively low importance of price to the target segment, maintaining a price advantage over Makita and Milwaukee Tools, while potentially beneficial, is not likely to be a key differentiating factor.

To improve its performance on the three dimensions on which it fails to create superior customer value—power, service, and brand image—Black & Decker needs to deploy resources necessary to improve its offerings to the tradesman. Analysis reveals that Black & Decker has the relevant resources, including its existing business infrastructure (manufacturing facilities), collaborator networks (suppliers and distributors), human capital (expert engineers, sales force, and customer service personnel), and access to capital. Furthermore, Black & Decker's brand portfolio contains DeWalt, a stationary woodworking equipment brand that, although relatively narrow in scope, is highly regarded by the tradesman. Accordingly, even though Black & Decker's current offering is not optimal for the tradesman segment, the company has the necessary resources to create value for this segment.

Step 8: Select the Strategically Optimal Segment

Following analysis of the attractiveness and compatibility of the identified segments is the selection of the most strategically viable segment. This involves selecting the target segment that best meets the attractiveness and compatibility criteria.

Deciding on the viability of each segment typically involves a binary (yes/no) decision indicating whether the company will pursue a particular set of customers. Note that in some cases a company might decide to pursue a strategically important segment even though it does not readily have the resources necessary to create superior value for these customers. In such cases, the company's decision to target this segment is predicated on its ability to build the deficient resources—a strategy that typically involves the investment of significant resources and/or a longer time horizon.

EXAMPLE: From a strategic perspective, tradesmen are the most attractive segment for Black & Decker. However, to successfully target the tradesman segment, Black & Decker must improve its offerings on two key dimensions—power and brand image. Improving the brand image is crucial because this is one of the attributes that target customers care most about and on which Black & Decker's brand is viewed to be vastly inferior to its top two competitors. Improving the power is also imperative given its primary importance to target customers and competitors' advantage on that dimension. Furthermore, because tradesmen view service as a top priority, Black & Decker might also consider improving its service even though it is at parity with the competition. Provided that it can improve its performance on these attributes, Black & Decker can go forward with allocating company resources to pursue this segment.

Tactical Targeting Analysis

Following the selection of a strategically viable segment is the identification of effective and cost-efficient ways to reach this segment. This step involves defining the readily observable characteristics (profile) of the strategically viable target segment and evaluating the tactical viability of pursuing this segment.

Step 9: Define the Profile of the Strategically Optimal Target Segment

The goal of this step is to identify the readily observable characteristics (profile) of the strategically chosen segment that can be used to communicate and deliver the offering in an effective and cost-efficient manner. This is important because without knowing the profile of its target segment a company faces the risk of not reaching all target customers and/or reaching them in a cost-inefficient manner.

The customer profile involves two types of factors: *demographic factors,* such as age, gender, income, level of education, ethnicity, social class, stage in the life cycle, employment status, household size, and geographic location, and *behavioral factors,* such as purchase quantity, frequency of repurchase, price sensitivity, promotion sensitivity (e.g., customer response to incentives), loyalty, communication format (e.g., the type of media most frequently utilized by customers), and distribution channel (e.g., the retail format preferred by the customer).

EXAMPLE: Black & Decker's goal here is to identify observable demographic and/or behavioral characteristics of the tradesman target segment that can be used to communicate and deliver its offerings. For example, tradesmen read industry magazines, such as *Builder* and *Electrical Contractor;* visit builder trade shows; and frequent home improvement stores.

Step 10: Assess the Tactical Viability of the Strategically Optimal Segment

Following identification of the target segment's profile is assessment of the tactical viability of serving this segment. Specifically, the goal here is to evaluate the overall feasibility of targeting a particular segment with respect to the company's ability to reach this segment in a cost-efficient manner. This step takes into account the availability of communication and distribution channels to reach this segment as well as the cost of gaining access to such channels. The tactical viability analysis ultimately produces a binary (yes/no) decision.

Note that for communication and distribution purposes the strategically selected segment can often be divided into subsegments reflecting different channels for reaching these customers with company communications and delivering the offering. Such fragmentation of the strategic target is likely to occur when this segment, although homogeneous with respect to the underlying needs and resources is, nevertheless, heterogeneous with respect to ways of reaching customers for communication and distribution purposes.

EXAMPLE: Black & Decker's goal is to assess the existence of effective and cost-efficient ways to communicate and deliver its offerings to the tradesman segment based on the profile of the segment. To accomplish this, Black & Decker might advertise in industry magazines, such as *Builder* and *Electrical Contractor,* that are favored by the tradesman, promote the product in trade shows, as well as use point-of-purchase displays at home improvement retailers. To make its products readily available to the tradesman, Black & Decker might further focus its distribution efforts on retail outlets catering to these customers, including large home improvement centers, such as Home Depot and Lowe's; smaller hardware chains, such as Ace Hardware; and independently owned hardware stores. Based on the cost-benefit analysis of these communication and distribution channels, one could conclude that this segment can be readily accessed via established communication and distribution channels

Customer Strategy Analysis

Once the strategic and tactical analyses have been completed, the next step is to articulate the customer strategy. This involves two key decisions: selecting the optimal target segment and developing a value proposition and positioning for this segment. Strictly speaking, only the first step—selecting the optimal target segment—pertains to identifying target customers, whereas the second step focuses on designing an offering that will fit the needs of the customers. However, because identifying target customers and defining the value the company will create for these customers are inseparable aspects of an offering's customer strategy, both aspects of the customer strategy are discussed here.

Step 11: Commit to Targeting a Particular Segment

Selecting the optimal target segment represents the culmination of the three preceding analyses—segmentation analysis, strategic targeting analysis, and tactical targeting analysis—which results in selecting the segment for which the company can develop strategically and tactically viable offerings. Selecting the optimal target segment yields the ultimate "go"/"no go" decision with respect to a particular segment. Because the strategic segments are defined by the varying needs of customers across segments, an offering can be truly optimized only for a single segment.

EXAMPLE: Given the market growth opportunity associated with the tradesman segment and Black & Decker's ability to develop a value proposition compatible with the needs of this segment, the company can develop an offering targeted to tradesmen. To pursue this segment, however, Black & Decker must allocate resources to develop offerings that are at parity with or superior to the competition in terms of power, brand image, and service.

Step 12: Develop a Value Proposition and Positioning for the Target Segment

The development of a value proposition involves determining the specific benefits and costs that the offering will create for target customers. The optimal value proposition stems from the value analysis conducted in Steps 2–4 and reflects the value characteristics of the target segment—the key value drivers and their relative importance. The offering's positioning builds on the offering's value proposition to define the primary benefit(s) that target customers should associate with the offering. A more detailed discussion of the specifics of developing a value proposition and positioning is offered in chapters 19 and 20.

EXAMPLE: To create value for the tradesman, Black & Decker must offer powerful and reliable tools from a trusted brand backed by dependable service (see Table 2). Given the relatively low importance of price and the relatively high prices of its key competitors, Black & Decker might consider raising its prices. This strategy not only can contribute to Black & Decker's bottom line but also can help build brand reputation by virtue of price-quality inferences, whereby buyers rely on price to infer an offering's performance on unobservable attributes. Furthermore, to create a distinct image of its offering in the minds of the tradesman, Black & Decker might position its offering by highlighting the individual attributes that are of primary importance to its customers and on which it could make a credible claim—power, reliability, and/or service. The specifics of Black & Decker's value proposition for the tradesman segment are outlined in Chapter 19.

The Targeting Matrix

The process of identifying target customers can be presented in the form of a matrix that encompasses the different aspects of the targeting decision (Table 4). This targeting matrix imposes logical structure on the targeting process, thus helping to streamline the process of deciding which customers to serve and which to ignore. The targeting matrix illustrated in Table 4 can also be used as a worksheet to guide the process of choosing a target segment.

Table 4. The Targeting Matrix

Steps 3,4 ⇨ **Customer value analysis** | Step 7 ⇨ **Compatibility analysis** | Step 6 ⇩

	Step 2 ⇩ Step 1 ⇨	Customer segments			Company offering	Competitive offerings			
		Segment A	Segment B	Segment C		Offering X	Offering Y	Offering Z	
Key value drivers	Attribute 1								
	Attribute 2								
	Attribute 3								
	Attribute 4								
	Attribute 5								
Strategic analysis	Segment attractiveness				⇦ Step 5				
	Segment compatibility				⇦ Step 7 ⟵ Resource alignment				
	Strategic viability				⇦ Step 8				
Tactical analysis	Segment profile				⇦ Step 9				
	Tactical viability				⇦ Step 10				
Customer strategy	Target segment				⇦ Step 11				
	Value proposition				⇦ Step 12				

Note that because articulating the key drivers of customer value is an integral aspect of targeting, the analysis underlying the selection of target customers can also serve as the basis for defining the offering's value proposition (Step 12). Thus, even though the development of a value proposition is a separate decision, it directly follows from targeting analysis, and can be considered as an integral aspect of the development of a sound targeting strategy.

Furthermore, even though for presentation purposes defining an offering's value proposition follows the identification of its target customers, in reality, the process of identifying target customers does not always precede the development of a value proposition. Thus, rather than starting with identifying an attractive customer segment and then developing a value proposition for this segment, a company might have an offering in advanced stages of development and seek to validate the viability of this offering by identifying a target market for which this offering can create superior value. Note, however, that regardless of the starting point of analysis—identifying target customers or designing a value proposition—the ultimate success of an offering is determined by the degree to which its value proposition is aligned with the needs and resources of its target customers. In this context, identifying target customers and designing a value proposition for these customers are the two aspects of an iterative process that culminates in the development of an internally consistent and viable marketing strategy.

The process of developing a targeting matrix can be further illustrated in the context of the Black & Decker case discussed this chapter. The targeting matrix summarizing the specific analyses and decisions made to identify the target customer and develop a value proposition for this customer is presented in Table 5.

Table 5. The Targeting Matrix: Black & Decker Power Tools

		Customer value analysis			Compatibility analysis			
		Customer segments			Black & Decker	Competitive offerings		
		Consumer	Tradesman	Industrial		Makita	Milwaukee	Ryobi
Key value drivers	Power	Low	High	High	Medium	High	High	Medium
	Reliability	Low	High	High	High	High	High	High
	Service	Low	High	Medium	Medium	Medium	Medium	Low
	Brand image	Medium	High	Low	Low	High	High	Low
	Price	High	Low	Medium	Medium	High	High	Medium
Strategic analysis	Segment attractiveness	Medium	High	Medium				
	Segment compatibility	–	High	–	← Improve on power, brand, and service			
	Strategic viability	–	High	–				
Tactical analysis	Segment profile	–	Behavioral profile	–				
	Tactical viability	–	High	–				
Customer strategy	Target segment	Tradesman						
	Value proposition	High performance tools backed by nationwide service						

For brevity, in Table 5 segment compatibility and the subsequent analyses (Steps 6–12) focus only on the most attractive segment (the tradesman). Assessments of the attractiveness and the strategic viability of the tradesman segment are based on the assumption that Black & Decker can develop the resources necessary to target this segment (power, brand, and service). The profile of the tradesman is defined by a set of specific behaviors, including reading industry magazines, such as *Builder* and *Electrical Contractor;* attending homebuilder trade shows; and frequenting home improvement and hardware stores.

EXAMPLE: Following the analysis of the needs of its customers in the tradesman segment, Black & Decker redesigned its offering by aligning the benefits of its offering to the needs of the tradesman. Specifically, it replaced its Black & Decker Professional brand with DeWalt, which was extended to cover Black & Decker's entire portfolio of offerings to the tradesman segment. DeWalt-branded tools were reengineered to strengthen their performance and reliability and were backed by a 30-day, no-risk satisfaction guarantee. To strengthen its service and further differentiate its offering from the competition, DeWalt offered a free one-year service contract, a 48-hour service/loaner tool policy, and toll-free technical support—attributes valued by the tradesmen (see Chapter 19 for more details). Launched in 1992, the DeWalt product line became an instant success, increasing its share in the tradesman segment from 10% to nearly 40% and becoming the market leader in fewer than three years.

NOTE

1 This example illustrates the main steps and the key considerations in the process of selecting target customers; it should not be used as a source of primary data about the company, customer segments, and/or market conditions. The reported data are based on "The Black & Decker Corporation (A): Power Tools Division" (595-057), "The Black & Decker Corporation (B): "Operation Sudden Impact" (595-060), "The Black & Decker Corporation (B): "Operation Sudden Impact" (596-510), and "The Black & Decker Corporation (C): Operation Sudden Impact Results, 1992–1994" (595-061), Harvard Business School: Harvard Business School Publishing, Boston, MA.

CHAPTER NINETEEN

THE BUSINESS MODEL WORKBOOK

Innovation is not the product of logical thought, although the result is tied to logical structure.

— Albert Einstein, theoretical physicist

An offering's business model defines the entities, factors, and processes involved in delivering and capturing value in the marketplace. The development of a business model involves analyses of the market in which the company operates and the value created by the offering. Building on the theory presented in Chapter 2, this chapter outlines the key aspects of the process of generating a business model.

The Key Components of a Business Model

The aim of a business model is to delineate a sustainable value proposition that optimizes the value for the relevant entities in a given market: the company, its customers, and its collaborators (Figure 1). The value proposition for each of these entities comprises two key components: strategy and tactics. The strategy identifies the market in which the company operates, defines the value exchanges between the key market entities, and outlines the ways in which an offering will create value for the relevant participants in the market exchange. Tactics, on the other hand, describe a set of activities—commonly referred to as the marketing mix—employed to execute a given strategy by designing, communicating, and delivering specific market offerings.

Figure 1: The Business Model as a Value-Creation Process

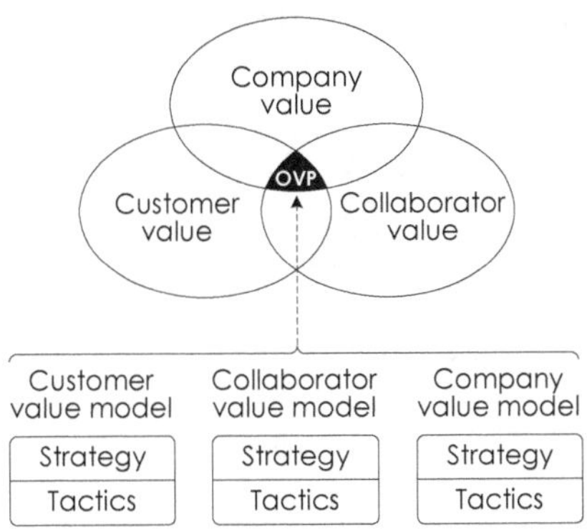

Defining an offering's business model involves articulating its four key aspects, including the target market and the value-creation models for each of the relevant market players: target customers, the company, and its collaborators. These four aspects of developing a business model are summarized below.

- The **target market** served by a given offering is defined by five key factors: target customers, collaborators, the company, competitors, and the market context.
- The **customer value model** outlines the ways (strategy and tactics) in which a given offering creates value for target customers.
- The **collaborator value model** outlines the ways (strategy and tactics) in which a given offering creates value for the company's collaborators.
- The **company value model** outlines the ways (strategy and tactics) in which a given offering creates (captures) value for the company.

The four aspects of a business model—target market, customer value model, collaborator value model, and company value model—are delineated in the following sections. The discussion of the key components of a business model is complemented by a company-specific example, which builds on the Black & Decker example introduced in the previous chapter. Specifically, the current chapter illustrates the process of developing a business model for the newly formed division of Black & Decker—DeWalt Industrial Tool Company.[1]

Target Market Analysis

The market in which a company's offering competes is defined by five key factors: *customers* for whom the company aims to create value, the *company* managing the offering, *collaborators* working with the company on this offering, *competitors* with offerings that target the same customers, and the *context* in which the company operates. These five factors defining the target market—often referred to as the Five Cs—are illustrated in Figure 2 and summarized below.

Figure 2: The 5-C Framework for Defining the Target Market

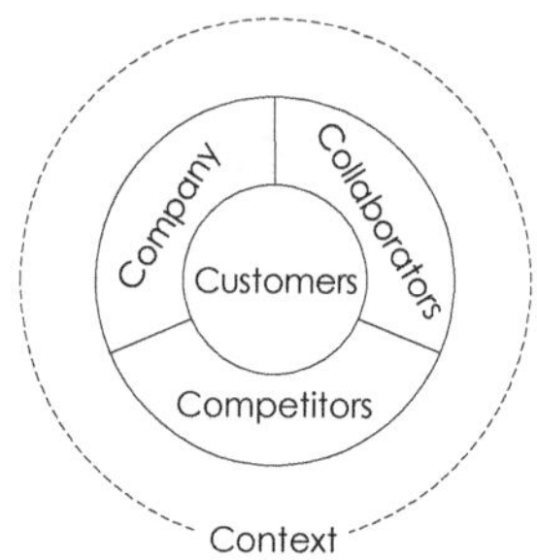

- **Customers**. Identifying target customers involves (1) defining the value sought and created by these customers (value drivers and value potential) and (2) identifying the profile of these customers (demographic and behavioral characteristics). Accordingly, identifying target customers involves the following aspects:
    - *Value potential* outlines the value these customers can create for the company and can involve factors such as market size, growth rate, disposable income, and brand loyalty
    - *Value drivers* outline the relevant benefits and costs that guide customer choice
    - *Demographic profile* defines the descriptive characteristics of the target customers, including age, gender, income, level of education, ethnicity, social class, stage in the life cycle, employment status, household size, and geographic location
    - *Behavioral profile* defines the key aspects of the behavior of target customers, including whether they have purchased the company's offerings in the past, their purchase behavior (volume, frequency, loyalty), and their information search behavior
- **Company**. Identifying the company involves defining the organizational structure and resources of the entity managing the offering. In the case of organizations managing a portfolio of diverse offerings, the term *company* refers to the particular organizational unit (often referred to as the *strategic business unit*) managing the offering.
- **Competitors**. Identifying competitors involves defining the entities that target the same need of the same customers. Because the competition is defined based on the company's ability to fulfill customer needs, it is not limited to the industry in which the company operates and might include cross-industry competitors (often referred to as substitutes). Accordingly, competitive analysis identifies both industry-specific and cross-industry competitors.
- **Collaborators**. Identifying collaborators involves defining the entities—suppliers, manufacturers, distributors (dealers, wholesalers, and retailers), research-and-development organizations, and service providers—that partner with the company to create value for target customers.
- **Context**. Identifying the context involves defining the relevant aspects of the environment in which the company operates. Specifically, there are six aspects of the environment that could be potentially important in defining target markets:
    - *Economic context*—the relevant economic factors, such as economic growth, money supply, inflation, and interest rates
    - *Business context*—the relevant aspects of the market environment, such as the emergence of new business models, changes in the market structure

(e.g., fragmentation), changes in the balance of power between market entities (e.g., manufacturers and retailers), and access to information

- *Technological context*—the relevant technological aspects of the environment, such as the emergence and/or proliferation of new technologies
- *Sociocultural context*—the relevant sociocultural aspect of the environment, such as demographic trends, value systems, and behaviors
- *Regulatory context*—the relevant regulatory aspects of the environment, such as import/export tariffs, taxes, pricing and communication regulations, and patent/trademark protection policies
- *Physical context*—the relevant aspects of the physical environment, such as natural resources, climate, and geographic conditions

EXAMPLE: Target market analysis outlining the above five factors in the case of DeWalt is illustrated in Table 1 below.

Table 1: The Target Market Worksheet: DeWalt

MARKET	KEY ATTRIBUTES
Customers	*Description*: Tradesmen—small businesses and independent contractors working in residential construction and using power tools on the job. *Value potential*: Tradesmen represent 28% ($420M) of the US power tools market and are the fastest growing (9%) segment of this market. *Value drivers*: Performance (power, precision, and ergonomics), reliability, service, and brand image *Demographic profile:* Small businesses and independent contractors (carpenters, plumbers, and electricians) working in residential construction *Behavioral profile*: Use power tools on the job; read trade press (*Builder* and *Electrical Contractor*), visit trade shows and home improvement stores, including large home improvement centers, such as Home Depot and Lowe's; smaller hardware chains, such as Ace Hardware and ServiStar; and independently owned hardware stores
Company	DeWalt Industrial Tool Company (a strategic business unit of Black & Decker, launched in 1992 to serve the tradesman segment)
Competitors	Makita Electric (50% market share), Milwaukee Tools (10% market share), Ryobi (9% market share)
Collaborators	Distribution channel partners: Wholesale distributors (serving smaller retailers), large home improvement centers (Home Depot, Lowe's), smaller hardware chains (Ace Hardware, ServiStar), and independently owned hardware stores.
Context	*Economic context:* Recession, resulting in high unemployment, limited money supply (credit), increased inflation, and slow GDP growth *Business context:* Rapid growth of new home construction and remodeling prior to the recession; consolidation of home improvement retailers and rise of big box home improvement centers, including Home Depot and Lowe's *Regulatory context:* Price dumping allegations against some of the Japanese manufacturers, including Makita, raising the possibility of imposing import duties on certain tools imported from Japan

Following the definition of the target market, the articulation of the business model involves defining the value for each of the three relevant entities: customer, collaborators, and the company. The key aspects of customer value, collaborator value, and company value analyses are discussed in the following sections.

Customer Value Analysis

Customer value analysis aims to define the offerings' value proposition for target customers. Specifically, customer value analysis articulates the way the offering's strategy is carried out by the marketing mix – product, service, brand, price, incentives, communication, and distribution – defining the offering's tactics (Figure 3).

Figure 3: Customer Value Model

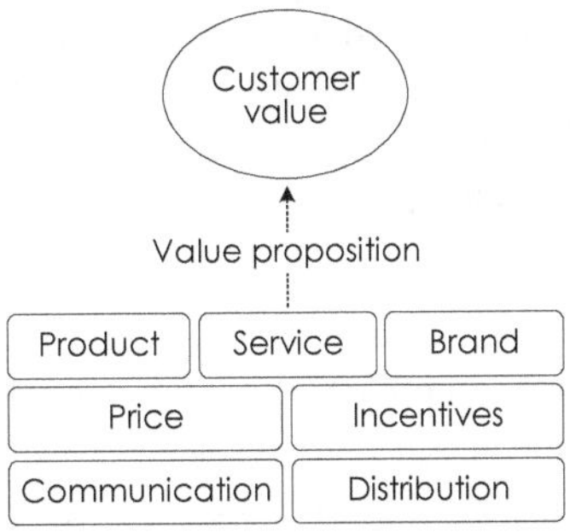

From a structural standpoint, customer value analysis comprises two aspects: strategy, defining the offering's value proposition and positioning, and tactics, defining the seven key marketing mix factors. The focus of strategic analysis is on the target customer and the fit between customer needs and the benefits and costs of the offering, whereas the focus of tactical analysis is on the company's offering and the specifics of the marketing mix with respect to the ability of the individual marketing tactics to create customer value.

- **Strategy**. Identifying the strategic aspect of the customer value of the offering involves identifying the offering's value proposition and its positioning for target customers. The customer value proposition defines all relevant benefits and costs of the company's offering for target customers. Building on the value proposition, the offering's positioning defines the key benefit of the company's offering that is designed to serve as the reason for choosing the offering.

- **Tactics.** Identifying the tactical aspect of customer value involves defining the key marketing mix variables – product, service, brand, price, incentives, communication, and distribution. Defining each of these marketing tactics involves (1) defining their key attributes and (2) defining the value (benefits and costs) they create for target customers. An important aspect of defining the offering's tactics is that the customer value of each marketing mix variable should be clearly articulated to ensure that all of the company tactics are consistent with the offering's value proposition.

EXAMPLE: The key aspects of the customer value analysis are illustrated in Table 2, documenting DeWalt's strategy and tactics targeting the tradesman market.

Table 2: Customer Value Worksheet (DeWalt)[2]

STRATEGY	Key attributes
Value proposition	High-performance, reliable tools backed by a national service and quality commitment unparalleled in the power tool industry
Positioning	"No downtime" performance (reliability and service commitment)

TACTICS	Key attributes	Value
Product	Thirty-three high-performing power tools (drills, saws, sanders, and plate joiners) and 323 accessories designed to maximize power, precision, ergonomics, and reliability	*Benefits:* Performance (power, precision, and ergonomics) and reliability
Service	*Loaner Tool Policy*: DeWalt will lend a tool during the repair period. *48-Hour Service policy:* If a repair is not completed within 48 hours, DeWalt will provide a new tool free of charge. *Technical Support*: Experts are available by phone at 1-800-4DeWALT to offer assistance regarding DeWalt products, service, repair, or replacement. *Free One-Year Service Contract*: DeWalt will maintain the tool and replace worn parts free any time during the first year of ownership *One-Year Warranty:* DeWalt will warranty materials and workmanship for one year. *Superior Diagnostics*. DeWalt Certified Service Centers use state-of-the-art testing equipment to diagnose problems quickly and accurately.	*Benefits:* Minimize downtime (fast service and loaner availability), professional training, technical support, accurate diagnostics
Brand	*Brand name*: DeWalt® (replaces the Black & Decker Professional brand) *Brand logo:* DEWALT *Brand color:* Yellow *Brand associations*: High-performance industrial tools; "no downtime" company *Brand hierarchy*: Free-standing brand (serviced at Black & Decker authorized service centers)	*Benefits:* Brand designed for professional (not consumer) use *Costs:* New brand with unknown reliability

Price	*Price:* Premium price tier (10% higher than Makita) *Returns:* DeWalt will accept returns for any reason within 30 days from the date of purchase.	*Benefits:* Peace of mind (30-day return policy) *Costs:* premium price
Incentives	*Loyalty programs:* Preferred Contractor Program	*Benefits:* Price discounts
Communication	*Message:* Create awareness of the new product line and service program; build the DeWalt brand to create customer brand loyalty. Taglines: *DeWalt. Guaranteed Tough* and *High Performance Industrial Tools** *Media:* Industry magazines (*Builder* and *Electrical Contractor*; $1M budget); trade shows; direct-mail catalogs ($300K budget), point-of-sale displays at home-improvement retailers; ten vans visiting job sites promoting DeWalt products ($1M budget)	*Benefits:* Awareness of the offering and its specifics
Distribution	*Product:* Large home-improvement centers (Home Depot/Lowe's), smaller hardware chains (Ace Hardware/ServiStar), and independently owned hardware stores *Service:* 117 Black & Decker authorized service centers with a dedicated DeWalt counter	*Benefits:* Product accessibility (wide distribution network), service accessibility (wide service network), convenience (returns processed in the store)

*A specific example of customer communications in the print media, featuring a plate joiner (a woodworking tool used to join two pieces of wood together), is outlined below. Under the headline: "The Joint Chief," the advertising copy reads: "The key to a plate joiner's performance is its fence. And that's what makes the DeWalt plate joiner a real stand-out in its field. Because the DeWalt fence lets you make a great variety of joints and move with speed and precision from one kind to anther. And the angles are covered with an integral fence which tilts 0°-90°. The fence is calibrated from 0-90 degrees so you can make the cut at exactly the proper angle. The fence can also be located on the inside or outside of a mitered joint, according to your preference. In addition, flush cuts can be made at 0 degrees without having to remove the fence. Rack and pinion control provides easy, accurate height adjustment and keeps the fence parallel to the blade. With this feature, the risk of making an inaccurate cut is virtually eliminated. And this rack and pinion control is a feature unique to DeWalt. So, if you haven't decided which plate joiner to get, you don't have to guess anymore. All you have to do is try DeWalt. You'll add it to your staff immediately."[3]

Collaborator Value Analysis

Collaborator value analysis aims to define the value of the offering to company collaborators. Specifically, collaborator value analysis articulates the way the offering's strategy is carried out by the marketing mix defining the offering's tactics (Figure 4) in order to identify the ways in which the offering creates superior value for the company's collaborators.

Figure 4: Collaborator Value Model

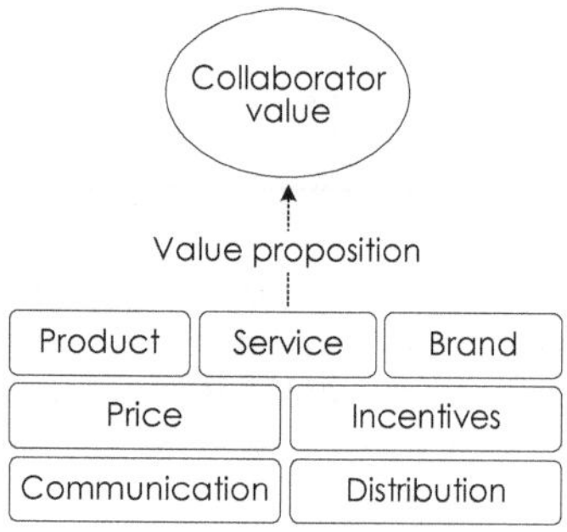

Similar to customer value analysis, collaborator value analysis comprises two elements: strategy, defining the offering's value proposition and positioning, and tactics, defining the seven key marketing mix factors. Here, the focus of strategic analysis is on collaborators and the fit between their needs and the value created by the offering, whereas the focus of tactical analysis is on the company's offering, the specifics of the marketing mix, and the ability of the individual marketing mix variables to create collaborator value.

- **Strategy**. Identifying the strategic aspect of the collaborator value of the offering involves identifying the offering's value proposition and its positioning for collaborators. The collaborator value proposition defines the total value of the offering for the company's collaborators. Building on the value proposition, the offering's positioning defines the key benefit of the company's offering that is designed to serve as the reason for collaborators to support the offering.
- **Tactics.** Identifying the tactical aspect of the collaborator value proposition involves defining the key marketing mix variables—product, service, brand, price, incentives, communication, and distribution. Defining each of these marketing tactics involves defining their key attributes as well as defining the collaborator value (benefits and costs) associated with each individual marketing mix variable. As in the case of customer analysis, an important aspect in defining the offering's tactics is that the collaborator value of each marketing mix variable should be clearly articulated to ensure that the company's tactics are consistent with the overall value proposition reflected in its strategy.

EXAMPLE: The key aspects of the collaborator value analysis are illustrated in Table 3, documenting DeWalt's strategy and tactics targeting the tradesman market.

Table 3: Collaborator Value Worksheet (DeWalt)

STRATEGY	Key characteristics
Value proposition	High-performance, reliable tools backed by a national service and quality commitment unparalleled in the power tool industry; supported by a large promotional budget to generate customer traffic; offering superior trade profits
Positioning	Profitable for the retailer

TACTICS	Key characteristics	Value
Product	Thirty-three high-performing power tools (drills, saws, sanders, and plate joiners) and 323 accessories designed to maximize power, precision, ergonomics, and reliability; aimed to replace the Black & Decker Professional product line	*Benefits:* Superior product line better tailored to the needs of tradesmen compared to the Black & Decker Professional line it replaces *Costs:* Discontinuing Black & Decker Professional products; stocking the DeWalt products
Service	Trade support provided by Black & Decker (ordering, inventory management, returns)	*Benefits:* Superior trade support compared to that for the Black & Decker Professional line
Brand	*Brand name*: DeWalt (replacing Black & Decker Professional) and Black & Decker (parent brand) *Brand promise*: Profitable *Brand hierarchy*: DeWalt as a sub-brand of Black & Decker	*Benefits:* Adding the DeWalt brand to a retailer's brand portfolio helps solidify its image as a go-to shop for tradesmen
Price	*Price:* Trade margins 5% higher than Makita *Returns:* DeWalt will accept returns for any reason within 30 days from the date of purchase *Price protection:* Price protection from discounters (e.g., halting supplies to price-cutting retailers) to prevent horizontal channel conflict	*Benefits:* Superior margins relative to Black & Decker Professional; price protection from discounters (not offered by Makita)
Incentives	*Point-of-sale promotions:* Trade incentives to ensure retailer "push"	*Benefits:* Trade incentives provide additional source of revenue
Communication	*Message:* Create awareness of the new product line and service program; build the DeWalt brand to create retailer loyalty. Tagline: *There's only one thing about DeWalt that's not tough: Making a profit.** *Media:* Trade shows (National Association of Home Builders trade show); Black & Decker sales force	*Benefits:* Increased store traffic from DeWalt customer communication
Distribution	*Product:* Distributed through the existing Black & Decker channels; direct distribution to home-improvement stores, and indirect (wholesaler) distribution to hardware stores. $20M inventory buildup at launch to ensure product availability and avoid stock-outs	*Benefits:* Distributed by the same vendor (Black & Decker); sufficient inventory available at the time of launch *Costs:* Ordering and inventorying the DeWalt product line;

	reverse logistics for the remaining Black & Decker Professional products

*A specific example of customer communications in the print media, featuring a plate joiner (a woodworking tool used to join two pieces of wood together), is outlined below. Following the headline: "There's only one thing about DeWalt that's not tough: Making a profit," the advertising copy reads: "In developing the complete line of DeWalt high-performance industrial tools and accessories, we've kept you in mind. By doing everything possible to make them profitable for you to sell. And this is what we've done. We've put together easy-to-understand pricing programs tailored to your specific needs. We've got a sales force dedicated to helping the tools sell through. They'll be out on job sites putting tools in your customers' hands, creating demand and sales for you. All tools come with a 30 Day No Risk Satisfaction Guarantee plus a full 1-year warranty. And with our quick-return repair service, which includes a free loaner program, your customers will never have a problem with down time. Why are we doing all this? Because at DeWalt, we believe selling tools that work hard shouldn't have to be hard work. And, above all, it should make you a solid profit."[4]

Company Value Analysis

Company value analysis aims to define the value of the offering to the company. Specifically, company value analysis articulates the way the offering's strategy is carried out by the marketing mix defining the offering's tactics (Figure 5). Thus, the company value worksheet aims to identify the ways in which the offering creates superior value for the company.

Figure 5: Company Value Model

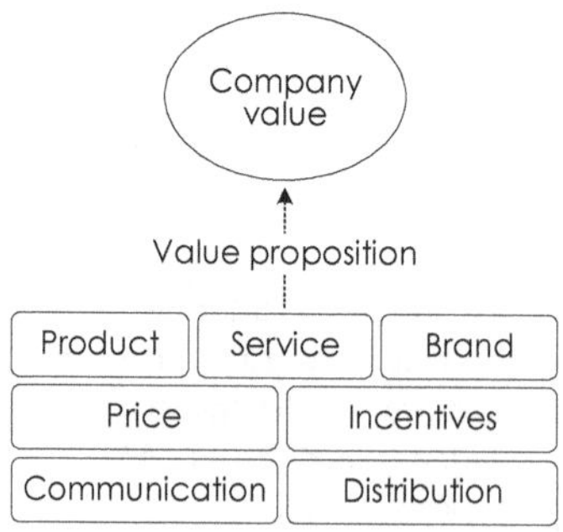

Similar to customer and collaborator value analysis, company value analysis comprises two elements: strategy, defining the offering's value proposition and positioning, and tactics, defining the seven key marketing mix factors. Here, the focus of strategic analysis is on the company and the fit between its goals and the value created by the offering, whereas the focus of tactical analysis is on the offering, the specifics of the marketing mix and the ability of the individual marketing mix variables to create value for the company.

- **Strategy**. Identifying the strategic aspect of the company value of the offering involves identifying the offering's value proposition and its positioning for the company. The company value proposition defines the value of the offering for the company, whereas the offering's positioning defines the primary benefit of the offering for the company.
- **Tactics.** Identifying the tactical aspect of the company value involves defining the key marketing mix variables—product, service, brand, price, incentives, communication, and distribution. Defining each of these marketing tactics involves defining their key attributes and defining the associated company value (benefits and costs).

EXAMPLE: The key aspects of the company value analysis are shown in Table 4, which illustrates DeWalt's strategy and tactics targeting the tradesman market.

Table 4: Company Value Worksheet (DeWalt)

STRATEGY	Key characteristics
Value proposition	*Monetary value:* Potential to increase market share from 8% to 50% and increase margins from 5% to 10%. Increase the valuation of the company by creating a new brand. *Strategic value:* Ensures leadership positioning in the growing tradesmen segment. Solidifies Black & Decker's relationship with retailers by offering an attractive product portfolio that enables retailers to have a single-source supplier for both consumer and professional segments.
Positioning	Organic profit growth

TACTICS	Key characteristics	Value
Product	Thirty-three high-performing power tools (drills, saws, sanders, and plate joiners) and 323 accessories designed to maximize power, precision, ergonomics, and reliability ("the banner of quality")	*Benefits (strategic):* R&D innovation can benefit other product lines; R&D challenges can help attract talent; the new product line establishes a quality benchmark for Black & Decker *Costs (monetary):* Product development and production costs
Service	*Customer service:* Loaner tool policy, 48-hour service policy, technical support, free one-year service contract, one-year warranty, superior diagnostics *Trade service:* Retailer support (ordering, inventory management, returns)	*Benefits (strategic):* Builds customer loyalty; offers sustainable competitive advantage over Makita *Costs (monetary):* Service implementation costs
Brand	*Brand name*: DeWalt® (replaces the Black & Decker Professional brand) *Brand logo:* DEWALT *Brand color:* Yellow	*Benefits (strategic):* Identifies the offering to create customer loyalty; captures some of the advertising expenses in the form of brand (DeWalt) equity

	Brand associations: High-performance industrial tools; "no downtime" company *Brand hierarchy*: Free-standing brand (serviced at Black & Decker authorized service centers)	*Costs (monetary):* Brand-building expense
Price	*Price:* Premium price tier (10% higher than Makita and Black & Decker Professional) *Returns:* 30-day return policy	*Benefits (monetary):* Captures customer value in the form of revenues *Benefits (strategic):* Premium price enables Black & Decker to invest in product development, service, brand building, and promotion
Incentives	*Loyalty programs:* Preferred Contractor Program *Point-of-Sale promotions:* Trade incentives to ensure retailer "push"	*Benefits (strategic):* Stimulates customer demand *Costs (monetary):* Incentives-related expenses *Strategic cost:* Monetary customer incentives could have detrimental impact on the DeWalt brand
Communication	*Customer communication:* $1M advertising in industry magazines (*Builder* and *Electrical Contractor*); $300K direct mail catalogs; $1M van promotion program; $200K point-of-sale displays; trade shows *Trade communication:* Black & Decker sales force; trade shows	*Benefits (strategic):* Creates awareness of the offering; builds the DeWalt brand *Costs (monetary):* Communication expenses
Distribution	*Product:* Distributed through the existing Black & Decker channels offering direct distribution to large home-improvement centers (Home Depot/Lowe's) and indirect (wholesaler) distribution to smaller hardware chains (Ace Hardware/ ServiStar) and independent hardware stores. $20M inventory buildup at launch to ensure product availability and avoid stock-outs *Service:* 117 Black & Decker authorized service centers with a dedicated DeWalt counter	*Benefits (strategic):* Solidifies Black & Decker's relationship with retailers by offering a comprehensive product portfolio *Costs (monetary):* Cost of making DeWalt available to the trade; cost of discontinuing Black & Decker Professional

Comparative Value Analysis

The discussion so far has focused on the intrinsic value an offering creates for the relevant market entities. Value, however, is not created in a vacuum: Offerings are commonly evaluated in comparative terms, using other offerings as a reference point. In this context, the intrinsic value of an offering is complemented by its comparison with referent offerings.[5] Therefore, to succeed, an offering must not only create intrinsic value for the relevant market entities but must also create value superior to that of the other market offerings, including competitive offerings as well as the other offerings in the company's product line.

The process of evaluating an offering's advantages and disadvantages relative to other offering(s) is referred to as comparative value analysis. Because the comparative analysis of the value of an offering for target customers and collaborators involves comparing that offering to the competition, comparative value analysis in this case is also referred to as competitive analysis. In the same vein, because the comparative analysis of the value of an offering for the company involves comparing that offering to other offerings in the company's product line, comparative value analysis in this case is also referred to as product-line value analysis.

An offering's success hinges on its ability to create value for each of the three market entities: target customers, the company, and its collaborators; thus, comparative value analysis can be performed with respect to each of these three entities. Furthermore, comparative analysis of the offering's value for each of these entities can be viewed as a process comprising the following three steps: (1) defining the key aspects (strategy and tactics) of the company's offering, (2) defining the key aspects (strategy and tactics) of the referent offering(s), and (3) evaluating the relative advantages and disadvantages of the company's offering compared to the referent offering(s). An example of a comparative value analysis is illustrated in Table 5.

Table 5: Comparative Value Analysis

	Company offering	Referent offering(s)	Comparative value analysis
Value proposition	Define the relevant benefits and costs of the company's offering	Define the relevant benefits and costs of the referent offering	Define the points of parity and points of difference in the company's and referent offerings
Positioning	Define the key benefit of the company's offering	Define the key benefit of the referent offering	Define the relative advantage of the company's benefit
Product **Service** **Brand** **Price** **Incentives** **Communication** **Distribution**	Define the key aspects of the company's offering on each marketing mix variable	Define the key aspects of the referent offering on each marketing mix variable	Define the relative advantage of the company's offering on each marketing mix variable

The comparative value analysis illustrated in Table 5 represents a scenario with a single referent offering. In the case of multiple referent offerings (e.g., multiple competitors and/or multiple offerings in a company's own product line), each referent offering should be represented in the comparative value worksheet.

NOTES

[1] This example illustrates the main steps and the key considerations in articulating a company's business model; it should not be used as a source of primary data about the company, customer segments, and/or market conditions. The reported data are based on "The Black & Decker Corporation (A): Power Tools Division" (595-057), "The Black & Decker Corporation (B): "Operation Sudden Impact" (595-060), "The Black & Decker Corporation (B): "Operation Sudden Impact" (596-510), and "The Black & Decker Corporation (C): Operation Sudden Impact Results, 1992-1994" (595-061), Harvard Business School: Harvard Business School Publishing, Boston, MA.

[2] "The Black & Decker Corporation (B): "Operation Sudden Impact," (595-060).

[3] "The Black & Decker Corporation (B): "Operation Sudden Impact," (595-060).

[4] "The Black & Decker Corporation (B): "Operation Sudden Impact," (595-060).

[5] The term *referent offering* denotes any offering—competitive or in a company's own product line—that is used as a reference when evaluating the focal offering.

CHAPTER TWENTY

POSITIONING STATEMENT WORKBOOK

Perfection is achieved, not when there is nothing left to add, but when there is nothing left to take away.

—Antoine de Saint-Exupéry, French writer, author of *The Little Prince*

The positioning statement is an internal company document that succinctly outlines an offering's strategy to guide tactical decisions. Thus, the positioning statement is a communication device that aims to share the offering's strategy with the relevant stakeholders involved in the development and management of a particular offering. The key principles of developing a positioning statement are the focus of this chapter.

Positioning Statement as a Means of Communication

The positioning statement is a succinct document—usually consisting of a single sentence—that outlines the key aspects of an offering's strategy. The primary purpose of the positioning statement is to guide tactical decisions related to the product, service, brand, price, incentives, communication, and distribution aspects of the offering. As such, the positioning statement aims to communicate the essence of the offering's strategy to all stakeholders involved in the development and management of a particular offering. The importance of the positioning statement as a communication device within the company is underscored by the fact that different entities within the company—research and development, marketing, sales force, senior management, finance, operations—often do not have the same level of understanding of the offering's strategy, such as who the offering's target customers are, why they would buy the offering, and what the company's stake is in ensuring this offering's success. Therefore, the positioning statement aims to provide a common vision of the offering's goals, strategy, and tactics to all relevant entities with the company.

In addition to making sure that different company entities are on the same page, the positioning statement plays an important role in ensuring that the company's external collaborators—including research and development and product design partners, advertising and public relations agencies, channel partners, and external sales force—correctly understand the company's strategy with respect to the particular offering. Communicating the offering's strategy to the company's collaborators is particularly important because they are often less familiar with the company's goal and strategic initiatives. In fact, many collaborator conflicts arise from the lack of clear communication regarding the strategy guiding the company's offerings.

The positioning statement is often confused with an offering's positioning. Although directly related, these concepts reflect different aspects of the marketing management process. An offering's positioning identifies the key aspect of the offering's value proposition. While the positioning statement incorporates the offering's positioning, it is broader in scope than the positioning and includes the offering's target customers (in the case of customer-focused positioning statements) in addition to the value proposition.

The positioning statement also can be confused with the brand slogan and communication tagline. This is because all three capture certain aspects of the offering's strategy. Despite their similarities, however, these concepts are very different on several important dimensions, including their primary focus, structure, and target audience. Unlike the positioning statement, which summarizes the offering's overall marketing strategy, the brand slogan and communication tagline focus on specific aspects—branding and communication—of the offering's marketing strategy. Furthermore, from a structural standpoint, the positioning statement also identifies the offering's target customers—unlike the brand slogan and the communication tagline, which capture only the offering's value proposition. Accordingly, the brand slogan and communication tagline are usually short phrases, whereas the positioning statement is typically a bit longer and is expressed as a sentence.

To illustrate, consider Gillette, the leading shaving brand in the United States. Its positioning statement can be written as: *For all men who shave, Gillette provides the best shaving experience because it uses the most innovative shaving technology.*[1] Gillette's brand slogan is much more succinct and memorable: *Gillette. The Best a Man Can Get.* Finally, one of Gillette's communication taglines for its Fusion ProGlide razor highlights a particular aspect of its razor: *Less Tug and Pull.* In the same vein, BMW's positioning statement can be articulated as: *BMW is the best vehicle for drivers who care about performance because it is the ultimate driving machine.* BMW's brand slogan is: *The Ultimate Driving Machine.* And a recent advertising tagline is: *BMW. We Make Only One Thing: The Ultimate Driving Machine.*

Another important distinction between an offering's positioning statement and the brand slogan and communication tagline is that they are written for different target audiences. The positioning statement is an internal company document aimed at company employees, stakeholders, and collaborators; it is not designed to be seen by target customers. In contrast, the brand slogan and the communication tagline are explicitly written for the offering's target customers. Consequently, the brand slogan and communication tagline use catchy, memorable phrases designed to capture customers' attention, whereas the positioning statement is written in a logical, straightforward manner.

Depending on its target audience, three types of positioning statements can be distinguished: (1) customer-focused positioning statement, which articulates the offering's value proposition for target customers, (2) collaborator-focused positioning statement, which articulates the offering's value proposition for the company's collaborators, and (3) company-focused positioning statement, which articulates the offering's value proposition for the company. These three types of positioning statements are discussed in more detail in the following sections.

Customer-Focused Positioning Statement

The customer-focused positioning statement is by far the most popular positioning statement format. A typical customer-focused positioning statement consists of three components: target customers, frame of reference, and reason for choice. These three aspects of the positioning statement are outlined in more detail below.

- **Target customers** are buyers for whom the company will tailor its offerings. These customers are defined by the key benefit(s) they seek to receive from the offering as well as by their demographic and/or behavioral profile. The selection of target customers is discussed in more detail in Chapter 4.
- The **frame of reference** identifies the reference point used to define the offering. Based on the choice of a reference point, five different frames of reference can be distinguished: (1) need-based framing, which relates the benefits of the offering to a particular customer need, (2) user-based framing, which relates the offering to a particular type of buyer, (3) category-based framing, which defines the offering through its membership in a particular product category, (4) competitive framing, which defines the offering by comparing it to the competition, and (5) product-line framing, which defines the offering by comparing it to the other offerings in the company's product line (see Chapter 6 for more details).

  Based on the nature of comparison, the above five frames of reference can be either noncomparative or comparative. *Noncomparative* framing relates the value of the offering to the reference point without explicitly comparing it to other offerings; in contrast, *comparative* framing defines the offering by contrasting it to other offerings. Need-based, user-based, and category-based frames tend to be noncomparative, whereas competitive framing and product-line framing are always comparative. Accordingly, positioning statements involving noncomparative framing are referred to as noncomparative, whereas those using comparative framing are referred to as comparative positioning statements.
- The **reason for choice** identifies the primary reason why customers will consider, buy, and use the offering. The primary reason for choice typically

highlights the key benefit—functional, psychological, and/or monetary—defining the value of the offering for target customers. Most positioning statements identify a single reason for choice, although positioning statements using multiple reasons are not uncommon. Positioning statements that use multiple reasons for choice often select reasons that are closely related and can be grouped into a single, more abstract benefit; using unrelated reasons for choice representing distinct benefits can present challenges because they might dilute the offering's positioning in the minds of its target customers (see Chapter 6 for more details). Examples of common customer-focused positioning statements are given below.

EXAMPLE A. This example illustrates a positioning statement that articulates the offering's key benefit and justifies its ability to deliver this benefit.

Noncomparative Positioning:

Template: For [target customers] who seek [key benefit], [offering] is an excellent [product category] because [justification of the benefit].

Example: *For the tradesman who uses power tools to make a living, DeWalt offers dependable professional tools that are engineered to be tough and are backed by a guarantee of repair or replacement within 48 hours.*

Comparative Positioning:

Template: For [target customers] who seek [key benefit], [offering] is a better [product category] than [competitive offering] because [justification of the benefit].

Example: *For the tradesman who uses power tools to make a living, DeWalt offers professional tools that are more dependable than any other brand because they are engineered to be tough and are backed by a guarantee of repair or replacement within 48 hours.*

EXAMPLE B. This example illustrates a positioning statement that articulates the offering's key benefit and justifies its ability to deliver this benefit. The format is similar to that in the first example except for the organization of the positioning statement.

Noncomparative Positioning:

Template: [Offering] is the [product category] that gives [target customers] [key benefit] because [justification of the benefit].

Example: *Mountain Dew is the soft drink that gives young, active consumers who have little time for sleep the energy they need because it has a very high level of caffeine.*

Comparative Positioning:

Template: [Offering] is the [product category] that gives [target customers] more [key benefit] than [competitive offering] because [justification of the benefit].

Example: *Mountain Dew is the soft drink that gives young, active consumers who have little time for sleep more energy than any other brand because it has a very high level of caffeine.*

EXAMPLE C. This example illustrates a positioning statement in which the product category serves as a reference point.

Noncomparative Positioning:

Template: [Offering] is an excellent [product category] for [target customers] because [the primary reason to choose the offering].

Example: *Aquafina is an excellent bottled water for health-conscious consumers because it is pure.*

Comparative Positioning:

Template: [Offering] is a better [product category] than [competitive offering] for [target customers] because [the primary reason to choose the offering].

Example: *Brita is a better source of drinking water than bottled water for price-conscious consumers because it costs less.*

EXAMPLE D. This example illustrates a positioning statement in which customers' needs serve as a reference point. This format is similar to that in the previous example except for using customer needs rather than the product category as the reference point.

Noncomparative Positioning:

Template: [Offering] is an excellent choice for [target customers] because [the primary reason to choose the offering].

Example: *Gatorade is a smart choice for athletes because it rehydrates, replenishes, and refuels.*

Comparative Positioning:

Template: [Offering] is a better choice for [target customers] than [competitive offering] because [the primary reason to choose the offering].

Example: *Gatorade is a smart choice for athletes because it rehydrates, replenishes, and refuels in ways water can't.*

Collaborator-Focused Positioning Statement

Delivering value for target customers, although important, is only one aspect of ensuring an offering's success. To succeed, an offering has to create value not only for its target customers but also for the company's collaborators. Accordingly, in addition to developing a customer-focused positioning statement, managers also need to develop a positioning statement outlining the offering's value for its collaborators.

The collaborator-focused positioning statement is similar to the customer-focused positioning statement, with the main difference that instead of identifying target customers and the key value proposition for these customers, it identifies the company's key collaborators and delineates the offering's key value proposition for these collaborators. The core question the collaborator-focused positioning statement must answer is: *Who are the offering's key collaborators and why would they support the company's offering?*

The typical collaborator-focused positioning statement consists of three key components: collaborators, the frame of reference, and the key reason for choice. The overall structure of the collaborator-focused positioning statement is similar to the structure of the customer-focused statement. The key differences involve using the company collaborators rather than target customers as the focal point, and defining the key benefit relative to collaborator value rather than customer value. Examples of common collaborator-focused positioning statements are given below.

EXAMPLE E. This positioning statement is similar to the one shown in Example C, with the key difference that it articulates the value for collaborators rather than for target customers.

Noncomparative Positioning:

Template: [Offering] is an excellent choice for [collaborators] because [the primary reason to choose the offering].

Example: *DeWalt power tools are a great choice for retailers because they are profitable.*

Comparative Positioning:

Template: [Offering] is a better choice for [collaborators] than [competitive offering] because [the primary reason to choose the offering].

Example: *DeWalt power tools are a better choice for retailers than Makita because they offer price protection from discount retailers.*

EXAMPLE F. This positioning statement is very similar to the one shown in Example A, with the key difference that it articulates the value for collaborators rather than for target customers.

Noncomparative Positioning:

Template: For [collaborators] who seek [key benefit], [offering] is an excellent [product category] because [justification of the benefit].

Example: *For mass-market retailers who seek to grow profits, Gillette Fusion offers a consumer staple that will generate high profit margins.*

Comparative Positioning:

Template: For [collaborators] who seek [key benefit], [offering] is a better [product category] than [competitive offering] because [justification of the benefit].

Example: *For mass-market retailers who seek to grow profits, Gillette Fusion offers a consumer staple that will generate higher profit margins than Gillette Mach3.*

Company-Focused Positioning Statement

Creating value for target customers and collaborators, although important, is not sufficient to ensure the market success of an offering. To succeed, an offering must create value for the company. Accordingly, in addition to developing a positioning statement outlining the offering's value for target customers and collaborators, managers also need to outline the offering's value for the company.

The company-focused positioning statement identifies the company's strategic business unit managing the offering and outlines its key value proposition for the business unit and the company. The core question this positioning statement must answer is: *Why should the business unit and the company invest in this offering?* The company-focused positioning statement aims to justify the viability of the offering to the senior management and/or the key stakeholders (e.g., company directors) by articulating how the offering will help the company achieve its goals.

A typical company-focused positioning statement consists of three key components: the company, the frame of reference, and the key reason for choice. The overall structure of the company-focused positioning statement is similar to the structure of the customer-focused statement. The key differences involve using the company rather than target customers as the focal point, and defining the key benefit relative to company value rather than customer value. Examples of common company-focused positioning statements are given below.

EXAMPLE G. This positioning statement is similar to the ones shown in Examples C and E, with the key difference that it articulates the value for the company rather than for target customers or collaborators.

Noncomparative Positioning:

Template: [Offering] is an excellent choice for [company] because [the primary benefit derived from the offering].

Example: *DeWalt power tools are a great choice for Black & Decker because they offer profit margins that are in line with the company's goals.*

Comparative Positioning:

Template: [Offering] is a better choice for [company] than [competitive offering] because [the primary reason to choose the offering].

Example: *DeWalt power tools are a better choice for Black & Decker than Black & Decker Professional power tools because they have a larger margin and generate greater sales volume.*

EXAMPLE H. This positioning statement is very similar to the ones shown in Examples A and F, with the key difference that it articulates the value for the company rather than for target customers or collaborators.

Noncomparative Positioning:

Template: [Offering] is an excellent choice for [company] because [the primary benefit derived from the offering].

Example: *Fusion is an excellent option for Gillette because it will assert Gillette's position as the leader in the wet-shaving market and will ensure high profit margins.*

Comparative Positioning:

Template: [Offering] is a better choice for [company] than [alternative offering] because [the primary reason to choose the offering].

Example: *Fusion is a better option for Gillette than Mach3 because it will assert Gillette's position as the leader in the wet-shaving market and will ensure higher profit margins.*

NOTE

[1] The examples used in this chapter are for illustration purposes only and might not adequately reflect the companies' actual positioning strategies.

INDEX

Terms listed in this index are grouped into four categories: (1) marketing concepts, (2) financial concepts, (3) marketing frameworks, and (4) companies, products, and brands.

MARKETING CONCEPTS

FINANCIAL CONCEPTS

MARKETING FRAMEWORKS

COMPANIES, PRODUCTS, AND BRANDS

FINANCIAL CONCEPTS

MARKETING FRAMEWORKS

COMPANIES, PRODUCTS, AND BRANDS

021515

CPSIA information can be obtained
at www.ICGtesting.com
Printed in the USA
LVHW102011160119
604153LV00013B/318/P